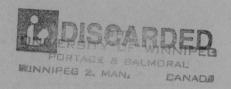

THE SEARCH
FOR ST. TRUTH

MARY CARRUTHERS

THE

SEARCH

FOR

ST. TRUTH

A Study of Meaning
in *Piers Plowman*

NORTHWESTERN UNIVERSITY PRESS

EVANSTON 1973

MARY CARRUTHERS formerly taught English at Smith College
and is now an Assistant Professor of English
at Case Western Reserve University.

Publication of this book was assisted
by the AMERICAN COUNCIL OF LEARNED SOCIETIES
under a grant from the ANDREW W. MELLON FOUNDATION.

To
JEANNE HUGO CARRUTHERS
and to the memory of
LYMAN BRUCE CARRUTHERS

❧ CONTENTS ❧

ᖇᖇ PREFACE ᖇᖇ

Any study of *Piers Plowman* undertaken at this particular moment faces the problem of a lack of modern editions of the text, and this will continue to be so until all three volumes of the new critical edition of the poem are completed. As of this writing, only the A-Text, edited by George Kane (London, 1960), has appeared, although the B-Text, edited by George Kane and E. Talbot Donaldson, is now at press. Professor Donaldson has very kindly made the readings of this new edition of the B-Text available to me, and it is mainly for this reason that I have felt secure in basing my reading of the poem on the B-Text. My choice of B was also influenced by the fact that most previous criticism of the poem has focused on this version. I have also occasionally drawn on passages in A and C to emphasize or clarify points in B. From this practice, it will be clear that I do not adhere to any multiple-authorship theory of the poem's composition, believing that the question has been answered, at least to my satisfaction, by George Kane's recent book, *The Evidence for Authorship* (London, 1965).

My textual quotations and the bulk of my general commentary are based on the most readily available published text of the poem, W. W. Skeat's parallel-text edition (Oxford, 1886). Line references are to this text, and I have also followed its spellings and punctuation, though I have omitted the medial point with which Skeat marks the caesura, and substituted for it my own punctuation when it seemed necessary to do so. The readings of the Kane-Donaldson text are indicated in square brackets in my quotations. Where Kane-Donaldson rearranges lines from the sequence found in Skeat, I have indicated this rearrangement by enclosing the reordered lines in square brackets. Omission of lines, phases, or words in Kane-Donaldson, which are included by Skeat, are indicated by omission points enclosed in square brackets. The changes I noted in the Kane-Donaldson edition did not affect in any significant way the general reading of the poem which I had evolved from Skeat's text, but I have taken these changes into account when they were relevant to my analysis of the passages I have quoted.

I would like to acknowledge here my large debt to the several persons and institutions who have aided this project in its various stages.

My warmest thanks go to Andrea Rosnick, whose insights into *Piers Plowman* and into poetry have enlarged, changed, and enriched my own thinking in ways too fundamental for me to begin to acknowledge adequately, and whose editorial good sense is reflected in almost every paragraph of this book.

I began the study of *Piers Plowman* under the direction of E. Talbot Donaldson, first in a graduate course and then as a dissertation. He very generously read the manuscript of this book, even though it deals with figuralism and St. Augustine, and saved me from many errors. His unflagging interest in *Piers Plowman* and in this study over many years has been a continuing source of enlightenment, encouragement, and education.

I would also like to thank friends, and colleagues of mine at Smith, who talked long hours to me about allegory, poetry, and *Piers Plowman*, especially Jackie Pritzen, Margaret Shook, John Hill, and William Oram. Elizabeth Kirk read the manuscript and made several valuable suggestions. I regret that her book, *The Dream Thought of Piers Plowman* (New Haven, Conn., 1972), appeared too late for me to make use of it in the preparation of my manuscript.

Thanks are also due to the editors of *Studies in Philology* and *Philological Quarterly* for permission to reprint parts of two articles published previously in those journals. Smith College provided me with two summer research grants and a grant-in-aid for manuscript preparation. The staffs of the Neilson Library of Smith College and of the Pontifical Institute Library of the University of Toronto made my life easier on many occasions. Hilda McArthur turned the typing of the manuscript into an editorial occasion, saving me much labor and embarrassment. Finally, I must thank the staff of Northwestern University Press, especially Janice Feldstein and Ralph Carlson, for their care and enthusiasm throughout the process of publishing this book.

Hadley, Massachusetts
June, 1973

THE SEARCH
FOR ST. TRUTH

ᔕ CHAPTER ONE ᔓ

"Mercy, Madame, what [may] this [by]mene?"

T he belief that *Piers Plowman* does mean something is one that its readers and critics have clung to tenaciously, sometimes vainly, often desperately, through the poem's many incongruities, twists, and turns. It is a belief to which I subscribe as well, though I admit to attacks of doubt along the way. Indeed, I sympathize wholly with the confession of one of the poem's chief editors, who looked forward "to a year when the many incidental problems of editing *Piers Plowman* will, I hope, constantly distract me from the effort of understanding its meaning." [1] Yet, in the effort to understand the problematical meaning of the poem, its readers have too often neglected the problem of meaning in the poem. For the meaning of *Piers Plowman* is at least as baffling to its characters as it is to its critics, and their efforts to understand what it all means give the poem its momentum and help to determine its form.

During the confessions of the Seven Deadly Sins in Passus V, the following exchange occurs between Repentance and Avarice:

> "Repentedestow [. . .] euere," quod Repentance, "[or] restitucioun madest?"
> "ʒus, ones I was herberwed," quod he, "with an hep of chapmen, I roos whan thei were arest and yrifled here males."
> "That was no restitucioun," quod Repentance, "but a robberes thefte,

---

1. E. T. Donaldson, "Patristic Exegesis: The Opposition," in *Critical Approaches to Medieval Literature*, ed. D. Bethurum (New York, 1960), p. 25.

Thow haddest be better worthy be hanged therfore."

[..]

"I wende ryflynge were restitucioun, [. . .] for I learned neuere
rede on boke,
And I can no Frenche in feith, but of the ferthest ende of Norfolke,"

(V. 232–39)

This conversation is an echo of a similar one earlier in the scene in which
Repentance is again misunderstood, this time by Envy:

> "ʒus, redili," quod Repentaunce and radde hym to [goode],
> "Sorwe [for] synne is sauacioun of soules."
> "I am sori," quod [enuye], "I am but selde other,
> And that maketh me [so mat] for I ne may me venge."

(V. 125–28)

These encounters are comic intensifications of a situation that is typical in
Piers Plowman. Neither Avarice nor Envy can understand what Repentance
is saying; they mis-take his words. Avarice, without comprehension, hears
in "restitution" only a mystifying French borrowing, and Envy understands
"sorry" in quite another sense from the one Repentance has intended.
Repentance uses a Latinate pedantry on the one hand and an ambiguous,
unintended pun on the other, neither of which successfully communicates
the intended meaning to its audience.

Neither of these misunderstandings involves a level of meaning more
exalted than that of the literal word itself. This is an important point to
ponder, since the temptation for the reader is to leap to "read the allegory"
of *Piers Plowman* without pausing to reflect upon the fact that *allegoria*
needs a solid base in *littera* before it can mean anything. And the *littera*
of this poem is slippery in the extreme. Verbal ambiguity, mistaken meaning, pun, hidden connotation, extreme compression or expansion of ordinary
syntax—such devices are the hallmarks of Langland's language, and they
define the situations which his characters face over and over again in the
poem.[2] I believe that this analysis of words as ambiguous tools of thought,
capable not only of revealing a true cognition but also of generating a
corruption of understanding, is the basic concern of the poem: *Piers Plowman* is an allegory which devotes its primary energies to redeeming its own

---

2. For an analysis of some of Langland's word play, see B. F. Huppé,
"Petrus Id Est Christus: Word Play in *Piers Plowman,* B-Text," *ELH,* XVII
(1950), 163–90.

littera. Poetry is a cognitive art, "in the service of wisdom," [3] but the verbal medium in which it is conducted is full of traps, and to assume that the words of this poem are not inherently problematical is the mark of a fool.

Overconfidence in his own interpretive abilities is certainly the mark of the poem's biggest fool, Will.[4] Indeed, it is the first mistake that he makes. After viewing the diverse procession of figures in the Prologue, Will assures his audience:

> What [þe] montaigne bymeneth and the merke dale,
> And the felde ful of folke I shal ȝow faire schewe.
>
> (I. 1–2)

The meaning is all perfectly evident to him. However, when Lady Holy Church approaches him, his confidence dissolves into a question about the very things he had been so sure of nine lines earlier: "Mercy, Madame, what [may] this [by]mene?" (I. 11). She proceeds to explain to him at great length and with considerable precision exactly what it all means, but as her explanation becomes fuller, Will's questions become more frequent and reveal less understanding. For instance, she states clearly that "treuthe is tresore, the triest on erthe" (I. 135). To which Will responds by asking, "By what crafte in my corps it comseth and where?" (I. 137). Lady Holy Church is angered at his dullness and tells him, "It is a kynde knowyng . . . that kenneth in thine herte / For to louye thi lorde" (I. 140–41). Yet her words to Will are less clear than she supposes—or than he does, for that matter. The "tresore" she refers to is spiritual treasure, the truth which is Truth. But by describing this treasure as the "triest on erthe" she creates a false impression of it, at least to an uninitiated listener. Lady Holy Church looks to the *allegoria* of words; Will cannot get beyond their *littera.* Will understands in the earthly sense; thinking of truth as knowledge of earthly things, he wants to know from what "craft" in his body it comes. In her

---

3. M.-D. Chenu, *Nature, Man, and Society in the Twelfth Century,* sel. and trans. J. Taylor and L. Little (Chicago, 1968), p. 100.

4. "Fool" is one of the poem's ambiguous concepts, exemplified in Will's gradual change from a foolish dolt to one of God's initiates, foolish in the eyes of the world. Not all of the poem's critics have realized that such a change occurs. The characterization of the dreamer as stupid is most fully made by Howard Meroney, "The Life and Death of Longe Wille," *ELH,* XVII (1950), 1–35. A somewhat overstated case for regarding Will as a "simple" or "natural" fool is made by Jay Martin, "Wil as Fool and Wanderer in *Piers Plowman,"* *TSLL,* III (1962), 534–48.

answer, Lady Holy Church again uses ambiguous words—*kynde* and *herte*. *Kynde* could mean simply the earthly nature of man, or it could mean his spiritual one, man as the image of God. Similarly, *herte* either could mean the bodily organ or could be a metaphor for the spiritual one. It becomes quite clear, in fact, that Will and Lady Holy Church are speaking two quite different languages, though they are using the same lexicon. And unless they can agree upon the significance of the word, come to understand the exact reference of the verbal sign, it is useless as a cognitive tool. Thus, the initial situation in the poem seems to me to present succinctly its basic concern with the problem of meaning, particularly of verbal meaning. The meanings of mountain, dale, and field seem perfectly clear to Will; yet, in the next moment he has no idea of what they mean. This is the cognitive situation typical of *Piers Plowman,* both for its characters and for its critics. And the heart of this dilemma lies in the problematical nature of words themselves, as the poem perceives them.

There are three words which are particularly troublesome in *Piers Plowman,* as its narrator and nearly all of its critics have rightly perceived. They are three of the simplest words in the poem—*Dowel, Dobet,* and *Dobest.* The morphemic gradation of the adverb-suffix suggests that the three words make up an orderly, progressive revelation of meaning. Dowel is not an isolated term—it has degrees and aspects. As graded compounds, their relationship implies that they are aspects of a semantically unified concept, whose meaning will be revealed by their progressive structural relationship, as "-well" is progressively revealed in "-better" and "-best." Meaning is thus inextricably linked to the graded structural progression in the relationship of the three words. Moreover, the poem promises that this gradation bears a real relationship to its whole structure, by naming the chief sections which follow the *Visio,* the *Vita de Dowel,* the *Vita de Dobet,* and the *Vita de Dobest.* Unfortunately, most critics of the poem have chosen to regard the relationship of these three terms as conceptual and thematic rather than structural and formal.

Since Henry Wells published his article on "The Construction of *Piers Plowman,*"[5] most of the poem's commentators have argued that its structure depends on a progressive thematic relationship among these three words. But the attempt to define just what the informing concepts are has been most unsatisfactory, partly because the poet gives us so many definitions of them. The problem which these various definitions presents can

---

5. Henry W. Wells, "The Construction of *Piers Plowman,*" *PMLA,* XLIV (1929), 123–40.

best be understood if one puts them together schematically. (The following list includes only the major definitions, and only those that emerge when all three terms are defined together by the various characters indicated).

	Dowel	Dobet	Dobest
Thought			
VIII. 78–106	lives righteously	helps others	wears a bishop's crown
Wit			
IX. 1–16	is lord of the castle, Caro	is his daughter	is a bishop's equal
Wit			
IX. 92–106	fears God	fear of God through love	wastes neither speech nor time
Wit			
IX. 199–203	obeys the law	loves friend and foe	cares for young and old, heals and helps
Wit			
IX. 203	dreads God	suffers	subdues wicked will
Clergy			
X. 218–30	believes in articles of Faith	acts in accord with belief	leads the sinful to righteousness
Drunken Doctor			
XIII. 118–32	does what clerks teach	teaches others	does as he himself teaches
Patience			
XIII. 136	*disce*	*doce*	*dilige inimicos*
Conscience			
XIII. 459 to XIV. 27	is contrition	is confession	is satisfaction

The differences between the three terms are more apparent than real. Wells attempted to classify them (and the divisions of the poem) into characteristics appropriate to the Active, Contemplative, and "Mixed" or Prelatical Lives; in this he was followed with varying degrees of enthusiasm by Chambers, Coghill, and more recently Dunning, and Robertson and Huppé.[6] But, as has often been pointed out, taken together, the definitions

---

6. Henry W. Wells, "The Philosophy of *Piers Plowman*," *PMLA*, LIII (1938), 339–49; R. W. Chambers, *Man's Unconquerable Mind* (London,

do not support this division.[7] For example, the command *dilige inimicos* applies to all Christians, not just bishops, and the virtue of not wasting time is surely an aspect of living righteously. Frank writes with considerable understatement that "the relationship between the terms and their meanings is not very stable." [8]

Other critics have more or less thrown up their hands at the prospect of wedding the definitions to the sections of the poem that bear their names and have attempted instead to characterize the sections themselves. Meroney has suggested that the terms refer to the mystic way of the Purgative, Illuminative, and Unitive states.[9] This division is followed reluctantly by Donaldson, on the grounds that Dowel, Dobet, and Dobest seem to refer more to inner states than religious vocations.[10] And, indeed, the definitions given in the poem describe states of the soul at least as frequently as they do religious actions; moreover, the *Vita de Dowel* and the *Vita de Dobet* are psychological and contemplative in nature. But, as Donaldson himself points out, "As it stands, Do-Best does not seem to contain much that is suggestive of the vision of God of St. Bernard." [11] Frank rejects this scheme entirely on the grounds that the chaotic social vision which concludes the poem "can hardly be the poet's dramatization of the contemplative union with God." [12] He suggests instead, as Wells did before him,[13] that the three divisions are governed by the gifts of the Father, the gifts of the Son, and the gifts of the Holy Spirit. This scheme is somewhat more satisfactory than the other two, since at least it does not require that the three divisions of the poem be seen as getting conceptually "better," although again the poem does not really reflect it. The *Vita de Dobest* depicts a society lacking divine gifts of *any* sort; the contemplative vision of divine mysteries which concludes the *Vita de Dobet* should technically be one of the gifts of the

---

1939), pp. 149 ff.; Nevill Coghill, "The Character of Piers Plowman," *MÆ*, II (1933), 108–35; T. P. Dunning, "The Structure of the B-Text of *Piers Plowman*," *RES*, N.S., VII (1956), 225–37; D. W. Robertson and B. F. Huppé, *Piers Plowman and Scriptural Tradition* (Princeton, N.J., 1951).

7. See especially R. W. Frank, Jr., *Piers Plowman and the Scheme of Salvation* (New Haven, Conn., 1957), pp. 34–44.

8. *Ibid.*, p. 38.

9. Meroney, "Longe Wille," pp. 10 ff.

10. E. T. Donaldson, *Piers Plowman: The C-Text and Its Poet* (New Haven, Conn., 1949), pp. 158–59.

11. *Ibid.*, p. 197.

12. Frank, *Piers Plowman and the Scheme of Salvation*, p. 95.

13. Wells, "Construction of *Piers Plowman*," *passim*.

Spirit;[14] and if knowledge is one of the gifts of the Father, Will has not received it during the course of the *Vita de Dowel,* as he complains to Anima at the beginning of Passus XV. We are left with a multitude of ill-matching definitions, three sections of the poem named, with apparent arbitrariness, for three terms, and no clear relationship among them. S. S. Hussey has stated the case succinctly when he writes that Dowel, Dobet, and Dobest represent an equation with "one unknown and two multiples of it." [15] Or as Piers Plowman himself says, reported by Clergy, "Dowel and Dobet aren two infinites, / Whiche infinites, with a feith, fynden oute Dobest" (XIII. 127–28).

It seems to me that all attempts to define the relationship among these terms clearly, or to relate them to the sections of the poem that bear their names, have been proceeding from the wrong assumptions. The important question is not how they are related. The fact that so much critical manipulation[16] has been required to answer that question should be enough indication that it is misdirected. The important question, rather, is why those definitions are there at all, and why there are so many of them. Dowel, Dobet, and Dobest are self-evident terms—or should be. It has always struck me as curious that Langland's terms are so much simpler than those of his critics; Dowel means *doing well,* a far more commonplace concept than the Active Life, or the Purgative State, or the gifts of the Father. That Langland should feel the need to define the term at all is curious; the Bible, the preachers, the Fathers had laid out quite clearly what the life of doing well should be for a Christian. Evidently, he has far less confidence in the meaning of the word than do those critics who use it as a springboard to discover other levels of allegory.

As we have seen, Langland not only defines Dowel but also redefines it and redefines it. He does so in ways that confuse more than clarify, and yet there is great urgency behind the definitions. Will keeps asking his question, though he has received many answers to it, all at least partially satisfactory. None of the definitions is rejected as wrong: the procedure suggests, rather, that they are all somehow inadequate, as though the verbal sign itself had no viable meaning for Will, pointed to no self-evident idea.

---

14. As John describes himself being "in the Spirit" at the start of his vision, Rev. 1:10.

15. S. S. Hussey, "Langland, Hilton, and the Three Lives," *RES,* N.S., VII (1956), p. 149.

16. For example, Dunning, "The Structure of the B-Text," characterizes two of the definitions of Dowel as "accidents" (p. 232).

It is surely significant that all of Will's teachers accept the fact that the term needs definition; not even the bluntest of them tells him that Dowel means doing well and that's the end of it. Such a process of continual definition suggests that the sign itself is being tested, explored, even stretched to the limits of its conceptual significance. In a very real sense Dowel is a word in search of a referent in this poem—hence the multitude of its definitions, the felt inadequacy of all of them, the confusion which results in a term which should be, by its very nature, perfectly clear.

Piers Plowman is a poem of searching, structured according to a series of pilgrimages—the pilgrimage of the folk on the field in the Visio, Will's pilgrimage in the Vita de Dowel and Vita de Dobet, which brings him at last to Unity-Holychurch, Conscience' pilgrimage at the end. And the pilgrimage motif early in the poem is cast in terms of a search for St. Truth. The central problem in Piers Plowman is not a moral one, though its moral application is apparent; it is one of knowing Truth. Doing well depends on knowledge, a knowledge which is no longer secure, as Will's persistent questions make clear. The cognitive concern of Piers Plowman is always basic to its moral and social concerns; even when the poem concentrates on social issues, these are inevitably recast as cognitive and perceptual problems, as the progress from the Visio to the Vita makes clear. This view of the problem of right action is venerably orthodox: "Ye shall know the Truth, and the Truth shall make you free." True understanding produces freedom of the will, which is the agent of moral action. Moreover, the interaction of understanding and will, according to Augustine, is God's image in the soul, an image man must fulfill and perfect in order to be saved.[17] Piers Plowman is not basically a moral poem, or a social one, or even an apocalyptic one; it is an epistemological poem, a poem about the problem of knowing truly. Will's question to Lady Holy Church at the beginning of Passus I is the question of the entire poem: "Mercy, Madame, what [may] this [by]mene?" (I. 11).

As Langland uses it, allegory is a cognitive mode, a means of discovering invisible and ineffable truth through the images and analogies of visible things. His understanding of the nature of allegory derives from the view that all visible things, including language, are signs which point to some-

---

17. In De trinitate X, Augustine argues that the soul is created in a trinitarian image of the triune God. He finds several trinitarian analogies in its operations, but the most important lies in the relationship of memory, understanding, and will, which he identifies as the true image of God in which the soul is created.

thing beyond themselves. A sign conveys knowledge; it is a cognitive form, the *sacramentum visible invisibilis formae*.[18] Yet, the new understanding which the poem seeks through signs is not a known goal to Langland; he regards his allegory as a tool of exploration, to be tested and proved, rather than as having a fixed, previously known referent. Langland's desire to achieve a new understanding expresses itself in his discomfiture with a corrupted rhetoric and his desire to forge a new one, to find new signs of Truth or at least to redeem the old ones.

The exploratory attitude toward the language of allegory is a unique feature of this poem, and is basic to it. However, it derives from two fundamental medieval perceptions: that cognition comes through signs, and that all signs are basically constructed on the model of verbal signs.[19] At the heart of all medieval theories concerning knowledge is the problem of signs.[20] God reveals himself in signs, true signs, which if properly interpreted can yield true, if partial, knowledge of him. The most complete

---

18. Chenu, *Nature, Man, and Society*, p. 126.

19. Chenu, *ibid.*, emphasizes the primacy of Augustinian understanding of the nature of signs as *"translatio verborum*, the transference of words" (p. 120), in the medieval conception of signs. He clearly distinguishes this view from the pseudo-Dionysian view, which was of lesser influence: "in Augustinian symbolism, it was literary method that dominated" (p. 121), whereas the pseudo-Dionysian view is more mystical, an instrument of the *via negativa*, "the means by which one could approach the mystery; [the *symbolon*] was homogeneous with mystery and not a simple epistemological sign more or less conventional in character" (p. 123).

20. Some particularly good recent discussions of this dominant characteristic of medieval thought are: E. Gilson, *The Christian Philosophy of St. Augustine*, trans. L. Lynch (London, 1961); Chenu, *Nature, Man and Society*, especially the chapter entitled "The Symbolist Mentality"; Marcia Colish, *The Mirror of Language* (New Haven, Conn., 1968). Two standard histories of medieval thought trace the development of the analysis of signs throughout the period: E. Gilson, *History of Christian Philosophy in the Middle Ages* (London, 1955), and F. C. Copleston, *A History of Philosophy*, Vol. II (1950; rpt. New York, 1957). For discussions of the problem of verbal signs as it applies to medieval developments in logic, see Philotheus Boehner, *Medieval Logic* (Chicago, 1952), and his essays on William of Ockham's "Theory of Truth," "Theory of Signification," and "Theory of Supposition and the Notion of Truth," in *Collected Articles on Ockham* (St. Bonaventure, N.Y., 1958); see also Desmond P. Henry, *The Logic of St. Anselm* (Oxford, 1967). Two works dealing with related fields, which shed a great deal of light on the medieval perceptions of the nature of signs, are H. de Lubac, *Exégèse médiévale*, 4 vols. (Paris, 1959–64), and E. de Bruyne, *Etudes d'esthétique médiévale*, 3 vols. (Bruges, 1946).

revelations have occurred in Christ, the Word made flesh expressed in earthly actions and language, and in Scripture, the Word of God expressed through the language of the Biblical writers. The nature of language, to the Middle Ages, is thus not a peripheral concern; it lies at the basis of God's revelation and of man's ability to understand it.

Ancient and medieval views of language begin with the premise that words are signs.[21] All signs, including words, are "things used to signify something," as Augustine defines them in De doctrina christiana, following Cicero and Aristotle.[22] There is a real relationship between sign and signatum, a thing which signifies and a thing which is signified. Understanding thus depends upon interpretation, the discovery of how the significator is revealed in the sign and what relationship the sign bears to that which signifies it. This analysis of the process of cognition presupposes that there exists an inherent and generally stable relationship between signs and what they signify. A sign is "a thing which causes us to think of something beyond the impression the thing itself makes upon the senses";[23] thus, the significance of the sign is inherent within it, either through God's agency or through the agreed-upon conventions of a particular human

---

21. One mark of this fundamental view of language is the curious status given to etymology by the ancients and by medieval writers, whereby the etymology is regarded as an acceptable proof of the real nature of the thing signified by the word. This attitude is best expressed among the ancients in Plato's dialogue, Cratylus. Cratylus, whose views are adopted with some major modifications by Socrates, argues that the name of a thing can express at least part of its real essence, if it is a "true" name (Cratylus, in The Dialogues of Plato, trans. B. Jowett, 4th ed., Vol. I. [New York, 1937], especially pp. 179–80, 228). It is thus possible to discover something of the true nature of the thing signified by examining the word carefully, by learning to read it correctly. In the Cratylus, Socrates proceeds to demonstrate how these names express the real essence of what they signify by indulging in a long series of etymologies. There is considerable argument over how seriously these are to be taken (see the discussion of A. E. Taylor, Plato, The Man and His Work [London, 1949], pp. 75–89, and P. Friedlander, Plato, trans. H. Meyerhoff [New York, 1964], II, 196–218). But there is no doubt that etymology was taken very seriously by the Latin grammarians, and that through them it became an essential branch of grammatica in the Middle Ages. Demonstration of the real nature of a thing through the etymology of its name is an accepted proof found among nearly all the theologians and poets of the Middle Ages. In Piers Plowman, Anima proves that the heathen are by nature unregulated by deriving the word from "heath," apparently correctly (XV. 450–51).

22. Augustine De doctrina christiana (trans. D. W. Robertson) I. 2. 2.

23. Ibid. II. 1. 1.

language, for the sign "causes" the thing it signifies to be understood or known in some way.[24] For Augustine, signification was accomplished through the recollection or understanding within the mind caused by the perception of the sign.[25] This understanding can be either right or wrong, depending on how well one has learned to read or interpret signs. Thus, all understanding, like all signs, is built on an interpretive linguistic model, the art of correct reading.

This emphasis on the primacy of the arts of reading was in part a phenomenon of medieval education.[26] Grammar and rhetoric were the basis of the medieval curriculum until the twelfth century. After that, dialectic achieved the position of primary importance. All three of these arts are concerned with the analysis of language: the relationships among classes of words as reflecting truthful relations among things; the relationship of verbal statement to truthful content; the truthful relationship among

---

24. The difference between this view of language and that of an influential modern school may be realized by contrasting Ernst Cassirer's remark that words are "not imitations, but *organs* of reality," *Language and Myth,* trans. S. Langer (New York, 1946), p. 8. Commenting on Adam's naming of the animals in Gen. 2:19, Augustine suggests that Adam spoke a truer tongue than any now spoken, pride having built the Tower of Babel and divided the languages of men: "Unam sane linguam primitus fuisse didicimus, antequam superbia turris illius post diluvium fabricatae, in diversos signorum sonas humanam divideret societatem. . . . Illa certe tunc loquebatur Adam, et in ea lingua . . . sunt istae voces articulatae" (*De genesi ad litteram* IX. 12 [Migne, *PL* XXXIV. 401]). Evidently, Augustine believed language to have been darkened by the Fall (or at least by the Babel incident) and does not seem to believe with others of the Fathers that Adam spoke Hebrew or any other known language. He also suggests that Adam's names spoke directly to the animals' comprehension, and that the name was understood by the animal as a true sign of its natural obedience to man: "Neque enim sicut indagant atque adigunt venantes vel aucupantes ad retia, quaecumque animantia capiunt, ita hoc factum esse credendum est; aut vox aliqua iussionis de nube facta est eis verbis, quae rationales animae audientes, intelligere, atque obedire assolent" (*De genesi ad litteram* [Migne, *PL* XXXIV. 402]).

25. Chenu's analysis of the Augustinian view of signs is pertinent: "Augustine's 'sign' belonged on the level of his psychology of knowledge and was developed with materials drawn from that psychology. . . . It was consequently the knower himself who was the principle and rule of the 'sign'; it was he who gave the 'sign' its value, over and beyond any objective basis in the nature of things. . . . In any Christian conception of 'signs,' therefore, the interior life of man, and above all faith, were primary" (*Nature, Man, and Society,* p. 125).

26. Colish, *Mirror of Language,* especially pp. xi–xii.

propositions expressed in language. "Grammatica est scientia recte loquendi," says Isidore of Seville, "et origo et fundamentum liberalium litterarum." [27] But right speaking, *recte loquendum,* and its corollary, right reading, *recte legendum,* are not simply the foundation of liberal letters. Since God has revealed himself in his Word, religious understanding itself takes on a predominately literary model. *Recte legendum,* the right interpretation of signs, is the foundation of all religious knowledge. The accepted etymologies in the Middle Ages of both "religion" and "intelligence" derive the words from the Latin *legere.* Thus, Isidore, following Cicero, derives *religio* from *relegere,* "to read again" or "to read aloud." [28] St. Thomas Aquinas derives *intelligere* from *intus legere,* which he explains as the science of correctly reading the truth concealed in the outward signs of God's revelation.[29]

No major Christian philosopher was more concerned with the problem of signs, particularly verbal signs, and of their use in truthful reading and speaking than Augustine, whose writings on this subject were deeply influential throughout the Middle Ages. For Augustine, the problem of Christian knowledge is centrally focused upon the nature of verbal sign and the proper use of language.[30] In large part, the *Confessions* trace his search

---

27. Isidore of Seville *Etymologiarum* (ed. W. Lindsay) Lib. I. 5.

28. *Ibid.* Lib. VIII. 2. Cf. C. T. Lewis and C. Short, *A Latin Dictionary* (Oxford, 1879), s. v. *religiosus.*

29. St. Thomas Aquinas *Summa theologiae* II–II^ae. A. VIII. a. 1. Edition of the Biblioteca de Autores Christianos (Madrid, 1961), reprinted from the Leonine text (hereafter cited as *ST*).

30. As Colish says, "Augustine projected a redeemed rhetoric as the outcome of a revealed wisdom. On the basis of this theory, a twofold linguistic transformation was in order; the faculty of human speech was to be recast as a Pauline mirror, faithfully mediating God to man in the present life; and the agencies appointed for the translation of man's partial knowledge by faith into his complete knowledge of God by direct vision were to be redefined as modes of verbal expression" (*Mirror of Language,* pp. 19–20). Her contention that Augustine's sign theory derives primarily from his consideration of verbal signs is also that of Chenu, *Nature, Man, and Society* (pp. 125–27 especially). A suggestive analysis of Augustine's rhetoric has been made by Erich Auerbach, "Sermo humilis," in *Literary Language and Its Public in Late Latin Antiquity and in the Middle Ages,* trans. R. Mannheim (New York, 1965), pp. 27–66. My discussion of Augustine's analysis of signs is greatly indebted to these works, and is based on Augustine's treatises: *De magistro,* ed. G. Weigel, *Corpus scriptorum ecclesiasticorum latinorum,* Vol. LXXVII (Vindobonae, 1961); *De doctrina christiana,* ed. G. M. Green, *Corpus scriptorum ecclesiasticorum latinorum,* Vol. LXXX (Vindobonae, 1963); and *De trinitate* (Migne, PL XLII, 819–1098; as well as the *Confessiones,* ed. W. H. D. Rouse, Loeb Classical Library (London, 1912).

for a new Christian rhetoric to replace the false rhetoric of the Latin schools, which had blinded him to the truths of God. Augustine's account of how he was seduced by Cicero's style from an appreciation of the simple style of Scripture illustrates this very well:

> For when I studied the Scriptures then I did not feel as I am writing about them now. They seemed to me unworthy of comparison with the grand style of Cicero. For my pride shrank from their modesty, and my sharp eye was not penetrating enough to see into their depths.[31]

On the other hand, he recounts how he was unable to be "swept away" by the *Hortensius,* the work which had so impressed him, because it did not contain "the name of Christ." [32] In both of these statements, Augustine attaches a cognitive value to language which is independent of its persuasive power. Indeed, the felicitousness of Cicero's style is seen to be a handicap, for it prevents Augustine, in his unconverted ignorance, from considering the inner truthfulness of Cicero's words as compared to those of Scripture. Scripture speaks correctly, Cicero eloquently; in this contrast of values lies the heart of Augustine's attitude toward language, suggesting as it does his sharp division of the superficial appearance of the literal words from their hidden *allegoria,* within which lies the cognitive value of language.

Ars recte loquendi is thus preeminent for Augustine, for without a true rhetoric reflecting a true intelligence (*intus legendum*) of the revealed Word there can be no salvation. His *De doctrina christiana* sets out the principles of this rhetoric as well as guidelines to the true reading upon which it must be based. Augustine defines his theory of signs in terms of a metaphor of pilgrimage:

> Thus in this mortal life, wandering from God, if we wish to return to our native country where we can be blessed we should use this world . . . so that the "invisible things" of God "being understood by the things that are made" [Rom. 1:20] may be seen, that is, so that by means of corporal and temporal things we may comprehend the eternal and spiritual.[33]

He assumes, with Paul, that corporal things, including language, can enable us to see the true nature of unseen things, if rightly understood and employed.

---

31. Augustine *Confessiones* (trans. Rex Warner) III. 5.
32. *Ibid.* III. 4.
33. Augustine *De doctrina christiana* I. 4. 4.

The purpose of language is to teach or rather to remind the listener of the truth. Words themselves do not teach, as Augustine tells Adeodatus in *De magistro*, but are known to be truthful by being referred to the Truth which dwells within both the speaker and the listener, which is Christ.[34] Thus, Christ is the true significator of all language, just as He is the source of all understanding. Augustine's doctrine of verbal sign is worked out most fully in his *De trinitate*, where he develops the analogy between the rational mind and the Trinity. He argues that the image of God in which man is created resides primarily in the "trinitarian" relationship between memory, understanding, and will. The mind's understanding is particularly the image of Christ, as Wisdom and as the Word. Man forms within himself an "inner word":

> with the eye of the mind . . . we perceive that eternal truth, from which all temporal things have been made, the form according to which we are, and by which we effect something either in ourselves or in bodies with a true and right reason. This true knowledge of things, thence conceived, we hear within us as a word, and beget by speaking from within.[35]

This "inner word" is an "enigma," or allegory, of the Word itself, a true, if partial, image of it. The Word is thus the significator of the inner word, which is the mind's understanding. This inner word is "the word which we speak in our heart, and it is neither Greek, nor Latin, nor any other language."[36] In turn, the inner word gives meaning to what the speaker says: "the word which sounds without is a sign of the word which shines within."[37]

Thus, the Christian speaker is under great obligation to use the signs of language with a constant regard for their true signification. Augustine assumes that there is a real relationship of significance between the spoken word and the inner word, as there is between the inner word and the Word. Good language observes this relationship; the task of Christian rhetoric is to discover in the sciences of language those forms which truly manifest this threefold signification. Nothing is worse to Augustine than a good orator on a bad subject; yet such a man is evil not because he is in himself

---

34. Augustine *De magistro* XI–XII.
35. Augustine *De trinitate* (trans. Stephen McKenna) IX. 7. 12.
36. *Ibid.* XV. 10. 19.
37. *Ibid.* XV. 11. 20.

a bad man (though he is likely to be that too) but because he distorts the real purpose of language and displaces it from its true significator. Signs displaced from their signification are worse than useless, for they then become signs of a corrupt understanding, an inner word begotten in *cupiditas* rather than in *caritas*.[38]

The Augustinian view that spoken language is a sign of the mind's understanding expressed in the inner word is amplified, in conjunction with other influences, in the work of the "speculative grammar," begun during the twelfth century but continuing through the fourteenth.[39] The speculative grammarians saw in the rules of grammar a structure which corresponded to the ways in which the intellect itself operates. This structure is independent of particular languages, a sort of "universal grammar" reflecting the essential nature of constructed speech as a mirror of the understanding.[40] One of these grammars, the *De modis significandi* of Thomas von Erfurt, analyzes language according to a passive and active aspect corresponding to the passive and active intellect. He speaks of the three "passions" of speech, by which he means "construction," "congruity," and "perfection," saying that

> voice-sounds which are significant upon utterance, such as grammatical sentences, are marks of the passions which are in the soul, *viz.*, signs of the concept of the mind or of the soul. . . . the construction or sentence in grammar is finally for the sake of expressing the concept of the mind.[41]

Thomas' treatise is only one of many attempts to demonstrate that grammatical rules are signs, or images, of the processes of thought and the

---

38. *Ibid.* IX. 8. 13.

39. A good though brief account of the general characteristics of speculative grammar is given by R. H. Robins, *Ancient and Medieval Grammatical Theory in Europe* (London, 1951), pp. 76–90. See also the remarks of Gilson, *History of Christian Philosophy,* pp. 312–14, especially his emphasis on the influential role played by Roger Bacon in the development of a philosophical study of grammar. I regret that I was unable to obtain the recent study of G. L. Bursill-Hall, *Speculative Grammars of the Middle Ages* (The Hague, 1971), in time to make use of it in my discussion.

40. I use the term "universal grammar" advisedly, for, although it belongs particularly to the Port Royal grammarians of the seventeenth century, it seems to me to be in part applicable to the medieval development under discussion, which bears some analogies to the later, rationalist theory.

41. Thomas von Erfurt, *De modis significandi sive grammatica speculativa,* trans. C. G. Wallis (Ann Arbor, Mich., 1938).

processes of Nature.[42] From the twelfth century on, grammar is frequently analyzed as an allegorical mirror, like the mirror of Nature and the mirror of history, a real correspondence to the processes of man's mind and to man's relationship with the things around him, including God.

This philosophical and literary *topos* is incorporated fully by Langland in the infamous "grammatical metaphor" of Passus IV of the C-Text, in which he develops the relationship of God, man, and Christ in terms of the grammatical accord between an antecedent and its adjective.[43] This accord is expressed by the term "rect" as contrasted to "indirect." These two terms of grammatical relationship are translated into ones of theological relationship. Thus, "man ys relatif rect yf he be ryht trewe; / He a-cordeth with Christ in kynde . . . / In case . . . / In numbre" (C. IV. 357–60). The "indirect" relationship, on the other hand, "ys inliche to coueyte / . . . With-oute resoun to rewarde, nauȝt recching of the peple" (C. IV. 373, 376). The concept of *rectitudo* as applied to the notion of truth is a scholastic commonplace.[44] Indeed, the standard definition of truth is based upon a conformity, *aedaquatio* or *rectitudo,* between a proposition and what it signifies.[45] Truth in logical statements is a matter, first, of the internal, grammatical correctness of the statement, and then of the rightness of what it signifies. But a proposition which does not fulfill the requirements of grammatical correctness can be neither true nor false; grammatical coherence is thus the first logical requirement for truth.[46] The notion of *rectitudo* was soon extended beyond the strictly logical realm of propositions to include moral theology as well.[47] (Indeed, the near-identity of moral

---

42. On the development of the literary motif of the grammatical metaphor, see E. R. Curtius, *European Literature and the Latin Middle Ages,* trans. W. R. Trask (New York, 1963), pp. 414–16. The most notable demonstration of the analogy between grammar and Nature is in John of Salisbury's *Metalogicon* Lib. I. 13–25 (Migne, *PL* CXCIX. 823–946).

43. A recent detailed study of this passage is that of Margaret Amassian and James Sadowsky, "A Study of the Grammatical Metaphor in 'Piers Plowman' C: IV: 335–409," *NM,* LXXII (1971), 457–76.

44. See Boehner, "Theory of Truth" and "Theory of Signification," in *Collected Articles on Ockham.*

45. "Veritas est adaequatio rei et intellectus, sicut generaliter adaequatio signi et significati." See the discussion of this maxim by Boehner, *ibid.,* p. 180.

46. See Henry, *Logic of St. Anselm,* pp. 230–31.

47. For the extension of the term *rectitudo* to apply to moral action, see Henry's interesting remarks, *ibid.,* pp. 230–39.

rightness and rightness of understanding and speaking is already contained in Augustine.)[48]

Thus, rightness of moral choice is dependent on rightness of will and of understanding, an idea whose relevance to *Piers Plowman* has been rightly emphasized before.[49] However, Langland also seems to have clearly realized that rightness as a moral term takes its significance from its use as a concept in logic—and before that, as a concept of grammar. *Rect* will and *rect* understanding are inseparably linked with *rect* language, as the C-Text passage makes clear. Langland evidently regarded language, properly used, as a truthful sign of divinity, and, in the tradition of Augustine, he was conservative in his understanding of verbal signs and their relationship to their ultimate significator, Christ.

The search for St. Truth is conducted in terms of a search for and an analysis of the signs that truly express him. This concern with the truthfulness of signs, analyzed in terms of verbal forms and images, is evident in the devices which the poet uses—personification of concepts, elaborate and fluid metaphor—and in the choice of dream vision, the most symbolic of literary modes, as the medium for his poem. The multitude of allegorizing devices bespeaks a concern with the very process of allegory-making itself, and with the verbal medium in which Truth dwells, especially in poetry. Langland is in his own way searching for a truly Christian rhetoric as urgently as Augustine did, and for much the same reason—out of a sense that a rhetoric has failed and has led men away from Truth rather than toward him. Language is continually remade and reexamined by the poet. Indeed, one reason why so many of the schemes imposed upon it fail to explain *Piers Plowman* adequately is that they derive from an outside rhetoric, instead of addressing themselves to the language being forged by the poem itself.

An example of how the poem makes its own language is Passus IX, which is devoted to the definition of Dowel. Wit begins his discussion of the term with a description of the castle of Caro, whose mistress is Anima, who in turn is served by Dowel, Dobet, and Dobest. This fable is followed

---

48. In *De doctrina christiana*, Augustine admits that good doctrine can be preached by a sinful man, but it is clear that the best understanding and speaking come from spiritually upright teachers (IV. 27. 59; IV. 29. 62).

49. Edward Vasta, "Truth, the Best Treasure, in *Piers Plowman*," *PQ*, XLIV (1956), 17–29, especially pp. 23–24. See also Vasta's book, *The Spiritual Basis of Piers Plowman* (The Hague, 1965), pp. 63–64.

by a discussion of Inwit, of unkind godparents and unkind bishops, and by three more definitions of Dowel, Dobet, and Dobest (IX. 94–97). Next, there is a discussion of true marriage, followed by the story of Cain, who first brought care upon earth, the Flood, more discussion of marriage, counsel to young men to wed rather than sin, counsel to married couples, a few remarks on bastardy, and finally two more sets of definitions of Dowel, Dobet, and Dobest. All these devices—moral counsel, Biblical lessons, allegorical fable—are methods of defining Dowel. The passus circles back in on the term continually, each new spiral being another perspective on its meaning, another context in which to place the term. The so-called digressions in this passus are not really digressions at all but different angles of vision producing modified or new understanding of its key term. In this way a word like Dowel is constantly explored, tried out in new contexts, new relationships. The definitions of Dowel in Passus IX occur not only in those lines in which Langland mentions the word—the whole section is about the term, each topic being a step in forging its meaning. And by the end of the section it is clear that Dowel is a word of manifold complexity. No outside source can possibly tell us what the word really means; the concept is being created by the text of the poem itself.

Nor is the desire to make a new rhetoric confined to the poem's key terms; it informs its entire structural development as well. *Piers Plowman* explores many different kinds of concepts and forms of allegory, rejecting those it finds overly imperfect or misleading, seeking constantly for a more truthful kind of sign. This explains the many different, often confusingly various, types of allegorical language found in the poem; the same things keep being said, but always in somewhat different form, each change of form also revealing a new cognitive slant. As the structure of the sign changes, so does the understanding it produces of that which signifies it, sometimes for the better, more often, at least in this poem, for the worse. One of the most original features of *Piers Plowman* lies precisely in the changing forms of the poem's allegory, from the rapid variations of the Prologue, through the predominance of conceptual personifications in the *Visio* and the *Vita de Dowel,* to the gradual attempts, using figural allegory and language, to forge a fully redeemed speech in the *Vita de Dobet,* which then collapse, drawing the world with them, in the apocalypse of the *Vita de Dobest.* And the change of form both signals and expresses a progressively fuller understanding in the poem of the ineffable nature of that which makes significant all language and all action, the Word itself.

To see the poem in this way is to insist that Piers Plowman be taken seriously *as a poem,* not merely as an allegory. One of the major difficulties with much recent criticism has been the underlying assumption that, because *Piers Plowman* contains allegory, it is enough to translate its various allegorical devices into their "second level" of meaning, without examining the ways in which those devices embody, explore, and modify the concepts to which they point, and the ways in which they bring various concepts into relationship within the poem. It is as if one were to attempt an understanding of one of Keats's odes by looking up all the words in the dictionary and simply listing their meanings. Such an exercise may have its uses, but it does not get one very far into the experience of the poem. To read *Piers Plowman* is to be immediately and continually confused by a barrage of topics, figures, words; and no appeal to schemes of the Active, Contemplative, and Prelatical Lives, or to Augustinian, or Thomistic, or monastic, or Joachite theology[50] will save the reader faced with the necessity of making sense of what he reads moment by moment. Any criticism of the poem which does not honestly start from this experience is doomed to failure, wholly or in part.

No one has yet denied that *Piers Plowman* is labyrinthine in structure, overly discursive, and badly organized. Yet, at least one of its apologists has insisted in the face of all the evidence that its author has "a strong architectural instinct for planning and carrying out a great composition. . . . It is not he who loses himself in a tangle of digressions."[51] This implied

---

50. The investigation which has sought to apply concepts of medieval theology to this poem has been most illuminating, and I do not wish to slight the many studies from which our knowledge of the poem has profited greatly, and to which I am much indebted. Augustinian theology has been used most notably, though in very different ways, by Robertson and Huppé, *Piers Plowman and Scriptural Tradition,* and by Sister Rosa Bernard Donna, *Despair and Hope: A Study in Langland and Augustine* (Washington, D.C., 1948). Thomistic concepts have been applied most successfully by T. P. Dunning, *Piers Plowman: An Interpretation of the A-Text* (Dublin, 1937), and Greta Hort, *Piers Plowman and Contemporary Religious Thought* (London, 1938). Monastic theology has often been applied, most judiciously, by Morton W. Bloomfield, *Piers Plowman as a Fourteenth-Century Apocalypse* (New Brunswick, N.J., 1961). Bloomfield's book also makes the most complete links between the poem and the mystical theology of Joachim of Flora. Popular mystical and devotional writings have been most thoroughly investigated in relation to the poem, since the suggestion was made long ago by J. J. Jusserand that the poem reflected mystical theology; see his *Piers Plowman: A Contribution to the History of English Mysticism* (London, 1894). A recent investigation of the poem in these terms is Vasta, *The Spiritual Basis of Piers Plowman.*

51. Nevill Coghill, "The Pardon of Piers Plowman" (Sir Israel Gollancz

negative judgment of the reader seems to me to be wholly misdirected. For the fact is that the confusion *Piers Plowman* produces is inherent in the very nature of the experience it records; it is reflected by the fluidity of all its constantly changing and various elements. Will's experience in this poem is not to realize a design, but to explore a vision; its various forms of personification, figuralism, fable, metaphor, exegesis, social satire, and sermon are not the building blocks of a cathedral but are often inadequate tools for charting unseen and perhaps unseeable terrain (or so the ending of the poem would imply). If T. S. Eliot's characterization of great poetry as a raid on the unknown is at all true, *Piers Plowman* must rank highly indeed.

It is important to realize that *Piers Plowman* records the process of a particular mind dealing with problems of meaning in the form of a visionary poem. There are few poems which express such a strongly individual, even eccentric, intelligence. The best argument against the multiple-authorship theory, to my mind, is the extreme improbability that two (let alone four or five) people who lived in England in the later fourteenth century could have been enough alike in their oddity to have jointly written this poem.[52] What is striking about the poem is the consistently extraordinary thought processes of its poet—how and why Langland thinks about things as he does, rather than what he thinks.

The poet's peculiarity is evident even in the simplest features of the narrative. For example, it is most unusual that Will wakes up and goes to sleep so frequently, at moments in the vision which often seem chosen out of pure whimsey. Indeed, the line between sleeping and waking becomes so hazy that the two blend into one another, as when Will, awake, meets the personification of Need in Passus XX of the B-Text, or is questioned by Reason at the beginning of Passus VI of the C-Text. But the fluidity of this relationship has a serious purpose, as it gradually merges dream with waking life, casting into doubt the ordinary perceptions of reality which are made possible only when there is a secure division between being awake and being asleep. This particular effect could not have been achieved without waking Will up and sending him back to sleep so many times.

In defense of the poem's often haphazard movement, which he thinks is nonetheless controlled, one critic reminds us that during the Middle Ages,

---

Memorial Lecture), *Proceedings of the British Academy*, XXXI (1945), pp. 8-9.

52. For a convincing review of the textual and historical evidence for authorship, which seems to have laid the multiple-authorship theories to rest, see George Kane, *Piers Plowman: The Evidence for Authorship* (London, 1965).

there may coexist in the work of art both a formidable simplicity of main design and a degree of minor graphic representation in which the eye loses itself in detail.[53]

The movement of medieval art tends to be circular or concentric, rather than linear. But this statement, useful though it is in defending Langland against a charge of total disorganization, does not account for the structural fluidity of *Piers Plowman.* The abundance of small sculptures in a cathedral like Chartres never detracts from the logically articulated movement of the building as a whole.[54] There is no question about which is subordinate, no sense of conflict between the main forms and the details of style. But there are important structural features of Langland's poem which work against the emergence of a general and simple design. Indeed, these features preclude the possibility of a dominant form for the poem, and thus exhibit a quality not common in medieval art.[55] In *Piers Plowman,* relationships of time and space, and of objects to one another, are indistinct. Things within the poem are not seen as coherent entities but are constantly in the process of changing into something else. The degree of distinction and coherence which marks characters and episodes in other medieval works, including allegorical visions, is simply not present in *Piers Plowman.*

Langland's disregard for naturalistic narrative structures can easily be seen when one examines the temporal progression of Will's visions, particularly of the two which contain inner dreams. The inner dream is not unique in medieval poems—what is remarkable is Langland's way of handling it. Dante, for instance, has several dreams during his ascent of the mountain of Purgatory. But Dante awakens exactly where he slept, after an appropriate time has elapsed. The inner dream is carefully distinguished from the main vision as a separate and distinct unit within it; it bears the same relationship to the main vision that a dream does to a person's waking hours. However, the secure structure which marks Dante's poem is not present in *Piers Plowman.* The first inner dream occurs in Passus XI. Scripture rebukes

---

53. John Lawlor, *Piers Plowman: An Essay in Criticism* (London, 1962), p. 236.

54. Cf. Erwin Panofsky, *Gothic Architecture and Scholasticism* (1951; rpt. New York, 1957), pp. 35–60.

55. Charles Muscatine has commented on the insecure structure of the poem, "The Locus of Action in Medieval Literature," *R Ph,* XVII (1963), 115–22. See also the comments of John Burrow, "Words, Works and Will: Theme and Structure in *Piers Plowman,*" in *Piers Plowman: Critical Approaches,* ed. S. S. Hussey (London, 1969), p. 124.

Will for his lengthy analysis of Dowel, and Will "for wo and wratth of her speche" (XI. 3) falls asleep. In the inner dream he receives instruction from several persons, one of whom is Scripture, the character in his main dream whose rebuke caused him to fall asleep in the first place. This may seem to be only a minor illogicality on Langland's part, but the point is that it is an illogicality which most poets—especially medieval ones—would never permit.

The second inner dream, the vision of the Tree of Charity, is even more interesting. When Will wakens from his first inner dream, he finds himself back in the time and place of the main dream. But the sequence of the second is continued into the main dream. Having witnessed the Incarnation and early life of Christ in the inner dream, Will awakens to meet Faith going to the Crucifixion, and his vision proceeds in time through the Resurrection. Inner dream and main dream have merged completely. The fact that Will wakes up at all seems to be a structurally unjustifiable concession to a conventional formula, since the two visions have ceased to be separate in any meaningful way. The blurring of these spatial dimensions within the vision is analogous to the hazy demarcation between sleeping and waking which I noted earlier, and it serves the same purpose. In contrast to *The Divine Comedy,* whose secure structural features provide solid ground for the reader's perceptions, even in a visionary world, *Piers Plowman* deliberately fuzzes the dimensions of reality. Time and space are the building blocks of Dante's cathedral; for Langland, they become the problematical dimensions of a world whose meaning is in the process of continual change.

The structural procedure typified in the handling of the inner dreams makes it difficult to tell one's physical location, something one rarely has trouble with in Dante or in Chaucer. Nor can the illogical progression of *Piers Plowman* be explained by "dream logic." The puppy which scampers from nowhere across the landscape of Chaucer's *The Book of the Duchess,* and abruptly disappears when his function is completed, may indeed be accounted for in that way, since dream characters have a way of entering without explanation and then suddenly disappearing when the dreamer is no longer thinking about them.[56] This is the manner of dreams, and the manner of medieval dream visions, and there are many instances of it in *Piers Plowman.* The fluidity of the poem's dimensions, however, is another

---

56. See the discussion by Bertrand Bronson, *"The Book of the Duchess Reopened," PMLA,* LXVII (1952), 863–81.

matter. For example, most medieval poets are faithful to some definite time sequence for their vision. Dante is the most scrupulous, of course, with his carefully orchestrated three-day vision, but even *The Romance of the Rose* is dreamed in one night.

Then, too, most dreamers are fairly careful to make clear the details of the physical progress of their dreams. The landscape itself may be peculiar, but its physical presence is always insisted upon, and the details of the dreamer's movement through time and space are accounted for with some regard to physical verisimilitude. Chaucer, for example, tells us how he gets places—there are gates through which he must walk (or be pushed), or there is an eagle to carry him around. But Langland's poem exhibits no regard at all for physical limitations. Scripture, for example, can hop between two visions without our being told how she got there. It is not just "dream logic" operating here, but Langlandian logic, or rather nonlogic, in which time does not impose a fixed sequence even upon visionary events, but is a fluid medium in which things can happen sequentially, or simultaneously, or take dizzying leaps backward and forward, however it suits the poet's thought. Indeed, nothing in this poem exists in solid dimensions. At any given moment, any given object is capable of extending itself in any direction, and frequently does.

Such fluidity of structure reflects the fact that *Piers Plowman* is not a designed poem, like *The Divine Comedy, The Parliament of Fowls,* or even *The House of Fame.* It is rather a poem of searching, the record of a mental wandering to find a way to the soul's native country. Dante's poem records a journey through known territory, known always to his guides and eventually to the pilgrim as well. Langland is searching through unknown territory, his guides being the fluid, partially understood, often inadequate verbal signs of an insufficient rhetoric. Both *Piers Plowman* and *The Divine Comedy* seek understanding of Truth through the understanding of those signs which reveal it. But Dante's *signatum* is an object of thought which can be securely, if partially, known, while Langland's St. Truth becomes less and less apprehensible as the signs that lead to him prove to be more confused, inadequate, unknowable. To put the comparison in other terms, Dante's pilgrimage leads to a destination, Langland's only to another pilgrimage.

Both the fluidity and diversity of the devices which the poem employs in its search for St. Truth also reflect Langland's concern with making a new rhetoric. *Piers Plowman* is continually becoming meaningful rather than being so. No one device is adequate; Landland employs them all. Allegorical forms are forged in response to epistemological problems as they develop in the consciousness of the poet and dreamer, a fluid associative intelligence,

whose reality is the movement of its own thought. If the poem lacks coherence, it is only because the Truth it so urgently seeks is not coherent in
terms of those signs which Langland employs to conduct his search. Though
its cognitive insecurity often results in tedium when the poem keeps
circling back and back on itself in trying to invest its symbols with real
meaning, this unsureness is also the source of its peculiar power. There
is a St. Truth—if only we knew the way to get there.

The sense of emerging into unknown territory is strong at the beginning
of the Prologue. It is clearly evident in its dream landscape and in the
curious character of the narrator, yet it is seen more subtly but importantly
in the fluid structural relationships created by the different kinds of symbols
which the poet uses to describe his vision. Nearly every form of allegory
used later in the poem is used also in the Prologue, and an examination of
these various allegorical structures in their relationship to one another indicates the way in which Langland uses the fluid medium of his poem to
raise and explore the question of meaning.

The poem opens in the familiar, conventional world of medieval dream
visions—a leisurely walk on a May morning ending with a little nap by a
burbling brook:

> In a somer seson whan soft was the sonne,
> I shope me in [to a shroud] as I a shepe were,
> In habite as an heremite vnholy of workes,
> Went wyde in this world wondres to here.
> Ac on a May mornynge on Maluerne hulles
> Me byfel a ferly of fairy me thou3te;
> I was wery forwandred and went me to reste
> Vnder a brode banke bi a [borne] side,
> And as I lay and lened and loked in the wateres,
> I slombred in a slepyng it [sweyed] so merye.
>
> (Prol., 1–10)

Yet certain details in this description ring curiously, introducing a note of
uncertainty. The dreamer characterizes himself as a solitary man, probably
a wanderer, "In habite as an heremite." This in itself is not so remarkable
—many medieval dreamers have their visions while walking by themselves
—but this dreamer is odd for two reasons. He suggests, first, that he is a
habitual wanderer and, second, that there is something shady about himself.
The phrase "as I a shepe were" has usually been taken to mean "I put on

rough clothes like those of a shepherd," [57] but it is quite possible that there is a pun on the word "shepe," in which case the phrase could also be a reference to the proverbial wolf in sheep's clothing. This additional meaning gains support from the next line, "In habite as an heremite vnholy of workes." Later on, Will consistently characterizes himself as a "lorel," a vagabond and an outcast from society, a role certainly suggested by these opening lines. He is a man who is not apt to be welcomed by, nor to feel at home in, ordinary society.

Will falls asleep at a particular time (though a conventional time, to be sure) "on a May mornynge," and in a particular place, "Maluerne hulles," but the dream occurs "in a wildernesse, wist I neuer where." Now, it is true that the unknown dream landscape is quite as conventional in this type of literature as is the May morning and the "brode banke bi a [borne] side." But the opposition here is sharply drawn. The reassuringly common and definite physical presence of the waking world makes more emphatic the indefinite nature of the dream world. The May morning, Malvern hills, the broad bank—these we know. They have definite shape and substance, and we have met them, or things very much like them, before, in countless other poems. But all we know about the dreamer is that he is not what he appears to be, and that this unknown character finds himself in his dream in an un-known landscape, "wist I neuer where." It is a world about which nothing is known; it could be, or become, anything at all.

Yet, this contrast is undercut by the fact that the unknown landscape is peopled with common contemporary folk, who are not at all unknown but are perhaps even more familiar than May mornings and burbling brooks. One is, after all, accustomed to meeting strange sights in visions, like the silver-leaved trees of Paradise in *Pearl* or the revolving wicker house of Rumor in *The House of Fame*. However, the field of folk is no stranger than a busy town street. Yet, the fact that it is part of the unknown landscape, "wist I neuer where," suggests that the everyday, known world itself is not nearly as reassuringly real as the opening contrast between waking and visionary, known and unknown worlds promises. The known world of contemporary life is called unknown; in light of this, the "real" world of literary convention with which the poem begins must also be called into

---

57. An excellent recent summary of the ambiguous meanings of this phrase, and of the initial appearance of the dreamer, is in David Mills, "The Rôle of the Dreamer in *Piers Plowman*," in Hussey, *Critical Approaches*, pp. 185–86.

question. Thus, Langland has doubly upset the conventional norms of reality, both literary and actual, bringing into focus the problematic nature of what things mean from the outset of his poem. Indeed, the strangeness of *Piers Plowman* is purely a function of the fluid nature of everything in it; it has no mysterious gates, strange gardens, mechanical birds, enameled meadows to signal to us that we are in a marvelous world. The opening world of *Piers Plowman* is, in fact, not marvelous at all, only profoundly ambiguous. Whatever structural lines it promises, it promptly dissolves.

The opening landscape of the dream is stark and unspecified:

[Ac] I bihelde in-to the est an heigh to the sonne,
I seigh a toure on a toft trielich ymaked;
A depe dale binethe, a dongeon there-inne,
With depe dyches and derke and dredful of sight.
A faire felde ful of folke fonde I there bytwene,
Of alle maner of men, the mene and the riche,
Worchyng and wandryng as the worlde asketh.

(Prol., 13–19)

In its visual spareness, this description is reminiscent of the manuscript drawing of the stage-set for *The Castle of Perseverance,* a high tower in the center of the playing area, and various *sedes* representing such places as "Mundus," "Deus," "Belyal," and "Caro." It is a wholly allegorical landscape, in which the objects plainly represent something of a spiritual nature and are intended to be considered as simple signposts for something else. The folk wandering on the field, however, are not allegorical in this way; they do not fit into a schematized drawing but are as lively and random as everyday life itself. And their placement between the tower and the dungeon upsets the order embodied in the stark oppositions of the opening scene, suggesting on the one hand the possibility that the allegorical landscape gives the folk meaning, yet on the other hand that it may be too simple and severe to quite contain them. It is peculiarly difficult to pinpoint where metaphorical reality ends and the commonplace begins, difficult even to tell whether the structural lines suggested by the opposition of these terms have real meaning for the poem. Indeed, I would suggest that this opposition is one cognitive structure which Langland tests and discards as inadequate in the course of the Prologue.

Next the poet brings certain groups of folk into focus:

Some putten hem to the plow, pleyed ful selde,
In settyng and in sowyng swonken ful harde,
And wonnen that [þise] wastours with glotonye destruyeth.

(Prol., 20–22)

The first group, plowmen, are typical of spiritual virtue, both by way of their place in the Christian exegetical tradition, and as they are described here. They win what wasters destroy through gluttony. And, to continue this opposition in even more specifically moral terms, the poet next contrasts those who apparel themselves after pride with those who live in prayer and penance. It is clear, however, that none of these types are specified—they inhabit a timeless, spiritual realm. They are "allegorical" in the simplest sense of the term, in which their physical relationships have total reference to another level of meaning.[58]

But in line 28 the poet suddenly refers these allegorical types of good by contrast to a condition both contemporary and English:

> In prayers and in penance putten hem manye,
> . . . .
> As ancres and heremites that holden hem in here selles,
> And coueiten nought in contre to kairen aboute,
> For no likerous liflode her lykam to plese.
> (Prol., 25, 28–30)

The effect of this contrast is to pull the reader out of the schematic allegory to which he has become accustomed and into a fourteenth-century scene. The reference to abuses of the hermit's life specifies the unknown and generalized landscape, thus changing the nature of the allegory and the bases upon which the poem must be read. The description refers to no "other level": anchorites who roam the countryside are not traditional iconographic types nor generalized figures of Everyman. They are busy wanderers belonging to a contemporary scene. This same rapid shifting between typological moral allegory, in characters like the plowmen, and literally intended social comment, in characters like the unruly anchorites, continues throughout the Prologue. Thus, some beggars are described in concrete detail:

> Bidders and beggeres fast aboute 3ede,
> [Til] her belies and her bagges [were bret] ful ycrammed;
> [Flite þanne] for here fode, fou3ten atte ale;
> (Prol., 40–42)

---

58. This other level of meaning I take to be a generalized spiritual one, nothing so specific as the "prelates" into which Robertson and Huppé wish to transform them (*Piers Plowman and Scriptural Tradition,* p. 19). For a judicious comment on their reading, see Donaldson, "Patristic Exegesis," pp. 8–11.

And yet these same beggars are next discovered consorting with personified vices:

> In glotonye, god [. . .] wote, gon hij to bedde,
> And risen [vp] with ribaudye, [as] Roberdes knaues;
> Slepe and [. . .] sleuthe seweth hem eure.
>
> (Prol., 43–45)

Shifts like these force a continuous change of perspective on the reader, from concrete description to metaphor and back again, without any clear borderline between them.

Some allegories can be relied upon to be consistently allegorical—that is, the narrative level points at all times to another level for which the story is the figure. Thus, in Alanus' *Anticlaudianus*, when Theology is made to conduct the chariot of the Seven Liberal Arts through the skies to Prudence, the reader makes the appropriate semantic translation of the literal level to its abstract meaning. The story demands that he do so and clearly directs him in the way to do it. But *Piers Plowman* defies most such efforts at the very level of the text, for it frequently varies the relationship between literal and metaphorical levels: literal statements change into metaphor, metaphors become different metaphors with startling and confusing ease.

Langland describes a pardoner preaching to the people:

> Lewed men leued hym wel and lyked his [speche],
> Comen vp knelyng to kissen his [bulle];
> He bonched hem with his breuet and blered here eyes,
> And rau3te with his ragman rynges and broches.
>
> (Prol., 72–75)

These four lines contain a rapid jump from a literal to a metaphorical statement. The unlearned men kneeling about the pardoner are first described in naturalistic terms, visual and wholly concrete. But then the pardoner hits them with his official letter, hard enough to make their eyes water. In literal terms, this statement is absurd, as is the next line, describing him as gathering in rings with his sealed patent. Clearly, the terms of the description have shifted from a literal to a metaphoric level. Lines 74–75 cannot be read in the same way as 72–73, yet they occur as part of the description of the same scene. And the change occurs with such sharp contrast that it confuses the reader's apprehension of the scene—is the description literal, or figurative, or does it "exist" somewhere between the two? This blurring of levels is neatly accomplished by the word "blered," a pun which means literally "watered" and metaphorically "fooled." [59] And the fact that the line makes sense either way dramatizes cogently the problem of meaning forced upon the reader by the verbal structure of the poem.

It is a strange group of people on the field, not only in terms of their mixed social class but also, more puzzlingly, at least to the reader, in terms of their degree of specificity. One never quite knows whether one is meeting an allegorical type or a particular figure drawn from Langland's familiar English scene. Those lean hermits going to Walsingham with their wenches are clearly in the latter mode, but the friars who succeed them in Langland's description, though they start as contemporary characters, end up by being assumed into an allegorical called Charity who is busily selling confessions to lords:

> Many of this maistres [. . .] mowe clothen hem at lykyng,
> For here money and [hire] marchandise marchen togideres.
> [. . .] Sith charite hath be chapman and chief to shryue lordes,
> Many ferlis han fallen in a fewe ʒeris.
> (Prol., 62–65)

After a description of more contemporary worldly clergymen (the pardoner, the lazy priests who neglect their parishes for soft livings in London, and churchmen who serve the temporal powers), the mode of the poem shifts again, this time to a wholly abstract level:

> I parceyued of the power that Peter had to kepe,
> To bynde and [. . .] vnbynde as the boke telleth,
> How he [it left] with loue as owre lorde hight,
> Amonges foure vertues, [most vertuous of alle],
> That cardinales ben called and closyng ʒatis,
> There crist is in kyngdome to close and to shutte,
> And to opne it to hem and heuene blisse shewe.
> (Prol., 100–106)

This is allegory on a level even more abstract than the schematized landscape with which the poem begins. There the poet perceived physical objects which stood for conceptual values; here he perceives the abstraction itself, Peter's *power* to bind and unbind, and the leaving of that power not

---

59. *MED*, s.v. *bleren*, v. (1).

to his successors but to the four cardinal virtues. Indeed, this statement can hardly be called allegorical at all; only the use of the verb "perceive" makes it a figure rather than an outright statement of doctrine. Except for that tenuous link to the narrative, the poem has left the realm of physical objects entirely and is contained within an abstract verbal frame.

The verbal nature of the allegory at this point is underscored by the fact that the poem proceeds to its next topic via a learned pun. "Cardinal" is related through the meaning of its Latin original, *cardo,* "a hinge," to the cardinals of the papal court. The pun serves here, as in the earlier pun on "blered," to effect a transition from a metaphorical statement to a literal situation (only in this case the transition is in the opposite direction). Once again the mode of the poem has shifted; these dozen lines cannot all be read from the same perspective, for we have on the one hand the abstract statement concerning the power of the keys (in itself a metaphor), and on the other a description of a historical situation. They are related to each other by means of a pun which itself plays off a literal against a more metaphorical meaning of a word.

Immediately following these lines, the Prologue describes a king, led by knighthood, whose clerks are counseled by Kynde Wit, and the *comunes* which he rules. The *comunes* contrive their crafts through the counsel of Kynde Wit, ordaining plowmen to till the land; and the king and Kynde Wit create law and loyalty. Then, suddenly, a lunatic looks up to beg the king to rule well, an angel leans down to him, speaking a warning in Latin, and a *goliardeys* shouts a verse in reply to the angel. The *comunes,* who have come together in some sort of parliamentary gathering (though this, like all the rest, is unclear) cry out to the king's council. And at that point a large herd of rats and mice rush out to consult among themselves on how best to deal with a cat that has been preying on them. After their debate ends in frustration, the dreamer describes sergeants of the law and others "in this assemble," though at this point it is very unclear *what* assembly is being referred to. The Prologue ends with a lively description of small tradesmen, diggers singing "Dieu [. . .] saue Dame Emme!," and cooks and taverners crying their wares.

The mysterious figures of the lunatic and the angel, the London taverners, and the parliamentary rats all coexist in the same visionary world. But the relationship of these figures is not at all clear. It is difficult to know how to read this allegory, what kind of sense, if any, it is supposed to make. Thus, the problem of meaning in the Prologue presents itself as a problem in reading, the task of finding an adequate interpretive structure for the multifaceted world which Langland presents to us, as his language constantly shifts its perspective among the temporal and eternal, literal and metaphorical, typological and specific modes of perception.[60] The search for St. Truth is a search for the signs that reveal him—in the Prologue Langland utilizes many possible types of sign, many possible kinds of language, and produces a kaleidoscopic mirror, every piece of which promises clear vision, and none of which produces it. And his procedure focuses attention on the signs of intellection themselves; the world of the Prologue demands to be understood, by the very fact of its confusion. The signs used to give it order and understanding are inadequate, in conflict with one another rather than in harmony. The leaves of Langland's universe are not only scattered; they seem to have come from unrelated volumes.

---

60. A good analysis of this problem in the reading of allegory is R. W. Frank, Jr., "The Art of Reading Medieval Personification-Allegory," *ELH*, XX (1953), 237–50. See also Priscilla Jenkins, "Conscience: the Frustration of Allegory," in Hussey, *Critical Approaches*, pp. 125–42, who suggests that Langland investigates the cognitive nature of allegory "through the juxtaposition of allegorical and literal" (p. 142).

ᑫᔊᕋ CHAPTER TWO ᔊᕋ

"Kenne me bi somme crafte to knowe the Fals."

E arly in Passus I, Lady Holy Church explains to Will what he has just seen in the Prologue. The Tower is the dwelling of Truth, the Dungeon that of Wrong. In the next two hundred lines, she gives a clear, full account of the traditional view of the world, of Truth, charity, and Falsehood. There is nothing remarkable in what she says; indeed, her teaching is based entirely on the Bible. What is remarkable about it is its apparent failure to guide or illuminate the rest of the *Visio*. Passus I should conclude the search for St. Truth, not initiate it. Lady Holy Church gives a comprehensive explanation of what the world in which Will finds himself has meant to Christians for centuries. Yet, her speech makes no apparent difference either to his understanding or to that of anybody else in the poem. There could be no more dramatic indication of what the poem sees as the failure of the orthodox rhetoric of the Church to make meaningful statements about the world to those who live on the field of folk. The world of *Piers Plowman* is the world Christians have always known—Heaven, Hell, and the earth between—but in Langland's view the traditional terms in which they have understood that world have become unintelligible.

Several critics have argued that Will's failure to understand Lady Holy Church reflects intellectual perversity on his part, a stubborn dullness due to his lack of wit rather than to any inadequacy in what the lady says.[1] This is

---

1. Chiefly, John Lawlor, *Piers Plowman: An Essay in Criticism* (London, 1962), pp. 20–21; Howard Meroney, "The Life and Death of Long Wille," *ELH*, XVII (1950), 9; and, more recently, David Mills, "The Rôle of the Dreamer in *Piers Plowman*," in *Piers Plowman: Critical Approaches*, ed. S. S. Hussey (London, 1969), p. 193.

true, to a point. But Will's dullness with respect to Lady Holy Church is shared by the poem, which insists on making its own journey to St. Truth rather than accepting her teaching. The Truth it seeks may be, in essence, the same as that which she has just defined, but the fact that her words are not understood and that she leaves the poem at its very inception suggests that we should not see the fault simply in Will's stupidity. Her words provide a problem for Will instead of a solution. At the start of Passus I he is confident of what his vision means; by the end of it, not only is he confused by the allegory but the language used by Lady Holy Church to explain it has become a barrier to him. Such words as *tresore, kynde, knowynge,* and *crafte* are differently understood by the two speakers, a difference which becomes all the more apparent as their dialogue progresses. At the beginning of Passus II, when Will turns to her to ask, "Kenne me bi somme crafte to knowe the Fals" (II. 4)—after all of Passus I has been devoted to defining the True and the False—it is clear that Lady Holy Church's "crafte," the elaborate conceptual system which she has just explained to him, is meaningless. Her words do not inform—they merely confuse— because the words no longer have a stable referent. Will's problem of understanding is located in language itself, its inexactness, ambiguity, and obscurity. However, this is the condition of the language which Will understands and speaks—the normal language of earthly men.

When Will turns from the Lady to look at the False, he immediately confronts a horde of ambulatory words, some good, some bad, most ambivalent. These words are among the signs that can, perhaps, lead to St. Truth, but their truthfulness must be tested and explored. The device Langland uses to do this is personification, one of the chief allegorical forms by which the poem explores the problem of meaning, and the one most ignored by its critics. I suppose personification-allegory often seems pedestrian in comparison to the rich symbolism of the allegorical images in Dante or Spenser because the personified figures are clearly labeled. The tendency of many commentators has been to regard personifications as wholly static figures, mere signposts pointing to the dictionary, instead of moving, acting characters in a long poem. This is a mistake, for such an approach is apt to limit the meaning of a personification to what the figure may denote at a single point in the poem rather than taking into account what is the fact— namely, that the personifications act, interact with each other, and reappear in different contexts in the poem, all of which can significantly affect the meaning they carry.

A personification gives the concept to which it refers significance by narrative means. The scenes in which it is placed, the people it talks to, the actions it performs, the descriptions that are given of it—these internal features of the poem give meaning to the personified concept. Thus, formal and structural considerations are just as important to meaning in personification allegory as they are in the more symbolical kinds of allegory—indeed, as they are in language itself. And it is precisely because personification reveals meaning through the structural design of its narrative that it is such an excellent device for exploring meaning: a personification enlarges the concept it signifies every time it moves from one place to another.

To see how this process works, it may be helpful to study its use in a less complex example taken from another allegorical poem, Guillaume de Lorris' part of *The Romance of the Rose.* If one contrasts the figures painted on the outside of the garden wall with the personification of Dangier, who guards the Rose against all comers, I think the significant quality of personification allegory will be clear. The obvious difference between the two kinds of figures is that one is painted on the wall as a static and flat emblem, while the other is walking about, coming into contact with different characters in dynamic relationships.

The figures on the wall of the garden are entirely typal. The Dreamer describes them in frozen attitudes, expressing through their physical attributes the concepts they represent:

> Amydde saugh I Hate stonde,
> That for hir wrathe, yre, and onde,
> Semede to ben a moveresse,
> An angry wight, a chideresse;
> And ful of gyle and fel corage,
> By semblaunt, was that ilk ymage.
> And she was nothyng wel arraied,
> But lyk a wod womman afraied.
> Yfrounced foule was hir visage,
> And grennyng for dispitous rage;
> Hir nose snorted up for tene.
> Ful hidous was she for to sene,
> Ful foul and rusty was she, this.
> Hir heed ywrithen was, ywis,
> Ful grymly with a greet towayle.[2]
> (ll. 147–61)

---

2. I have used Chaucer's translation of *The Romaunt of the Rose, Works,* ed. F. N. Robinson, 2d ed. (Boston, 1957).

Sometimes these figures are described as causing an action, but the action is inferred by the Dreamer from the physical form which he sees before him:

> Ful croked were hir hondis two,
> For coveitise is evere wod
> To gripen other folkis god.
> (ll. 202–4)

The *visibilia* thus express the corresponding *invisibilia* in a simple, one-for-one manner; this is what I have termed *allegory of equivalence,* in which the allegorical language comes closest to being just rhetorical ornament, devoid of cognitive content. Seeking the normative exemplariness of definition, it lacks process or change; such a figure is more successful as it is more static and two-dimensional.

Dangier, however, moves about both temporally and spatially. Thus, although he is always Dangier, he takes on very different shades of meaning in response to various situations and contexts in the poem. There are four such situations in de Lorris' part of the poem. First (ll. 3010–3180), when the Lover and Bel Aceuil approach the Rose, Dangier springs up suddenly, beating Bel Aceuil for allowing the Lover to approach. Both Bel Aceuil and the Lover are frightened and run off, the Lover remarking especially on Dangier's rudeness and churlish aspect. Then (ll. 3395–3792), the Lover begs Dangier's pardon, and, because of his good behavior, is allowed to stay near the Rose. At the climax of this section, Franchise and Pity, aided by Venus, persuade Dangier to allow the Lover to kiss the Rose. Dangier agrees, moved by Pity's description of the plight of the Lover, and because it would be "to gret uncurtesie" (l. 3587) not to do so. This behavior is in direct contrast to the first situation, when the Lover calls attention to Dangier's lack of manners. Thirdly (ll. 3999–4108), Shame and Fear, aroused by Jealousy, rebuke Dangier for his carelessness with the Rose. Dangier jumps up at once and shows himself to be much nastier than he was before (l. 4103). This state is more than a regression; it is an extreme reaction to his earlier mood. Finally (ll. 4145–4211), Dangier is made a captain of Jealousy's castle, imprisoning the Rose and Bel Aceuil.

In each of these four contexts, Dangier's nature and function—his meaning, in short—change from what they were before. In the first situation, he is the lady's guardian, rude and churlish to the Lover and distrustful of Bel Aceuil. He is overzealous out of ignorance, for he does not know the Lover. His is the mistrust of the ignorant and inexperienced, and, while he may be a churl and a boor, he is not an actively vicious character—he can be educated. This is exactly what happens during the second episode. As he gets to know the Lover, he becomes less suspicious. By the end of this section, his relationship to the Lover has changed completely. He has become docile, even an ally, albeit by default. He proves susceptible to Franchise and Pity and shows an appreciation of courteous behavior. Then in lines 3999–4108, his nature abruptly changes again. His nastiness here is a result not of ignorance but of outrage, of an experience which causes shame. It is no longer the result of innocent chastity, but verges on that of prudery. In the end, he degenerates into mere prudishness, a harmful and wicked creature, and the lieutenant of Jealousy.

Thus, Dangier's significance changes from situation to situation. This is not simply a process of accreting different meanings. Dangier's various functions reflect his various meanings, each of which signifies an aspect of Dangier but none of which, singly or together, completely defines him. Dangier in the end means *dangier,* and there is no reason to suppose that he could not respond to a dozen situations in as various a manner as he does to the four in this poem. The figure, as Guillaume has personified him, has a degree of fluidity and flexibility which the exemplary figure of Hate, frozen on the wall, cannot possibly have. One cannot simply read off what Dangier means in the same way that one can read what Envy or Hate or Avarice means, because his meaning is qualified by the context in which he is placed.

Personification gives a definite narrative shape to language; the word becomes a character in a story, which is the vehicle for the expression of its meaning(s). A personification is, at all times, a word; it is given human shape and activities, but its anthropomorphic form does not make it a person.[3] The action of the personification expresses its meaning as a word,

---

3. A fundamental confusion over the nature of personification, which treats personifications as human characters rather than as words, has been responsible for many misconceptions in *Piers Plowman* criticism about the poem generally and these passus in particular. This confusion certainly lies behind J. M. Manley's famous blast against the B-Text poet for his gross inconsistencies of characterization and plot, such as making Lady Meed the wife and daughter of False (*Cambridge History of English Literature* [New York, 1908], II, 1–48). It is also responsible for G. R. Owst's complaint that the figures of the Seven Deadly Sins are "inadequately harmonized" (*Literature and Pulpit in Medieval England,* 2d ed. [Oxford, 1961], p. 88). It has persisted, usually in less evident forms, among those critics who see the poem's paramount interests as social and moral. As I have argued, however, cognitive and therefore verbal issues are prior to their social expressions in this poem; it is most important to remain conscious of the verbal nature of personification when reading it. An essay

and the degree of responsiveness which the personification exhibits in various narrative contexts in exactly the same as that of the word, no more and no less. Dangier, the personification, and *dangier*, the concept, share exactly the same range of expressiveness and of possible meanings. The full range of meanings and semantic connotations are simply given narrative expression. An allegory conducted in personification, therefore, is an allegory wedded to language; it can have no meaning beyond that created by the conceptual boundaries of the words it personifies. Personification is a narrative made up entirely of *littera*, of language itself; it is thus the obvious tool for exploring the nature and limitations of human language. In *Piers Plowman*, personification is used most extensively to examine the nature of the False, which is embodied in a language that has lost its proper structure just as it has lost its proper reference.

The essential nature of evil, to medieval thinkers, is formlessness, lawlessness, meaninglessness. St. Thomas Aquinas, following Augustine, describes evil as entirely negative: "it must be said that by the name of evil is signified the absence of good." [4] Evil, however, is not merely illusory; it must be said to exist, though only as a privation in something:

> As the Philosopher says (*Metaph.* V, text. 14), being is two-fold. In one way it is considered as signifying the entity of a thing, as divisible by the ten *predicaments;* and in that sense it is convertible with thing, and thus no privation is a being, and neither therefore is evil a being. In another sense, being conveys the truth of a proposition which unites together subject and attribute by a copula, notified by this word *is;* and in that sense being is what answers to the question, *Does it exist?* and thus we speak of blindness as being in the eye; or of any other privation. In this way even evil can be called a being.[5]

The False has no real form of its own, and works to negate and empty coherent structures of all kinds, cognitive, moral, and verbal.

The assault of False is seen in the poem as an assault on language, a displacement of words from their "rect," spiritual referents. The result is pure chaos; the semantic outrage produces moral chaos, and is mirrored exactly by a formal outrage in the narrative structure of the poem. When False

---

which is a judicious reminder of this necessary step in the poem's analysis is R. W. Frank, Jr., "The Art of Reading Medieval Personification-Allegory," *ELH,* XX (1953), 237–50.

4. St. Thomas Aquinas, *ST* (trans. Fathers of the English Dominican Province) I². Q. XLVIII.

5. *ST* I². Q. XLVIII. a. 2.

uses words, they have no fixed meaning at all but can be used in direct viola-
tion of their proper meanings in order to cheat, deceive, and trick the intellect. This particular power of False is made explicit in the marriage
charter he and Meed are given. The charter grants them the freedom to
perform all seven of the deadly sins, but it concentrates on sins of a particular sort:

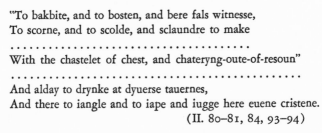

> "To bakbite, and to bosten, and bere fals witnesse,
> To scorne, and to scolde, and sclaundre to make
> ....
> With the chastelet of chest, and chateryng-oute-of-resoun"
> ....
> And alday to drynke at dyuerse tauernes,
> And there to iangle and to iape and iugge here euene cristene.
> (II. 80–81, 84, 93–94)

These are sins against language; False and Meed are given the freedom to
speak falsely and maliciously, and to use words without any regard for
truth. Their freedoms are granted to them, fittingly, by Favel, "with his
fikel speche." False and all his followers take full advantage of them in the
scenes that follow.

False is conceptually indistinct and slippery from the outset. He always
appears together with a rabble of indistinct and semantically undifferenti-
ated synonyms: false, favel, false witness, guile, liar, and wrong—the number of closely related words obscures rather than distinguishes meaning.
Semantic anarchy prevails throughout Passus II–IV; meaning is made to be
deceptively fuzzy, and there are too many words under foot that have no
order, rule, or number. For example, in the marriage charter, Meed and
False are to backbite, lie boastingly, bear false witness, scold, scorn, and
slander. The distinction of meaning among these words becomes less clear
as synonym is piled on synonym. The multiplicity of words used does not
refine the meaning of the action to which they refer but obscures it in a
cloud of verbiage, which is only seemingly meaningful. For all six words
refer essentially to the same activity; they are pleonastic, like so many of
False's followers, cloaking and smothering meaning in mere redundancy.[6]

---

6. John Burrow has recently commented, adversely, on the use of pleonasm
as a typical feature of the alliterative style, *Ricardian Poetry* (New Haven,
Conn., 1971), pp. 26–27. But even typical stylistic features can be used ex-
pressively by good poets; Marie Borroff comments on the meaningful use of
pleonasm by the *Gawain* poet, *Sir Gawain and the Green Knight: A Stylistic
and Metrical Study* (New Haven, Conn., 1962), pp. 70–73.

Not only is meaning concealed by hosts of synonyms and near-puns, but words denoting virtues are also used in ways that disrupt their accepted meanings. Law, for example, is represented by Simony and Civil; the sacrament of marriage, which should unite two persons, is a means of disruption, of sowing discord and contention; the binding oath of the charter is the oath of Guile. The most outrageous distorter of language is Meed herself, who is fond of perverting words like "love," "pity," and "mercy." She uses these concepts as window dressing for her own activities—for example, letting lechers off the hook in the name of pity. Her courtesy is merely polite show, her pity piteousness, her mercy sentimentality. She counsels mayors, for example, to wink at retailers who overcharge their customers:

> "For my loue," quod that lady, "loue hem vchone,
> And suffre hem to selle somdele aȝeins resoun."
> (III. 91–92)

Lady Meed makes Christian charity synonymous with cheating, in a systematic perversion of language which allows her to retain her vicious hold on society. As long as cheating the law can be seen as love, and church decoration as penance, bribery can be made to seem the same as rightful reward. Meed gives to every word, including herself, a double meaning, a false reference which masks and perverts.

And the semantic chaos of these passus gives rise to a narrative chaos as well, as distinctions of form and decorum are totally lost. Passus II–IV contain more personifications than any other part of *Piers Plowman;* they multiply like weeds everywhere Will looks, synonyms, puns, pleonasms, words with ambiguous relationships to their referents. Will no sooner perceives one figure than it multiplies itself by three or four vaguely similar, yet vaguely different, characters. This phenomenon happens the moment Lady Holy Church tells Will to look at False:

> "Loke vppon thi left half and lo where he standeth,
> Bothe Fals and Fauel and [hise] feres manye!"
> I loked on my left half as the lady me taughte,
> And was war of a woman [wonderliche] yclothed.
> (II. 5–8)

The grammatical logic of this passage is startlingly unclear. Will asks how he can know "the Fals." Use of the article indicates that he is talking about an abstract concept: the False is of the same order as the Good or the True. Yet Lady Holy Church bids him look and see where "he" stands, the personal pronoun indicating that the False has undergone a transformation from abstract noun to personified figure. "He" is most likely singular here, and could be either masculine or feminine.[7] But that "he" promptly becomes multiple, since Favel and his many companions are standing with False at Will's left. Thus, "the Fals" for which Will asked is first referred to as a single character, and then split up among many characters, the chief of whom is named False, but each of whom, in the context of this passage, must represent parts or aspects of the concept which Will asks to know. It is as though all one has to do is mention the word False and a host of ill-defined personifications, most of them *f*-alliterating, spring up. Yet, the oddest turn of all in the passage comes at the end. Having finally been promised many characters, Will sees only one when he actually looks to his left, and that one is a female—and she is not called False at all but Lady Meed.

Thus, "the Fals," that abstraction with which Will began, has in the course of four lines been personified, split among a troop of characters, and then gathered together again in the single figure of the woman wondrously clothed. This formal amorphousness does not end here. "Fals and Fauel and [hise] feres manye" wind through the language of Passus II in a welter of forms sharing each other's characteristics and epithets, at times even each other's bodies, until it becomes almost impossible to tell who is who, or who is doing what at any particular time. First, we are told that False, "that hath a fykel tonge," is the father of Meed (II. 25). Meed is also about to be married to a certain False Fickle-tongue (II. 40), who sounds suspiciously like her father.[8] False's chief cohort is Favel (flattery) who "thorw his faire

---

7. *He* is a native form of the 3d nominative plural, as well as of the masculine and feminine 3d nominative singular. Langland uses *he* for the feminine singular pronoun (as well as the masculine); see XIII. 46–49, where *he* is used to refer to Scripture. I have not discovered any instances in which he uses *he* as the 3d nominative plural pronoun—*hii* or *thei* seems to be his preference. The plural of the verb could end in *-eth*, like the 3d singular, and is so used occasionally by Langland (cf. Prol., 32–33), though a plural in *-e* or *-en* is more common to him. Thus, there is really no way of knowing whether the pronoun in B. II. 5 is singular or plural, though, given Langland's common usage, it is likely to be singular. Kane and Donaldson read *hise* for Skeat's *here* in II. 6, making the whole construction plainly singular and masculine.

8. Cf. the debate over this point: in Manly, *Cambridge History*, p. 37, and in *MP*, VII (1909–10), 117–21; and the rejoinders of J. J. Jusserand in *MP*, VI (1908–9), 303–5, and *MP*, VII (1909–10), 316–17. Manly was, of course, looking for evidence of multiple authorship; Jusserand was arguing

speche" (II. 41) has persuaded the people to allow Meed to marry False
Fickle-tongue (II. 42). Then, at line 78, we read of "Fauel with his fikel
speche," a quality previously predicated of False, *père* and *mari*. At line
129, the epithet is again applied to False—he is "[feyntless] and fikel in his
werkes." In the marriage charter, Meed and False are given privileges of
slander and false witness, which really belong to Favel. Finally, at line 146,
a character is introduced called False-witness; Favel, who should be a master
of the game himself, feels he needs to buy him over to his side in order to
persuade Meed to marry False. The confusion is increased by the presence
of Guile with his great oaths (II. 69), obviously a close relation of the others.
Nor is Guile allowed to keep his oaths all to himself, for in Favel's deed
of marriage Gluttony is associated with great oaths (II. 92), and, to cap
the whole confusing picture, Theology accuses Civil of giving Lady Meed
"to a gyloure" (II. 120), by whom he means not Guile but False.[9]

The formal slipperiness of these personifications is a mirror of their
referential instability. As their semantic distinctions are unclear, so is their
distinctiveness as figures in the narrative. They can even slide into one another's bodies, as Donaldson noted of Simony and Civil, who speak with
"one set of vocal-chords." [10] Given the verbal nature of personification, it is
necessary that, when the words have become ambiguous and unstable in
meaning, the figures in which they are embodied will exhibit exactly the
same characteristics. In the early part of the *Visio,* a continuously reciprocal
relationship exists between the intellectual confusion in the folk's understanding, the verbal confusion in their language, and the structural confusion of the narrative. It is as difficult to tell just what Will sees in
Passus II as it is in the Prologue. One good example of this occurs when
the whole band of False takes off for the court at Westminster:

> "And maketh of Lyer a longe carte to lede alle these othere,
> As [fobbes] and faitours that on here fete [iotten]."
> [. . .] Fals and Fauel fareth forth togideres,

---

against this, but neither combatant was willing to allow Lady Meed her in-
cestuous match, on moral grounds. All of which raises the interesting question of
whether words can commit incest—perhaps, in a sorry way, they can, at least
in Passus II.

9. Theology is more confused in the C-Text, where he gives Meed False for
a father and Fickle-tongue for a sire, while her mother remains the virtuous
lady Amends (C. III. 120–21). See E. T. Donaldson, *Piers Plowman: The
C-Text and Its Poet* (New Haven, Conn., 1949), p. 69.

10. *Ibid.,* p. 71.

And Mede in the myddes and alle thise [meynee] after.
. . . .
Ac Gyle was forgoer and gyed hem alle.

(II. 181–84, 187)

Determining the line of march here is an exhausting process, because every time one looks at it, it acquires a new leader. And the mounts of this procession are more extraordinary than its multiheaded leadership:

> [Thanne] Fauel fette [. . .] folus [of the beste];
> [. . .] Sette Mede vpon a schyreue shodde al newe,
> And Fals set on a sisoure that softlich trotted.

(II. 162–64)

Language has become the master of men; there could be no more emphatic depiction of the complete divorce of language from its proper function and relationship to things than this Bosch-like picture of triumphant words trotting off on the backs of their docile human horses.

The figure who epitomizes the semantic looseness and ambivalance which is the image of the False is Lady Meed. I have already discussed the ways in which she subverts the meaning of other concepts, yet she herself has a dangerously unclear double meaning. Lady Meed corrupts society by taking advantage of the linguistic accident that she, "meed," has two opposite, irreconcilable meanings, which Conscience identifies as follows:

> "Prestes and persones that plesynge desireth,
> That taketh mede and mone for messes that thei syngeth,
> [Shul haue] mede [on þis molde þat] Mathew [haþ graunted];
>   *Amen, amen, receperunt mercedem suam.*
> That laboreres and lowe [lewed] folke taketh of her maistres,
> It is no manere mede but a mesurable hire."

(III. 250–54)

The confusion over the nature of Lady Meed occurs from the start of Passus II. Lady Holy Church describes Meed to Will as the bastard daughter of False. She shows no sympathy for Meed in any form at all; Meed, she says, takes after her father, who "neuere sothe seide sithen he come to erthe" (II. 26). But Theology defends Meed, and rebukes Civil for allowing her to contract a marriage with False:

> "For Mede is moylere of Amendes engendred,
> And god [graunted] to gyf Mede to Treuthe,

[45]

. . . .

For *dignus est operarius* his hyre to haue,
And thow hast fest hire [wiþ] Fals, fy on thi lawe!

. . . .

Wel ʒe witen, wernardes, but if ʒowre witte faille,
That Fals is [feyntless] and fikel in his werkes,
And [as] a bastarde y-bore of Belsabubbes kynne.
And Mede is moylere, a mayden of gode,
[She] myʒte kisse the kynge for cosyn, an she wolde."
                    (II. 118–19, 122–23, 128–32)

Obviously, Theology and Lady Holy Church are not talking about the same woman at all. Theology's Meed is the daughter of Amends, marked out for Truth, and her pure and elevated background is contrasted with False's bastardy. Lady Holy Church's Meed is herself a bastard, false through and through. Theology has, in fact, failed to recognize a pun, for this Lady Meed, as she reveals plainly by her actions at court in bribing the judges and clerks, is actually what Lady Holy Church says she is, but she is masquerading as what Theology takes her to be and enjoying the advantages of the confusion she has created.

Thus, the problem of recognition and of understanding presented by Lady Meed is essentially verbal.[11] Meed herself is perfectly aware of her dual nature and consistently poses as rightful reward, while her association with False plainly demonstrates her real corruption. Thus, she argues in her defense:

"It bicometh to a kynge that kepeth a rewme,
To ʒiue [hise men mede] that mekelich hym serueth,
To alienes and to alle men to honoure hem with ʒiftes;
Mede maketh hym biloued and for a man holden."
                    (III. 208–11)

---

11. Other discussions of Lady Meed have noted her dual character, especially A. G. Mitchell, "Lady Meed and the Art of 'Piers Plowman,'" Third Chambers Memorial Lecture (London, 1956); John A. Yunck, *The Lineage of Lady Meed* (Notre Dame, Ind., 1963), p. 10; and Donald R. Howard, *The Three Temptations: Medieval Man in Search of the World* (Princeton, N.J., 1966), pp. 171–72. These critics, however, have tended to see her only as a social and moral vice; while certainly not denying her social significance, I believe that it is her dual verbal nature which gives rise to her corruption of society. In other words, her verbal nature is prior to and causative of her moral viciousness.

But her words are false-seeming, guileful, and lying. So Conscience, a concept who has not yet succumbed to False, and who understands the nature of words and the problems of semantic reference, kneels to the king to reveal that Lady Meed is not the word the king thinks she is: "There aren two manere of medes, my lorde." Lady Meed is a pun, and therein lies the source of all the king's difficulties with her.

Semantic difficulties of this sort abound in these three passus. A similar confusion involves Wit. Theology, who seems particularly prone to dullness in these matters, cautions Civil:

> "[. . .] Worcheth bi wisdome and bi witt [after],
> [. . .] Ledeth hire to Londoun there lawe is [yhandled],
> . . . .
> ȝet beth war of [þe] weddyng for witty is Truthe,
> [For] Conscience is of his conseille and knoweth ȝow vchone."
>   (II. 133–34, 137–38)

And sure enough, two characters prominent in engineering Lady Meed's trial are called Waryn Wisdom and Witty, or Wit (IV. 76 and 81). Wit, true wit, identified with Kynde Wit, also appears on the side of Reason and Conscience. The girth of Reason's saddle is "wit[ful]" (IV. 20), and [Kynde] Wit concurs in Reason's judgment of Meed (IV. 158). Both Wit and Meed are puns in these passus,[12] and it is significant that these rather dangerous puns should be particularly evident in Passus II–IV. False thrives upon this kind of semantic confusion. Even good concepts, most notably Peace, are subverted by False's influence. Peace is one of the Four Daughters of God in Passus XVIII; here, however, he meekly accepts Meed's golden present in exchange for his broken head and lost wife—peace at any price, rather than the peace that passeth understanding.

The effect of False's assaults on language is a paralysis of understanding on the part of the folk on the field, especially of the king. The king is told twice over, by Conscience and then by Reason, exactly what Lady Meed is, but he cannot understand the verbal nature of the cognitive problem she presents. To him, she is a lovely courtly lady, who has gone astray because she hasn't a decent husband; he mistakes her personified, apparently human form for her real nature, which is verbal and not human. Similarly, when

---

12. For an excellent discussion of another personification built around a pun, appearing later in the poem, see the analysis of Recchelessnesse in Donaldson, *The C-Text and Its Poet*, pp. 170–74.

he hears of Meed's proposed marriage to False, he is outraged and orders his constables to

"attache tho tyrauntz for eny [tresor], I hote,
And fettereth [Falsenesse faste] for enykynnes 3iftes,
And gurdeth of Gyles hed, [. . .] lat hym go no furthere."
(II. 199–201)

To the king, False and Guile are obviously felons, wicked persons—cut off their heads and all will be well. But the slippery, formless False can scarcely be contained by fetters. False is not a man, he is a concept; not a thing, but the verbal manifestation of an inner falseness of understanding. Since False attacks words and is a word himself, he can only be dealt with linguistically, as Conscience deals with Lady Meed, by making clear distinctions and definitions, reaffixing the word to a stable, clear referent. The king, however, never comes to understand the cognitive nature of his problem. He treats the personifications as human creatures throughout these passus. He will lock Meed up in prison and govern his kingdom with the aid of his knight and counselor, Conscience and Reason. He does not perceive these personifications as words, signs, which have meaning only in reference to spiritual, inner states.

It is a fitting clue to the verbal nature of False and Meed that the narrative in these passus takes the form of a trial—a war of words, a battle of definitions, the doubletalk of Meed opposing the rational distinctions of Conscience. Meed's license for "chaterynge-withouten-resoun" is to be replaced by law based on reasoned speech. As the king says: "I wil haue leute in lawe, and lete be al 3owre Ianglyng" (IV. 180). Though Lady Meed may be purged by definition, False cannot be. Lack of definition, slipperiness, are his essence. Trials deal with externals, such as evidence, and arrive at fine distinctions through reason, but they cannot get at inner truths. Lady Meed may be exposed at court, but her spirit is very much abroad in the hearts of the folk in the guise of the Seven Deadly Sins. Backbiting, lying, anger, gluttony, and envy, the marks of False, appear again in the folk on the field—indeed, the Seven Deadly Sins are the patrimony and legacy of Meed, as her marriage charter in Passus II promised.

The Seven Deadly Sins share all the characteristics of the other false concepts in these passus. They use words in the same solipsistic and corrupted way. The Seven Deadly Sins are a distillation of the folk on the field, a concentrate of their concerns, occupations, families, and limited, sinful understanding. Their language, and the language used of them, has a stub-

[48]

born tendency toward the literal, away from any kind of spiritual or meta-phorical meaning. One result of this is the vividness of their commonplace stories, and the concreteness of their appearance. Avarice, for example is dressed

> in a [torn] tabarde of twelue wynter age,
> [...............................]
> But if [. . .] a lous couthe [lepe, I leue and I trowe],
> She sholde nouȝte [wandre] on that welche, so was it thredebare.
>
> (V. 197–99)

The most memorable aspect of this description is not the inner depravity of the sin, but the image of that solitary louse, forced to jump long distances between the threads of his shabby garment. The language describing the in-sect's plight is vividly pictorial and concrete. But Avarice is a sin. One would expect that the things typical of Avarice would be evident signs of his spiritual state, continually illuminating the inner man, as, for example, the earthly appearance and activities of Hate refer entirely to spiritual states in Guillaume's icon. However, the description of Avarice does not work in this way. We should see the hidden nature of avarice, but instead what we see vividly is a threadbare coat and a desperate louse. The language em-ployed, typical of the descriptions of all the Seven Deadly Sins, has no spiritual resonance. Tavern games, the clinical details of Gluttony's drunken-ness, the merchandizing tricks of Avarice, Envy's withered cheeks, like a leek dried out in the sun—these details do not reverberate with hidden sig-nificance as the iconographic features of a spiritual type. The descriptions are wonderfully vivid, but they lack spiritual context or content. On the contrary, their context is emphatically worldly and specific, as in the follow-ing lines:

> Thanne goth Glotoun in and grete othes after;
> Cesse the [sowestere] sat on the benche,
> Watte the warner and his wyf bothe,
> Tymme the tynkere and tweyne of his [knaves]
> Hikke the hakeneyman and Hughe the nedeler,
> Clarice of Cokkeslane and the clerke of the cherche,
> [Sire Piers of Pridie and Peronelle of Flaundres,
> Dawe the dykere and a dozeine other;]
> A ribibour, a ratonere, a rakyer of Chepe,
> A ropere, a redyngkyng, and Rose the dissheres,
> Godfrey of Garlekehithe and Gryfin the Walshe,

[Of] vpholderes an hepe, erly bi the morwe
Geuen glotoun, with glad chere, good ale to hansel.

(V. 314–26)

The effect of this description is to make Gluttony only one of the many ordinary individuals in a common tavern—no more iconographic in nature than Rose the dish seller or Godfrey of Garlichithe. The very particularity of the language robs it of a spiritual dimension; the sin is set in a context which precludes allegory. Indeed, it is often hard to remember that the Seven Deadly Sins are allegorical representations of sin at all, so specific and particular, so literal, is their appearance and behavior. As depictions of an inner state—sin—they are remarkably concrete, visual, and earthbound.[13]

What is true of the language used of the sins is also true of the language they use. Avarice' conversation with Repentance, which I have referred to before, reveals his constant bent toward completely literal concerns and literal understanding, away from abstract, or spiritual, or metaphoric language. His understanding of words is analogous to the king's perception of personifications as people, literal things rather than signs with a metaphoric or spiritual referent. Avarice cannot make any sense of the word *restitucioun* —it is too learned, too abstract, for a man who has never been beyond Norfolk. He does understand usury, having used it once in his youth, but he has now learned a better trick:

> "To wey pens with a peys and pare the heuyest,
> And lene it for loue of the crosse to legge a wedde and lese it."
>
> (V. 243–44)

---

13. Rosemond Tuve has perceptively commented on this aspect of the later medieval depiction of vices in her comments on Guillaume de Deguileville's *Pélerinage de la vie humaine:* "What is so characteristically allegorical about these figures is not the element of an abstraction personified, doing actions, but the fact that the suffocating, piled-on concretions define and realize a universal that has a life and a nature of its own" (*Allegorical Imagery* [Princeton, N.J., 1966], pp. 176–77). As is evident from the context of her remarks, Miss Tuve is using the term "allegorically" to mean "typical of moral allegory," as she defines it (pp. 3–55), in distinction to allegory which refers to a second level of meaning. Miss Tuve was among the first to recognize a firm distinction between allegory which is significant in terms of itself (like moral and personification allegory, and fable) and allegory which is significant in reference to a hidden meaning, related metaphorically and analogously to the *littera* of the text (like figuralism). In his depiction of the Seven Deadly Sins, Langland is using the "suffocating, piled-on concretions" typical of the personified vice in order to emphasize the wholesale literalness and lack of any spirituality in these figures.

The pun on *crosse* reveals the essence of Avarice' literal-minded under-standing. Hard, golden metal is the only cross that moves him. Spiritual reali-ties have no meaning to him at all; they are as foreign to his tongue as *restitucioun*.

Their inability to understand language in any way beyond the level of literal statement and worldly references stamps the Seven Deadly Sins as followers of False, perverters of language, who are unable to give to words their true, spiritual reference. And, like the other false personifications, they also lack formal coherence and distinction. Envy, for example, is described as wrathful:

> His body was [bollen] for wratthe that he bote his lippes.
> (V. 84)

Repentance counsels Wrath against a form of Gluttony:

> "And drynke nou3te ouer delicatly ne to depe noyther,
> That thi wille [ne þi wit] to wrath my3te torne."
> (V. 184–85)

Gluttony, after his drinking bout, has "an accidie" (V. 366); and Sloth says he never tells his beads, "but if it be in wrath" (V. 407). Sloth also con-fesses to two sins which he shares with Covetise and Gluttony:

> "I nam nou3te lured with loue but there ligge au3te vnder the
> thombe,"   (V. 439)

and,

> "Bothe bred and ale, butter, melke, and chese
> Forsleuthed in my seruyse til it my3te serue noman."
> (V. 444–45)

Finally, both Sloth and Covetise suffer from wanhope (V. 286, 452), though the condition properly belongs only to Sloth. Even within themselves, the Sins shift their human shapes about. Sloth is both priest and layman. Wrath has been a friar, in fact the convent gardener (V. 137), and still walks about with the friars (V. 147). He has also cooked for his aunt, an abbess (V. 155), and for monks (V. 156).

The lack of cohesion among the Seven Deadly Sins identifies them with the formlessness of False, of which they are, indeed, another manifestation. Their confessions are abortive without the absolution which would give them meaning. By the end of them, human language has been pretty well discredited: even Repentance cannot use it without being misunderstood. Detached from a meaningful referent, words have become solipsistic, devious, and wicked; Passus II–IV demonstrate plainly that language is as much in need of redemption as society and suggests, moreover, that the two can only be accomplished together. For without understanding, there can be no reform, no change in human society, no development of man's relationship with God. These early passus of the *Visio* seem to me to present a test of language and to discover that it is as corrupt and ambivalent, in the same ways, as the world Will is first presented with in the Prologue. The trial of Lady Meed is more of a trial of language and of true verbal comprehension than it is of the value of bribery, or of reward, in society. The corruption it reveals is not monetary greed or social vice; these disorders of the soul and of the kingdom are themselves symptoms of a greater disorder, a fundamental displacement of earthly images of all kinds from the divinity which should inform them. The corruption of language demonstrated in these passus is indeed of greater significance than is the corruption of society which the language generates, especially through personifications like Lady Meed. Langland seems to demonstrate that words in his language have lost their inherent and generally stable relationship to those things which should signify them—the spiritually upright heart and the divine Word, which is the faith upon which Christian rhetoric is based. Lady Holy Church, Reason, and Repentance can no longer speak meaningfully to the folk on the field. And as the relationship between sign and significator becomes unstable and ambiguous, the whole foundation of knowledge—God's revelation of himself in signs—is also jeopardized.

ᘒ CHAPTER THREE ᘒ

"This were a wikked way, but who-so hadde a gyde
That [myꝫte] folwen us eche a fote"; thus this folke hem mened.

omeone obviously is needed to lead the folk through the multiplicity
of traps set by False. The *Visio* is full of would-be guides—the
king, Lady Holy Church, Reason, Repentance, the veteran of the
pilgrimage-tour in Passus V who has never heard of the "corseint" called
Truth. But only two of the many guides in the *Visio* achieve any measure of
success—Conscience and Piers Plowman. These two figures dominate the
action of the *Visio*. They are differently structured as characters: one is a
personification, the other a typological figure. And they achieve their success
in ways commensurate with their own allegorical natures. The understanding which Conscience produces in Passus II–IV is quite different in kind
from that produced by Piers Plowman, and an examination of the ways in
which these two figures solve the problem of meaning—indeed, the ways in
which they perceive the nature of meaning—clarifies many of the problems
in understanding which are basic to the structural progression of the rest
of the poem.

The search for a guide is a formal expression of the problem of finding
a true perspective, a reliable ground upon which to create in the poem a
structure meaningful for the world. The Prologue and Passus II present a
world ruled by the False, an ambivalent, formless, random world. The im-
possibility of determining any perspective in the Prologue, produced by its
rapid shifting between literal and metaphorical statement, finds a visual
counterpart in the extreme randomness with which its figures pass before
Will's eyes. The composition of the Prologue is very much like the crowded
groups of figures in a Brueghel canvas—*Children's Games,* for example, or
Dulle Griet—in which, although each individual group is clearly drawn,

the whole picture has no over-all coherence or design, no perspective, no definable point of view.

Like the structural problems in this poem, the problems of social order are expressions of cognitive problems. Indeed, the linking of order with understanding is apparent from the start of the poem; societies are established under the guidance of cognitive faculties, and the quality of the order is itself an expression of the adequacy of the cognitive faculty which supports it. Thus, in the Prologue, a king appears in the maze of folk and tries to establish an order based on Kynde Wit, a feudal order in which he is guided by knighthood and supported by the "comunes." [1] This is the first of several attempts to impose a structure on the folk, and it is not an auspicious beginning. Kynde Wit, by itself, is an ambiguous and unreliable guide. It is the same faculty as the scholastic *vis cogitativa,* an intelligent power which man shares with animals.[2] Middle English *kynde wit* is "native sense," "horse sense," or, as in the Prologue, "mouse sense." Social order under Kynde Wit turns into the rout of rats and mice, and the only law that "mouse sense" produces is self-interest. The rats want to restrain the activities of a cat which has been preying on them. The mouse reminds the rats of the "rules" governing the natural state of affairs: if they killed this cat, another one would come, and if cats didn't kill rats, the rats would soon destroy everything themselves. In such a world, the mouse reasons, self-interest is the only sense: "For-thi vche a wise wiȝte I warne, wite wel his owne" (Prol., 207). Yet self-interest produces the fragmentation and isolation which govern the structures, both social and poetic, of the Prologue and of Passus II. Of course, one figure does plead for just rule under *leaute* at the king's inauguration—but he, alas, is a lunatic. "Leaute," [3] the loyalty

---

1. The orthodoxy of the social order described in these lines has been established by E. T. Donaldson, *Piers Plowman: The C-Text and Its Poet* (New Haven, Conn., 1949), pp. 104–8.

2. Randolph Quirk, "Langland's Use of *Kynde Wit* and *Inwit,*" *JEGP,* LII (1953), 183–85.

3. *MED,* s. v. *leaute,* defines the word as "uprightness, honorableness, honesty; truth; justice, fairness," or "loyalty" (its modern derivative), or "allegiance." These definitions fall somewhere between Donaldson's contention (*The C-Text and Its Poet,* p. 66, n. 4) that the word means "legality," and that of P. M. Kean, "Love, Law, and *Lewte* in *Piers Plowman,*" *RES,* XV (1964), 255, that it means "virtue . . . living well, in a wide sense." As glossed by the *MED,* the word carries with it the idea of binding obligations, like those of allegiance to an oath, as well as the idea of faithfulness to those incurred responsibilities; it seems peculiarly well suited to express the whole

of subject to king and king to subject, and of both to God, presupposes a world in which all understand their true functions, their place in the order of things. But an order of things is precisely what the Prologue lacks—and Kynde Wit is insufficient to supply it.

The lack of structure which marks society in the Prologue and language in Passus II stems from the same cause—the False, self-interest, the displacement of God's image from the Word which should inform it, and the consequent confusion of all things. The guides of the *Visio* are primarily cognitive guides, secondarily moral ones; they lead the way to St. Truth. The emphasis on the primacy of the problem of meaning is the reason why the routing of Lady Meed is so important in the *Visio*. Lady Meed is a social vice, but she acquires her hold in the first place because even the best of the folk do not possess the intellectual means to discern her true nature. Within the context of this poem, she gains her vicious ascendance because she is a pun, and only when Conscience reveals the pun can he purge the vice.

Conscience' role in his confrontation with Lady Meed is a complex one, just as it is in the poem as a whole.[4] Along with Will and Piers Plowman, he is educated in the course of the poem; the nature of his understanding when we first meet him is considerably more limited than it is later. In Passus III he is called in by the king to wed Meed and make her respectable, since by her marriage to False she is threatening to undermine the precarious order he has established. The king sees her error as due only to ignorance.[5]

> "Vnwittily, [wye] wrouȝte hastow oft,
> Ac worse wrouȝtestow neure than tho thow Fals toke."
> (III. 105–6)

What she needs is a good husband to guide her, namely, the king's knight, Conscience. It is quite clear, however, that it is the king, not Lady Meed, who needs the guide, and Conscience sets out to perform this task with help from his two allies, Kynde Wit and Reason.

The concept which Conscience embodies has several possible meanings,

---

system of obligation, allegiance, and responsibility, which underlies medieval political thought.

4. See my article, Mary C. Schroeder, "The Character of Conscience in *Piers Plowman*," *SP*, LXVII (1970), 13–30.

5. As does A. G. Mitchell, "Lady Meed and the Art of 'Piers Plowman,'" Third Chambers Memorial Lecture (London, 1956), p. 22.

each of which comes into play as his role develops.[6] In Passus III–IV, his primary quality is psychological; conscience as judge of right and wrong blends the scholastic terms *synderesis* and *conscience*.[7] He is the moral agent of reason (or the *practical intellect*, in scholastic terminology); this, of course, is why he appears in these passus in company with Kynde Wit and Reason. Conscience as "moral sense" has a clear role in the scholastic analysis of human psychology.[8] St. Thomas (unlike Langland)[9] distinguishes between synderesis and conscience.[10] Synderesis is a habit, a natural disposition of the practical intellect, by means of which the intellect is inclined to the good. Conscience is formed by a number of secondary habits, all derived from and based upon the primary habit of synderesis; it is defined by St. Thomas as the act by which these intellectual habits are applied to something:

> Conscience, according to the very nature of the word, implies the relation of knowledge to something. . . . But the application of knowledge to something is done by some act. Wherefore . . . it is clear that conscience is an act.[11]

Thus, Conscience, in the scholastic conception of it, becomes the judge of right and wrong:

---

6. *MED,* s. v. *conscience,* gives the following major meanings of the word: "1) the mind or heart as the seat of thought, feeling, and desire; attitude of mind, feelings; 2) the faculty of knowing what is right . . . moral sense . . . awareness of right and wrong; 3) a sense of fairness or justice; scrupulousness, conscientiousness; 4) tenderness of conscience, solicitude; anxiety."

7. See Quirk, "Kynde Wit," p. 188, and Morton W. Bloomfield, *Piers Plowman as a Fourteenth-Century Apocalypse* (New Brunswick, N.J., 1961), pp. 167–69.

8. *MED,* s. v. *conscience,* 2.

9. Bloomfield, *Piers,* p. 111. Cf. Quirk, "*Kynde Wit,*" pp. 186–88, who says that for Langland conscience is "inwit in action," *inwit* being defined as "human . . . comprehension," not only of the intellect but also of feeling. See also *MED,* s. v. *conscience,* 1.

10. St. Thomas Aquinas discusses synderesis in *ST* (trans. Fathers of the English Dominican Province) I*. Q. LXXIX. a. 12. He implies that many habits form conscience: "Habitus autem ex quibus conscientia informatur, esti multi sunt, omnes tamen efficaciam habent ab uno primo principio, scilicet ab habitu primorum principiorum, qui dicitur synderesis" (*ST* I*. Q. LXXIX. a. 13).

11. *Ibid.*

For conscience is said to witness, to bind, or incite, and also to accuse, torment, or rebuke. And all these follow the application of knowledge or science to what we do.[12]

The perfection of conscience-synderesis depends upon the perfection and accuracy of one's knowledge. Conscience thus is closely connected with knowledge. Randolph Quirk notes that *inwit* (which he defines as synonymous with *intellectus agens,* the practical intellect) is frequently confused with conscience, as in Michael of Northgate's famous treatise, *The Ayenbyte of Inwyt,* for *inwit* is "concerned with the apprehension of truth, [and] it is therefore concerned with the distinction between true and false, good and evil; hence its functions can come near to, and be confused with, those of conscience."[13] But if *inwit* could be confused with conscience, conscience could also be confused with *inwit* and mean "consciousness," "inward knowledge," or "mind."[14] Conscience functioned not only as moral judge but also as intellectual judge, distinguishing between truth and falsehood. Indeed, such an extension of meaning is almost implicit in the scholastic definition of the term, since the action of conscience implements the knowledge of the *intellectus agens,* or *inwit.*

Conscience is associated with truth from the start. Theology warns Civil to beware of trying to wed Meed to False because "witty is Truthe, / [For] Conscience is of his conseille and knoweth зow vchone" (II. 137–38). Being of Truth's counsel he knows the false when he sees it, and, unlike the king, he is not confused by it. His victory over Meed begins when he is able to distinguish her two opposite meanings, meed as rightful reward, and meed as bribery. Clearly then, Conscience' role involves more than a simple blend of the scholastic synderesis and conscience. He is a fully conscious figure, his effectiveness being directly dependent upon the refinement of his comprehension.

But the kind of comprehension that Conscience must possess in order to be a reliable guide to Truth involves far more than mere intellectual acumen. This becomes evident during the course of his debate, when, in trying to explain to the king what Meed is, he gives as an example Saul's ill-fated expedition against the Amalekites:

---

12. *Ibid.*
13. Quirk, "Kynde Wit," p. 187.
14. *OED*, s. v. *conscience,* 1. The etymological note states that "in ME. *conscience* took the place of the earlier term INWIT in all its senses." See the discussion of this meaning of conscience by Günter Spitzbart, *Das Gewissen in der mettelenglischen Literatur* (Cologne, 1962), pp. 9–40.

"Such a myschief mede made [. . .] the kynge to haue
That god hated hym for euere and alle his eyres after."
(III. 276–77)

The issues shift from the comparatively limited ones of the court at Westminster to the ultimate battle itself, in which the enemy is still Meed, but a Meed so powerful that she can be routed only by "loue and lowenesse and lewte togederes" (III. 289). Conscience' role in this apocalyptic description is central. He is the companion of "kynde loue" (III. 297). Together they will set up a millennial society of peace and perfect truth.

Conscience' program sounds like everything Lady Holy Church could wish for, but if one examines his words carefully it is apparent that this is not the case. All Conscience foresees here is a social harmony and order based upon law, the reign of reason, as he calls it in III. 283, and, though he says that the world will be ruled by one Christian king (III. 287) and that priests will be made to behave themselves (III. 309–312), the element of *grace*, necessary for any genuinely Christian society, is entirely lacking. What Conscience envisions is no reign of the saints on earth, but a society of enlightened, reasonable men. The love which sustains it is not Christian *caritas* but "kynde loue," natural love, and Conscience' acknowledged instructor is Kynde Wit (III. 282). Langland regards Kynde Wit rather more highly than some critics would have us believe,[15] but it is never more to him than a purely natural mental power.

After listening to Conscience' arguments, his emphatic and entirely reasonable rejection of Meed, the king still does not perceive the danger. He interrupts at the beginning of Passus IV, tired of the argument, and commands Conscience to shut up and kiss Meed, for they shall both serve him. Conscience responds rudely to this silly request and decides to call in Reason as his ally. In doing so he is not so much appealing to a higher authority as simply getting a second voice to support him. The king has not been convinced—perhaps if he hears it from somebody else he will be. After having been instructed by Conscience concerning the situation at court (IV. 33–41), Reason's argument, to which the king favorably responds, turns out to be no more than a summary of what Conscience has already said,

---

15. D. W. Robertson and B. F. Huppé, *Piers Plowman and Scriptural Tradition* (Princeton, N.J., 1951), pp. 27–29. For a criticism of their understanding of the term, see a review of their book by Morton W. Bloomfield, *Speculum*, XXVII (1952), 245–46.

even to an echo of his own words.[16] The relationship of Conscience and Reason seems to be one of equals rather than of servant and master. This emphasizes not only Conscience' importance but, by what it leaves out, his limitations. His guides are only Reason and Kynde Wit. His is a wholly natural consciousness, human comprehension in a form that is eminently rational, but lacking the illumination of grace.

In these scenes, Conscience' psychological function is translated allegorically into a social function. He is the king's chief knight. Just as the function of conscience is to protect the soul and guide it to truth, so the function of a knight is to protect the kingdom. Knights also, in a more spiritual role, protect Truth itself; as Lady Holy Church teaches Will, they are to "holden with him and with hir that [asken þe] treuthe" (I. 100). But Conscience' knightly role is also linked with two less exalted meanings of the word, "scrupulousness" and "tenderness of conscience." [17] This is the meaning of conscience which is especially applicable to knights of courtly romance, models of courtesy and gentle practice.

This aspect of knights and of Conscience is a distinct liability as far as Langland is concerned. The only time he even approaches the style of the courtly romances is in the Lady Meed episodes. The *descriptio* of her in Passus II—the only example of that form in the poem—is pure convention in its emphasis upon the brilliant color and richness of her jewelry and costume:

> Fetislich hir fyngres were fretted with golde wyre,
> And there-on [riche] rubyes as red as any glede,
> And diamantz of derrest pris and double manere safferes,
> Orientales and ewages enuenymes to destroye.
> Hire robe was ful riche of red scarlet engreyned,
> With ribanes of red golde and of riche stones;
> Hire arraye me rauysshed suche ricchesse saw I neuere.
>
> (II. 11–17)

---

16. Compare Conscience' words in describing the millennial society:

> "And make of lawe a laborere suche [. . .] loue shal arise,
> And such [. . .] pees amonge the peple and a perfit trewthe."
>
> (III. 298–99)

Reason's words are a direct echo of this:

> "Lawe shal ben a laborere and lede a-felde donge,
> And Loue shal lede the londe as the lief lyketh!"
>
> (IV. 147–48)

17. *MED,* s. v. *conscience,* 3 and 4.

When she arrives at Westminster she is treated as befits a courtly heroine:[18]

> Curteysliche the clerke thanne as the kyng hight,
> Toke Mede bi the middel and brouʒte hir in-to chaumbre,
> [Ac] there was myrthe and mynstralcye Mede to plese.
> [. . .] That wonyeth [at] Westmynstre [worschipeþ] hir alle;
> Gentelliche with ioye the justices somme
> Busked hem to the boure there the birde [dwelleþ].
>
> (III. 9–14)

Everyone including the king bends over backward to be nice to her. Adverbs like *curteysliche* and *gentelliche* in the above passage are paralleled by Meed's responses, *mildeliche* (III. 20) and *hendeliche* (III. 29). When Meed comes before the king he speaks to her *curteisliche* (III. 103), and his whole treatment of her is velvet-gloved—"The kynge graunted hir grace with a gode wille" (III. 171).

That is much too nice a way to handle someone like Lady Meed. The king's anxiety to avoid a quarrel and effect a reconciliation makes it extremely difficult for Conscience to win his argument; as we have seen, he has to bring in Reason to repeat what he has already said before the king will believe it. The court, in fact, is so courtly that its concern for the outward forms of polite, conscientious behavior has blinded it entirely to the truth about the woman standing before it. Meed may be introduced in the most elegant terms, but the fact is that she is clothed in scarlet and closely allied to False. Meed is not only the dangerous pun which Conscience is at pains to define, but a rhetorical flourish as well. The ambiguous nature of the word *"quen"* (*queen-quean*)[19] which ends the A-Text's version of her

---

18. John A. Burrow has noted the high percentage of courtly vocabulary found in this passage, "The Audience of *Piers Plowman*," *Anglia*, LXXV (1957), 81.

19. I have used George Kane's edition of the A-Text (London, 1960). There is perhaps no phonological pun here, although there is some evidence to indicate that in certain dialects of the West Midlands which derive from West-Saxon and Mercian such a pun might have been possible. ME *quen* ("quean"), from OE *cwene,* had ẹ̄, due to the lengthening of the vowel in open syllables. The regular form of ME *quen* ("queen"), from OE *cwēn,* had ẹ. The vowel of OE *cwēn* developed by i-mutation from Prim. OE ō, the normal development of Prim. OE nasalized ā. There are, however, a number of spellings in WS and Mercian texts for *cwēn* and words of similar derivation with ǣ instead of ē (see Alastair Campbell, *Old English Grammar* [Oxford, 1957], § 198, and n. 4). Indeed, Bosworth-Toller lists *cwǣn* as an alternate spelling for *cwēn.* If these

descriptio puts the situation most succinctly: "*þere* nis no quen queyn*tere þat* quyk is o lyue" (A. II. 14). The king and his court see only the gorgeous romance queen before them and not the quean beneath all the layers of rhetorical ornament.

In Passus III, Conscience sees much more clearly than the court, but he does not lack courtesy toward Meed. He speaks harshly to her in his argument, not mincing terms and consistently addressing her in the familiar form, "thow." But when he has won the victory (or so he thinks), he switches to the polite form of address, "ȝe," and calls her "lady" and "madame" (III. 333–49). One critic interprets this as "exaggerated deference," which "parodies the respect paid her at . . . first." [20] But this is surely not parody. Conscience' deference is not particularly exaggerated; it is the way in which a courteous knight would address a lady. The trait is, however, a liability. Since courtesy is expressed by polite forms of speech and behavior, it is apt to be blinded by outwardly polite forms of speech and behavior. The king, though not himself a corrupt man, is fooled by Meed's rhetorical shimmer, both of speech and dress, and by her courteous behavior.

Thus Conscience is by no means an infallible figure. He has no divine qualities or guides in Passus III–IV, only his own natural comprehension and intellect, and he is inclined to be too polite and tender-hearted. He is very nearly bested by Lady Meed, though she is a relatively simple foe in comparison to the False itself, who has so many confusing forms. Conscience' aides, who are the natural faculties of Kynde Wit and Reason, are no better than he. Indeed, the triumph of Conscience lasts a very short time, for the field of folk soon collapses into confusion once again.

After the exposure of Lady Meed, Reason urges the folk to seek "seynt Treuthe" (V. 58), a command which moves the confession of the Seven Deadly Sins. Like so much else in the *Visio,* this confession is more interesting because of what it does not accomplish than what it does. For, while

---

graphs are phonologically significant, and their status is somewhat dubious (see Campbell), WS and Mercian *cwǣn* would give West Midlands *quen* with ę̄, the same sound as ME *quen* from OE *cwene.* Until the evidence is more complete, however, the possibility of a true pun on linguistic grounds must remain doubtful. Yet there can be no doubt that Langland had noted the similarity of the two words and used them in a punning fashion. An example occurs in the C-Text.

At church in the charnel cheorles aren vuel to knowe,
Other a knyght fro a knaue, other a queyne fro a queene.
(C. IX. 45–46)

20. John Lawlor, *Piers Plowman: An Essay in Criticism* (London, 1962), p. 34.

Repentance is present, Absolution is not, as in the confessions of the Old Testament sinners before the advent of Christ.[21] There is no indication that the people's prayers for forgiveness are answered—indeed, quite the contrary is true. Robert the Robber prays to Christ that he be saved, but, as Will comments, "What bifel of this feloun I can nouȝte faire schewe" (V. 479). What happens to the folk after Repentance' more eloquent prayer is plainly shown:

> A thousand of men tho thrungen togyderes;
> Criede vpward to Cryst and to his clene moder
> To haue grace to go [to truþe god leue that they moten].
> Ac there was [wye] non so wys the wey thider couthe,
> But blustreden forth as bestes ouer [baches] and hilles.
>
> (V. 517–21)

Once again, the folk are reduced to a lawless, bestial state, like the rats and mice of the Prologue.

By the time Piers Plowman pops his head into the poem, it is evident that Reason and Conscience are not sufficient to meet the problem of False. I suggested earlier that what Langland is seeking in *Piers Plowman* is a redeemed rhetoric, a new language to replace the outworn, imprecise formulations of the old. The key to this redemption of language lies in the Word, the resurrected Christ as redeeming Word, which alone can revivify and save man's language just as He alone can save man's soul. The inherent limitations of the old language and the need for a more truthful rhetoric are focused sharply for the first time at this point in the poem by a change in the mode of allegory between Passus V and Passus VI.

Passus I–V are peopled mainly by personifications. Personification allegory depends entirely on language in and of itself. It works with words, extending, exploring, refining their meaning, but the range of meaning possible in such allegory is never greater than that of the word personified. As an epistemological tool, such allegory is absolutely circumscribed by the limits of human language, of the concepts with which it is dealing. It can-

---

21. Cf. Chaucer's "Parson's Tale," where, in reference to Ps. 32:5, the Parson comments: "I seye that somtyme contricioun delivereth a man fro synne; / of which that David seith, 'I seye,' quod David (that is to seyn, I purposed fermely) 'to shryve me, and thow, Lord, relessedest my synne'" (*Works*, ed. F. N. Robinson, 2d ed. [Boston, 1957]). But the example of David was an exception rather than the rule for Old Testament sinners, as the Parson's "somtyme" indicates.

not, in short, create a new language from the ashes of the old. If the language on which the allegory is based is fallen and incapable of discovering truth, then the allegory itself must be subject to the same flaw. Unaided, language cannot redeem language.

This is why Conscience and Reason are finally unable to purge False. The medium in which False dwells is language—the concealed pun, the proliferation of pleonastic synonyms, the ambiguous phrase, the sophistical proposition. Thus, since Meed is a pun in English, the word itself is inherently susceptible to a misunderstanding which will lead to falsification and sin. No matter how hard Conscience tries to distinguish between the two meanings of the word, he cannot purge away the fact of their existence. And the poem's complete adherence to the most literal level of language, which is made up of puns, synonyms, and homonyms, complements its social and spiritual state in these early passus; the characters' reliance on natural law and on natural faculties finds its proper expression in a language limited to the *littera*. But, as Paul has said, "the letter killeth." The chief fault of personification allegory is that it makes the word, which should be a sign of something beyond itself, into its own significator; all the action and discourse of even the most complex word can ultimately express only what the word itself means to begin with. So, for example, Gluttony expresses himself in gluttinous ways which mean gluttony. There is a deadening circularity to personification when it is unrelated to any other kind of allegorical statement: it is simply *littera*, cut off from the spirit which giveth life, or "the word that shines within." Instead of being an epistemological tool, language has become a trap.

The structural change from Passus V to Passus VI can best be understood by contrasting the two kinds of pilgrimage to Truth which Piers sets for the folk. When they ask him to guide them, he first gives them a map. The path lies through Meekness and Conscience; it then takes a turn through several oddly-named places:

> And so boweth forth bi a broke, Beth-buxum-of-speche,
> [For to] ȝe fynden a [ford], ȝowre-fadres-honoureth,
> > *Honora patrem et matrem, etc.*
> Wadeth in that water and wascheth ȝow wel there,
> And ȝe shul lepe the liȝtloker al ȝowre lyf-tyme.
> [. . .] So shaltow se Swere-nouȝte-but-if-it-be-for-nede-
> And namelich-an-ydel-the-name-of-god-almyȝti.
> Thanne shaltow come by a crofte, [ac] come thow nouȝte there-inne;
> That crofte hat Coueyte-nouȝte-mennes-catel-ne-her-wyues-
> Ne-none-of-her-serauntes-that-noyen-hem-myȝte;

Loke [þow] breke no bowes there, but if it be [þyn] owne.
Two stokkes there stondeth, ac stynte [þow] nouȝte there,
They hatte Stele-nouȝte, Ne-slee-nouȝte; stryke forth by bothe;
And leue hem on thi left halfe, and loke nouȝte there-after;
And holde wel thyne haliday heighe til euen.
Thanne shaltow blenche at a berghe, Bere-no-false-witnesse,
He is frithed in with floreines and other fees many;
Loke thow plukke no plante there for peril of thi soule.

(V. 575–91)

This map is a fine example of personification allegory. Each of the commandments is embodied in a certain place, a stage on the journey to Truth. But the map doesn't help the folk on the field at all—it simply confuses them. They complain that the only way they can hope to get to the court of Truth over such complicated terrain is to have a guide who "wolde folwen vs eche a fote" (VI. 2). And they are right to be confused, since this kind of language has been confusing from the start of the *Visio*. Piers's map to Truth is, in fact, a misrepresentation, inherent in the nature of the allegory he employs. The Ten Commandments are commands to action; one either does them or not. They are not really like brooks or towns or crofts, to be waded through or avoided. And to make substantives of them, things rather than actions, is to distort their real nature and to employ a false analogy. Yet, allegory of this sort requires precisely this structure; concepts must be embodied in persons, in things, in the subjects of actions, and, as such, must necessarily become treated as nouns, even when they are imperative verbs. Thus the very allegorical structure which Piers has chosen is flawed; it leads to a misapprehension of Truth rather than providing a reliable sign of it. It is, however, a type of allegory entirely in keeping with the personification allegory of the earlier part of the *Visio*, and I believe that it is intended to emphasize the inadequacy of those structures as truthful epistemological signs. They are not accordant, "rect" signs, but discordant, "indirect," and distorting.

What is needed is a new relationship, a new form, in which to reestablish the meaningful connections of images with Truth. When the folk of the field cannot understand the allegory of the map to Truth, Piers provides them with an alternative route, a different structure for their pilgrimage: they can help him plow his half-acre.[22] "Perkyn and his pilgrymes" go

---

22. John Burrow, "The Action of Langland's Second Vision," *Essays in Criticism,* XV (1965), 247–68, argues convincingly that the real pilgrimage for Piers is the plowing of the half-acre.

forth to plow. The narrative, in this allegory, derives its meaning not from personified language but from figural action. Figural allegory is designed to perceive actions and things, events and persons as aspects of a spiritual pattern revealed in time and in particular occasions. It relates letter to spirit; it is the means by which one can learn to read the inner truths hidden within things, and thus gain a true intelligence of them.

The nature of this allegory can be seen in the following passage:

> "And I shal apparaille me," quod Perkyn, "in pilgrimes wise,
> And wende with 30w [þe wey], til we fynde Treuthe";
> [He] cast on [hise] clothes yclouted and hole,
> [Hise] cokeres and [hise] coffes, for colde of [hise] nailles,
> And [heng hise] hoper at [hise] hals in stede of a scrippe;
> "A busshel of bredcorne brynge me ther-inne;
> For I wil sowe it my-self, and sitthenes wil I wende
> To pylgrymage as palmers don pardoun forto haue.
> Ac who so helpeth me to erie or [any þyng swynke],
> Shal haue leue, bi owre lorde, to lese here in heruest,
> And make [hym] mery there-mydde, maugre who-so bigruccheth it.
> And alkyn crafty men that konne lyuen in treuthe,
> I shal fynden hem fode that feithfulliche libbeth.
> Saue Iakke the iogeloure, and Ionet of the stues,
> And Danyel the dys-playere, and Denote the baude,
> And frere [. . .] faytoure, and folke of his ordre,
> And Robyn the rybaudoure for his rusty wordes."
>
> (VI. 59–75)

In the course of this passage, Piers gives a new meaning to his role in the poem. Piers's entrance into the poem comes right after the palmer, a professional pilgrim, has admitted ignorance of Truth; the two figures are a complete contrast. The palmer is a pilgrim, Piers is a plowman; the palmer is a traveler, Piers is a stay-at-home; the palmer doesn't know the way to Truth, Piers does. Obviously, being a pilgrim and being a plowman are sharply opposed activities, as, in fact, the literal meaning of the words indicates. But Piers's plowing is a pilgrimage. He dresses himself "in pilgrimes wise" in the clothes of a plowman, with a seed basket around his neck instead of a palmer's scrip. He thus conflates the meanings of plowing and pilgrimage. Only after he has gone on pilgrimage with his plow will he go on pilgrimage "as palmers don"; and, indeed, in the narrative of the poem, he never goes on the palmers' sort of pilgrimage, for the pilgrimage of his plow brings about the pardon he hopes to receive.

The act of plowing and the act of pilgrimage are really the same, in

Piers's logic, because they are directed toward the same spiritual end—the attainment of pardon. They are thus both expressions of the same spiritual state, a penitent heart, indicated by the poor, penitential clothing that both plowmen and pilgrims wear. Plowing is seen to be a sacramental act, like pilgrimage, an outward and visible sign of an inner and spiritual state, or the *sacramentum visibile invisibilis formae*. The two actions, which are incompatible in literal terms, the terms in which they are first perceived by the folk, are resignified by reference to a spiritual state, and are thus seen to be true signs of the same thing, the same indwelling spirit or "inner word." Indeed, in these spiritual terms, Piers's plowing is the true pilgrimage, since it expresses a penitent heart desirous of serving Truth, while the pilgrim-palmer, despite the outward trappings of his many journeys, is really no pilgrim at all, since he has never heard of Truth.

Moreover, as he redefines himself in spiritual terms, Piers loses his specific timeliness. No one could mistake the figure of the palmer for anything but a fourteenth-century character. But as Piers makes himself into a spiritual plowman, he introduces a changed sense of time into the poem, which is an important feature of its figural allegory. As he is a spiritual plowman, his seed becomes spiritual seed, his harvest spiritual as well. He is thus associated with the figures from the parables of Jesus, with the plowmen of Christian iconology. Piers becomes a genuine *figura*,[23] linking in his own person one specific time with a pattern which encompasses all time. He is the atemporal and omnitemporal true pilgrim and true plowman, the Biblical sower of the seed, the lord of the future harvest, who refuses to feed some vividly contemporary folk—Daniel the dice-player, Donet the bawd, and Robin the dirty-joker. He thus relates present time to all time and to timelessness, as he is an aspect of the ongoing revelation of the figural pattern.

The perception that all time is in some sense present time through the continuing process of revelation is basic to a true Christian understanding. Time is the medium of revelation, within which events are joined as aspects of the all-encompassing divine pattern. Thus, the perception of time as figural in nature is basic to the cognitive concerns of this poem. Figural time makes possible a Scripturally-based, fourteenth-century, apocalyptic

---

23. In the sense developed by Erich Auerbach, *"Figura,"* in *Scenes from the Drama of European Literature* (New York, 1959), pp. 11–76. See also the interesting discussion of figural allegory in the introduction to *Piers Plowman,* ed. Elizabeth Salter and Derek Pearsall, York Medieval Texts (Evanston, Ill., 1967).

allegory like *Piers Plowman*. Basic to its conception of history is a theory of the nature of time itself; figural time assumes that the process of past, present, and future in human history is actually the progressive manifestation of a timeless pattern in eternity. This view of time thus brings the past recorded in the Bible into an essentially present relationship with the life of every Christian in all time, as past and present bear a revelatory relationship to each other. The present reveals and fulfills the past, the past prefigures the present, and both prefigure and are revealed and fulfilled by the future.

One of the best texts for illustrating a clear and conscious use of figural time is Augustine's *Confessiones*. For Augustine, his own life is a figural document; he is a living illustration of what the Psalmist and the Apostle have said. This self-perception is strikingly apparent at the moment of his conversion:

> So I spoke, weeping in the bitter contrition of my heart. Suddenly a voice reaches my ears from a nearby house. It is the voice of a boy or a girl (I don't know which) and in a kind of singsong the words are constantly repeated: "Take it and read it. Take it and read it." At once my face changed, and I began to think carefully of whether the singing of words like these came into any kind of game which children play, and I could not remember that I had ever heard anything like it before. I checked the force of my tears and rose to my feet, being quite certain that I must interpret this as a divine command to me to open the book and read the first passage which I should come upon. For I had heard this about Antony: he had happened to come in when the Gospel was being read, and as though the words read were spoken directly to himself, had received the admonition: *Go, sell all that thou hast, and give to the poor, and thou shalt have treasure in heaven, and come and follow me.* And by such an oracle he had been immediately converted to you.[24]

The example of St. Antony gives full significance to the voice Augustine hears in the garden, prompting him to pick up the Book. This is not to say that the moment of his conversion validates the past events of the saint's life in the way that an example validates a hypothesis; rather, it suggests that Augustine's life can only be understood fully in terms of those past

---

24. Augustine *Confessiones* (trans. Rex Warner) III. 5.

actions. In this way, the Bible and the saints' lives are continuously present documents for Augustine, a perception which accounts for his stylistic trait of incorporating large sections from the Bible into his narrative account of his life. And just as his life is a *figura* which must be understood in the full historical context recorded in the Bible, so he suggests the ongoing nature of his conversion by his sudden break into the present tense. This suggests that he views the story of his conversion in exactly the way he views the events of the Bible and of the lives of the saints, as moments which, though past, have a continuing present significance, even a present being, when figurally perceived—the present being they have in the eyes of eternity. The sudden shift in this passage from past to present tense is a perfect formal representation of this figural conception of time.

Since figuralism recognizes the divine Word as the source of its meaning, it is a richer and more complex instrument of understanding than personification can possibly be. Figural allegory relates the human world to its validating, divine pattern. But in order to be properly interpreted, it requires spiritual understanding, a right understanding proceeding from a rightly ordered will.[25] The figural nature of Passus V–VII is revealed by means of a test of understanding, just as the nature of the earlier part of the *Visio* is uncovered through the much simpler test provided by Lady Meed. In order to understand the structure and significance of the world in which they find themselves, the king, Conscience, and Will must understand the nature of Lady Meed: she is the key to the conceptually (and morally) lawless nature of False. The key to the nature of the world in the later part of the *Visio* is the figural enigma of the pardon from Truth.

Its position in the text makes clear the conclusive importance of the receiving of the pardon, for it turns the argument from the *Visio* to the *Vita de Dowel* in all three versions of the poem.[26] The pardon dispenses

---

25. The differences between scholastic philosophers over the primacy of reason to will, or will to reason, are settled for Langland (if he was even aware of them) in favor of will, as evidenced by the name of his chief character. Will moves the cognitive processes of the poem, and until will is in order knowledge is impossible. For an account of the differing theological positions, see E. Gilson, *History of Christian Philosophy in the Middle Ages* (London, 1955), especially his accounts of "The Golden Age of Scholasticism" (pp. 327–83) and of Duns Scotus' voluntarism (pp. 463–64).

26. Some of the material in the following pages was published in my earlier article, Mary C. Schroeder, *"Piers Plowman:* The Tearing of the Pardon," *PQ,* XLIX (1970), 8–18.

saving grace to the folk of the field; it brings about a radical change in Piers's way of life, and Piers rips it apart when the priest tells him that it is no pardon:

> [. . .] In two lynes it lay and nou3t a [lettre] more,
> And was writen ri3t thus in witnesse of treuthe:
> *Et qui bona egerunt, ibunt in vitam eternam;*
> *Qui vero mala, in ignem eternum.*
> "Peter!," quod the prest tho, "I can no pardoun fynde"
> . . . .
> And Pieres for pure tene pulled it [asonder].
>
> (VII. 110–12, 116)

The chief problem in this scene lies with Piers's apparently perverse tearing of the document on which the pardon is written. By ripping it up, he must mean to reject the pardon itself including the way of life upon which it is based, the life of Dowel. It has been argued, therefore, that the pardon is deficient and that, having been stung by the priest, Piers accepts something different and, presumably, "higher." Yet no one has come up with a satisfactory explanation of the pardon's deficiencies.

John Lawlor has recently made an attempt to do so; he agrees with the priest and suggests that the pardon is lacking in mercy. It is, he says, "a statement . . . of rigour. It records Law," that is, the natural moral law written in all men's hearts.[27] But this is surely not the case. The lines of the pardon come from the Athanasian Creed, a document "as familiar as the Psalms to the poet and his contemporaries." [28] One might accuse the statement of being succinct, but not of being morally insufficient or spiritually inadequate, for what it says is fundamental to the Christian moral scheme. It is also fundamental to *Piers Plowman,* since the attempt to understand Dowel, a concept introduced by the pardon, occupies most of the rest of the poem. For Piers to reject Dowel as "deficient," as he must if he rejects the pardon, belies the entire structural development of the poem.

Furthermore, the pardon, despite the priest's scorn, is a genuine pardon —as is evident from the words used to describe it at the beginning of Passus VII—and thus must be based on the law. God's grace, though necessarily unmerited, is not arbitrary. Perfect mercy is perfect justice, as the

---

27. Lawlor, *Piers Plowman: An Essay in Criticism,* p. 77.
28. R. W. Frank, Jr., *Piers Plowman and the Scheme of Salvation* (New Haven, Conn., 1957), p. 26.

Atonement demonstrates, and to accuse the pardon of "rigour" is to disregard the effects of Original Sin. If the pardon were a statement of conditions under the Old Law, as Lawlor and others have implied, there could be no Dowel at all, no release from sin and death.[29] As a gift from Truth, the pardon is an act of grace. And doing well at all requires grace, as Will emphasizes in his meditation on the value of Dowel—"god gyue vs grace here ar we gone hennes, / Suche werkes to werche" (VII. 197–98).

Yet all of this serves only to make the tearing of the pardon more inscrutable than ever. If the pardon represents a promised infusion of God's grace, why should Piers tear it up? For there can be no doubt about the importance of the action; it dominates all of Passus VII in the B-Text. Piers's action makes no literal sense; indeed, it is even contradictory to sense —just as equating plowing and pilgrimage is nonsense in literal terms. Evidently, it must be understood in other terms, as a figural action with a spiritual significance commensurate with the spiritual nature of Truth's pardon. The Biblical event which most closely resembles Piers's action is the similarly angry destruction of the written words of an earlier covenant of God with man—Moses' breaking of the tables of the Law in Exod. 32.[30] Moses returns from Mt. Sinai bearing the stone tablets upon which God has inscribed the Law of the Covenant and discovers the Israelites, led by Aaron the priest, worshipping the Golden Calf. In the words of the Vulgate, "iratusque valde, projecit de manu tabulas, et confregit eas ad radicem montis" (Exod. 32:19).

There are four narrative parallels between this action and the tearing of the pardon in Piers Plowman. First, the two principals, both lawgivers and leaders of a folk, are extremely angry; second, their anger is occasioned by the misguided and stupid religious counsel of a trusted priest; third, their anger causes them to destroy documents of supreme value; and finally, the destruction of the written words in no way negates or rejects the promises

---

29. Lawlor was anticipated chiefly by Nevill Coghill, "The Pardon of Piers Plowman" (Sir Israel Gollancz Memorial Lecture), Proceedings of the British Academy, XXXI (1945) and by R. W. Chambers, Man's Unconquerable Mind (London, 1939), pp. 117–19, though Lawlor states the pardon's inadequacies most strongly. The deficiency of the pardon as a document has again been argued by Rosemary Woolf, "The Tearing of the Pardon," in Piers Plowman: Critical Approaches, ed. S. S. Hussey (London, 1969), pp. 50–75.

30. A hint in this direction is given by Howard Meroney, "The Life and Death of Longe Wille," ELH, XVII (1950), who refers to Piers as "a ridiculous Adam-Moses" (p. 17) and links the tearing of the pardon to Moses' wrath at the faithlessness of the Israelites (p. 18).

contained in them. In breaking the tablets, Moses in no way invalidates God's covenant. The only consequence of his action is that he has to go back up the mountain and get a new set. Neither does the tearing of Truth's pardon negate the promise written upon it. The tablets are broken and the pardon torn not because they are theologically faulty, but because both Moses and Piers are suddenly enraged and vent their anger on the object that happens to be nearest. That they should destroy things of such value is only a measure of their rage and disgust, their "pure tene," occasioned in Moses' case by the blindness of the Israelites and his priest, Aaron, to God's care for them and in the case of Piers by the similar blindness of the niggling Christian priest.

A long and common exegetical tradition makes the breaking of the tablets in Exodus a type of the change from the Old Law to the New. Rabanus Maurus interprets it as follows:

> Iratusque quidem Moyses videtur tabulas testimonii digito Dei scriptas, collisisse atque fregisse; magno tamen mysterio figurata est iteratio testamenti, quoniam vetus fuerat abolendum, et constituendum novum.[31]

Both Isidore of Seville and Walafrid Strabo give only a slight variation of this reading,[32] and the figural significance of the episode would have been commonplace knowledge to any educated fourteenth-century reader.

Moreover, the text describing the pardon sent to Piers describes it as a type of the Atonement itself:

---

31. Rabanus Maurus *Commentaria in Exodum* (Migne, PL CVIII. 224). ["And indeed Moses, full of wrath, seems to have dashed together and to have broken the tables of the testament written by the finger of God: thus by a great mystery is figured the iteration of the testament, for the old was to be abolished and the new established."]

32. Isidore of Seville suggests that Moses' return for the second set of tables, which are not broken, figures the New Law: "Aliae vero, ad instar priorum iteratim incisae, Novi Testamenti habuere figuram. Istae non franguntur, ut ostenderentur Novi Testamenti eloquia permansura" (*Quaestiones in Exodum* [Migne, PL LXXXIII. 307]). Walafrid Strabo quotes Rabanus and Isidore, favoring the details of Isidore's reading (*Glossa Ordinaria* [Migne, PL CXIII. 287]). The tradition is generally clear, and slight disagreements about details should not detract from the value of these texts in illuminating *Piers Plowman*. Poets are not Biblical exegetes; the justification for and limits of the typological allusion in the tearing of the pardon scene come from the text of the poem itself, not from the words of the commentators.

Treuthe herde telle her-of and to Peres he sent,
To taken his teme and tulyen the erthe,
And purchaced hym a pardoun *a pena et a culpa*
For hym, and for his heires [. . .] euermore after.

(VII. 1–4)

The use of the verb "purchace" suggests the sacrificial death of Christ which paid for Adam's sin "euermore after," and released man *a pena et a culpa* from the major effect of Original Sin, making it possible for him to receive God's grace and to do well.

Piers's actions thus perfectly express the nature and meaning of the pardon. He realizes at once that the pardon is a figural allegory, a type of the New Law, and he demonstrates his understanding of it by an action which figures the change from the law of the letter to that of the spirit. The fact that Piers's response puzzles Will is Will's own fault. Piers sees all things more perfectly, even his own errors, and he reveals in a figure the spiritual significance not only of the pardon but also of the world of the *Visio*, which he himself helped to establish, prior to Truth's gift. Figurally speaking, that world is graceless, fallen, and false. As a fallen world, it cannot redeem itself any more than its language is capable of self-renewal. It needs an infusion of spiritual grace, a gift from Truth, in order to be redeemed.

The spiritual meaning of the *Visio* is best expressed by the Pauline concepts of *vetus homo* and *novus homo:*

> That ye put off . . . the old man, which is corrupt according to the deceitful lusts; And be renewed in the spirit of your mind; And that ye put on the new man, which after God is created in righteousness and true holiness.
>
> (Eph. 5:22–24)

The "old man" and the "new man" are two states of the soul, one of which has not received the grace of salvation and one of which has. These states not only determine the progress of Christian history from the Old Law to the New, but also govern the movement of each individual Christian soul from its natural state of sin to the state of grace. It is important to realize that the relationship embodied in the phrase *vetus homo* between man in the historical past under the Old Law and a man morally limited because he lacks the effecting power of God's grace is a typological one. The typology implicit in Paul's letter to the Romans is clearly defined by Augustine, who says that the historical progression from Old Law to New is (or should be) recapitulated in the life of every Christian in every age.[33] Any fourteenth-century man who tries to live simply according to law and justice without the sustaining power of grace is a moral type of the ancient Hebrews under the Old Law who also lacked grace. Thus, no matter how often the name of Christ is invoked in the *Visio,* no matter how Christian the surface of the poem may seem to be, the significant point is whether the grace of Christ is a meaningful factor in the society depicted in it.

All the efforts at order in the *Visio* seem to be based upon justice and law but lacking in grace. At their best they incorporate a rationally enlightened order governed by the Ten Commandments, but they know of divine wisdom and charity only through promise, not fact. The world of the *Visio* is a natural one, relying for its support wholly on the qualities of reason, conscience, and kind wit, all faculties of man's natural soul, and as such subject to the effects of Original Sin. In his fallen state, man may know the Law of God (as the Israelites did), but Original Sin prevents him from doing anything effective to save himself. He can only know what sin is; he cannot live sinlessly. He needs sanctifying grace, the grace given by God for salvation, to free him from his bondage to death. As the Samaritan tells Will in Passus XVII:

> "May no medcyn [vnder mone] the man to hele brynge,
> Neither Feith ne fyn Hope, so festred ben his woundis,
> With-out the blode of a barn borne of a mayde."
> (XVII. 91–93)

This unredeemed quality can be seen even when Piers sets the folk of the field to their various tasks in his half-acre. In Passus VI, Piers is a type of the lawgiver, a *figura,* who, like the plowman-pilgrim, has many spiritual antecedents. Two Biblical characters especially come to mind—the Old

---

33. "Ex quo comprehendimus quatuor esse differentias etiam in uno homine, quibus gradatim peractis in vita aeterna manebitur. Quia enim oportebat atque id justum erat, ut posteaquam natura nostra peccavit, amissa beatitudine spirituali, quae paradisi nomine significatur, animales carnalesque nasceremur; prima est actio ante Legem, secunda sub Lege, tertia sub gratia, quarta in pace" (Augustine, *De diversis quaestionibus* I. Q. LXVI. 3 [Migne, *PL* XL. 62]). The rest of this discussion defines the various states of the soul and their historical analogues in detail, relating the argument to Paul's discussion of the Law in Romans.

Testament figure of Moses, and the New Testament figure of the Holy Spirit giving spiritual gifts to the community of Christians. The Christian context of this scene would seem to suggest that Piers should be a New Testament type, but ironically, as the action progresses, he is shown to have more in common with Moses. Indeed, the spiritual deficiencies of this scene are deliberately evoked by the parallel scene in Passus XIX, when Grace distributes to the folk that divine gift of renewing grace which is exactly what Piers lacks in this earlier scene. Piers cannot order the folk on the field; and the nominally Christian context of Passus VI–VII has only an ironic ring as Piers's society fails so abjectly to be effective in any way at all.

Piers's understanding is still bounded in Passus VI by the terms of his allegorical map, the Ten Commandments of the Old Law. The directions which he gives to the folk are to obey the Commandments; if they do so, then they will be let in to the court of Truth by Grace, his gateward. Grace is a tough inspector of the custom, making sure that one's papers are in order. But this counsel does not recognize the fact that redeeming, sanctifying grace is not God's reward for obeying the Ten Commandments, as the spiritual history of the Old Testament teaches. Piers shows a blunted understanding of the nature of divine justice and of divine grace in the allegorical map which he gives to the pilgrims; the insufficiency of its form mirrors an insufficient understanding. And though he gives it over for a better, more truthful form, he still carries some of his limitations with him as he seeks to order society for the plowing of his half-acre. The basis for Piers's order in Passus VI is a natural and mutual covenant, a contract based simply on *mesurable hire,* equal pay for equal work. As Piers tells the knight:

> ". . . I shal swynke and swete, and sowe for vs bothe,
> And [. . . laboure ek] for thi loue al my lyf-tyme,
> In couenaunt that thow kepe holikirke and my-selue
> Fro wastoures and fro wykked men that [wolde me destruye]."
>
> (VI. 26–29)

The knight binds himself, but it is a purely human bargain which he pledges to uphold. What binds him is his unaided oath, and no matter how honorable or noble he may be, the fact remains that the basis of his bond is his limited natural strength. No one in this part of the poem, even Piers, ever asks for or mentions the need for divine grace to effect what he is trying to do. There are no everlasting arms maintaining Piers and his helpers—only the human ones of the knight.

Piers works for hire and is not ashamed to say so. He takes only what is just and asks no more: there is an absolute correspondence between his effort and his reward. Such a morality is the best that can be devised by Conscience and Kynde Wit operating without divine aid, but it is at best a poor approximation of the Christian ideal of labor without thought of reward, as embodied in figures like the Good Samaritan, St. Francis, or Chaucer's plowman. After setting the pilgrims to work on their tasks, Piers oversees them as if with a tally book in his hand:

> ". . . and who-so best wrou3te,
> [. . .] Shulde be huyred ther-after whan heruest-tyme come."
> (VI. 115–16)

Such an attitude is very different from that expressed in the peculiarly Christian parable of the Laborers in the Vineyard (Matt. 20:1–16), in which every man gets the same reward no matter how long he has worked. Under Piers's system, "Eche man in his manere made hym-self to done" (VI. 112). And that, of course, is the trouble with it.

Waster decides "in his manere" that he will not work, and there is nothing to coerce him except the threat of starvation. The knight tries to fulfill his oath:

> Curteisly the kny3te thanne as his kynde wolde,
> Warned Wastoure and wissed hym bettere,
> "Or thow shalt abugge by the lawe, by the ordre that I bere!"
> (VI. 166–68)

But the knight's "kynde" is powerless to change Waster's "kynde," no matter what order he serves. Without divine aid, each man is bound to live only within his natural limits; he can effect a spiritual change neither in himself nor in anybody else.

Nor can nature itself make a change. Hunger, to whom Piers calls for aid when the knight fails, is a purely natural, nonspiritual agent, dealing out strict justice based solely on natural cause and effect. Those who do not work do not eat. Hunger's philosophy is purely mundane, a philosophy of the belly, as one would expect. Its concern is with the procurement of food and the sustenance of life, concerns which are not evil but so natural that they are almost outside the moral sphere. To blame Hunger for glutting himself in a time of plenty, as he does at the end of this passus, would be absurd. None of his actions is moral; they simply fulfill his own unchangeable nature.

Piers, however, does try to deal with Hunger's advice in moral terms, for he does know the moral law of the Ten Commandments. After Hunger concludes his discourse with the text, *"Facite vobis amicos de mamona iniquitatis"* (VI. 230), Piers asks, "Miȝte I synnelees do as thow seist?" (VI. 232). This is clearly a moral question, but Hunger proves incapable even of Piers's level of moral understanding. He replies:

> *"Piger [propter frigus]* no felde [wolde] tilye
> [. . .] He shal [go] begge and bidde and no man bete his hunger."
> (VI. 238–39)

In essence all this says is "You can't change human nature." But the whole Christian ethic presupposes that, with God's help, you can and must. If man cannot be changed, he cannot be saved. Piers and his helpers, lacking God's grace, are unable to effect such a change, even though Piers wants to; his society has run up against the limits of its own unredeemed nature. There can be no progression toward goodness in such a world, no moral value. The rule of nature is a meaningless cycle of want and plenty in which the only constant is work and the only justice the blind actions of physical causation. It is the world of the Fall, purposeless and incapable of effecting true goodness because it is incapable of change. Doing well in such a world consists only in feeding oneself sufficiently and not overeating, and sin is a bellyache. The concluding picture of Hunger, fast asleep and glutted with good ale while wastrels and beggars swarm over the half-acre, provides the final satiric comment on the rule of unaided natural law, and gives an ironic cast to Piers's thanks for Hunger's instruction—"thise aren profitable wordis . . . !" (VI. 277).

This sense of entrapment in nature gives rise to Will's despair at the end of this passus, and the prophetic language in which it is couched merely adds to it a sardonic note.

> Whan ȝe se the [mone] amys and two monkes hedes,
> And a mayde haue the maistrie, and multiplie bi eight,
> Thanne shal Deth withdrawe and Derthe be iustice,
> And Dawe the dyker deye for hunger,
> But if god of his goodnesse graunt vs a trewe.
> (VI. 328–32)

The society of natural law, effected by Piers under the tutelage of Conscience and Kind Wit (V. 546), has failed, as it must, for it is sustained only by Nature. Death reigns, and dearth, the natural cycle personified in Hunger, is its law. Even Piers, the most honest and just man in the *Visio*, has failed to escape this cycle; only God "of his goodnesse" can redeem the unchanging pattern of the Fall and open the way to Truth. And Truth's response to this cry from Will is the pardon he sends at the beginning of Passus VII.

The receipt of the pardon touches off a controversy over its nature which dogs the poem and Will throughout the passus of the *Vita de Dowel*. Piers says that the pardon is a pardon; the priest says it is not. Evidently, they understand the word in different ways. Piers uses the word "pardon" in a way exactly parallel to his earlier use of the word "pilgrimage"; he says that plowing is a pilgrimage, but it is obvious to the folk that it isn't the sort of pilgrimage they are used to, the kind that palmers make.[34] And neither is the pardon the sort of pardon that pardoners hand out.[35] In arguing that the pardon is no pardon, the priest is considering its form alone. This is clear from his promise to Piers, "I [shal] construe eche a clause, and kenne it the on Engliche" (VII. 107). He is offering Piers, who being a plowman is ignorant of Latin, a grammar lesson; he will transliterate the pardon into English, clause by clause. And when he cannot discover the word "pardon" in the Latin statement, he says that it is no pardon at all. The priest is absolutely bounded by the literal statement of the words; they have no other significance to him.

Piers, however, sees the literal words as signs of a spiritual meaning, hidden within them, which can only be understood in relationship to the whole divine pattern governing men, events, and time. For Piers, the word has no meaning apart from the heart, the inner understanding, the spirit, which informs it. This is clear in his replies to the priest. He first tears up the pardon, thereby expressing as plainly as possible his contempt for the literal words themselves, but also performing a figural action which, when properly interpreted, reveals the spiritual meaning hidden within the pardon. Then, Piers announces that he will adopt the Christ-like life of patient poverty:[36]

---

34. This point is well developed by John Burrow, "Words, Works, and Will: Theme and Structure in *Piers Plowman*," in *Critical Approaches,* ed. Hussey, p. 115. See also Robertson and Huppé, *Piers Plowman and Scriptural Tradition,* pp. 93–94.

35. As was first pointed out by Frank, *Piers Plowman and the Scheme of Salvation,* pp. 27–28.

36. See Frank's discussion of the doctrine of *ne solliciti sitis* and of patient poverty, *ibid.,* pp. 30–33.

"*Ne solliciti sitis,* he seyth in the gospel,
And sheweth vs bi ensamples vs selue to wisse.
The foules on the [firmament], who fynt hem [. . .] at wynter?
[Whan þe frost freseþ fode hem bihoueþ]
Haue thei no gernere to go to but god fynt hem alle."

(VII. 126–29)

Patient poverty is a form of *imitatio Christi,* the modeling of one's actions on the life of Christ in order to become Christ-like. To undertake the imitation of Christ is to see oneself as a potential figure or image of Christ; having been a type of Moses, Piers will become a type of Christ. In doing so, Piers also demonstrates that he understands perfectly the inner, spiritual nature of man as created in God's image. He sets his decision in a fully Biblical context, beginning with the verse from Psalm 22 and ending with the example of the birds from Luke 12. He thus makes himself a part of the figurally revealed, divine pattern, in exactly the same stylistic manner Augustine uses in the *Confessions.* Piers's new way of life is thus an expression of his more perfect understanding.

The figural mode of life is an allegorical equivalent in narrative terms to Piers's figural use of language, since he sees the hidden, spiritual meaning of all things. Piers translates even the most concrete and literal words into metaphors of a spiritual reality. He has already equated his plowing with the spiritual action of pilgrimage; now, his plow will be "of preyers and of penaunce" (VII. 119), his bread will be tears: *"Fuerunt michi lacrime mee panes die ac nocte."* Piers's speech is the first example in the poem of redeemed language, in which the literal words are entirely given significance by reference to spiritual and divine reality, even though this means distorting their ordinary, literal meanings.

It is clear that Piers and the priest understand the pardon differently; in fact, they understand language itself differently. Though the words they use are English words, they cannot understand each other—or, rather, the priest cannot understand Piers, and Piers has only scorn for the priest's understanding. It is a situation similar to that which pertains in the conversation of Will and Lady Holy Church; the two principals do not speak the same language, though they use the same words. And their argument produces an impasse; there is no way for them to resolve their debate. The priest believes that Piers is only a pretentiously learned plowman. Obviously he hasn't the Latin to be able to read the "pardon" correctly, since if he could he would know it was no pardon. Therefore, says the priest, the only text Piers is fit to preach on is *dixit insipiens.* Piers, for whom the issue is not learning but understanding, calls the priest a "lewed lorel," who, however much he may know his Bible, has clearly not understood it. And as they square off, eyeball to eyeball, Will wakes up to muse upon his curious dream. The priest and Piers have called each other fools, with equal conviction, and at this point in the poem, it is not at all clear to Will which one is correct.

The problem presented by the pardon is essentially a problem of correct reading. And right reading can only come about as a result of a true understanding of the relationship between written words and their spiritual meaning—or, to use the Augustinian triad, the figural relationship between the expressed word, the "inner word" of the soul's spiritual understanding, and the Word. Unfortunately, only Piers understands the pardon as an interpretive, cognitive problem; to the priest it is simply a formal, almost a grammatical, problem. And Will also misses the real nature of the pardon: he sees it as a problem of words versus works:[37]

> [. . .] Al this maketh me on this meteles to thynke;
> And how the prest preued no pardoun to Dowel,
> And demed that Dowel indulgences [passeþ],
> Biennales and triennales and bisschopes lettres,
> [. . .] Dowel at the day of dome is dignelich vnderfongen,
> [He] passeth al the pardoun of seynt Petres cherche.
>
> (VII. 167–72)

The structure of these sentences opposes Dowel to pardon, indulgences, and bishops' letters, works to words. Will casts the problem in terms of a moral choice between empty, though learned, words and good, though unlearned, works. This simple-minded opposition leads him directly to the anti-intellectual position he takes throughout most of the *Vita de Dowel*, a position from which he must be extricated with great difficulty by Imaginatyf. It also leads him to his overweening pride of intellect, since he, knowing that works are better than words, is obviously cleverer than all those clerks who are wasting their time in fruitless learning, which is useless for salvation.

---

37. Many of the poem's commentators have followed Will's opposition of words and works, only to discover that, without considerable redefinition, it leads, as it leads Will, to an anti-intellectualism which is not supported by the poem. See, for example, the comments of Coghill, "The Pardon of Piers Plowman," and the corrective remarks of T. P. Dunning, "The Structure of the B-Text of *Piers Plowman*," *RES*, N.S., VII (1956). The opposition has been applied to the poem with better success by Burrow, "Words, Works," as a metaphoric device for defining certain structural features within the poem.

But the problem of the pardon is not moral, it is interpretive—a problem of understanding. Works are better than words, in the sense that words without works are dead, but this does not alter the problem of knowing what works to do, since words and works together are dead without the spirit that giveth life. Will has not yet realized that the problem of doing well is related to the problem of interpretation; words and works together are signs, images, mirrors, enigmas of the spirit. The problem of *intus legendum,* of inward reading, is as pertinent to works as it is to words, for true works express an inner, spiritual meaning just as true words do. Thus, the formulation which Will employs is a false one: it treats words and works as things in and of themselves, which can be judged absolutely on a moral scale, rather than understanding both as signs of a spiritual reality. And by casting the problem in terms of an irreconcilable conflict between words and works, Will demonstrates that he is just as wedded to a purely literal understanding as the priest is. He must understand, as Piers does, the true nature of words and works as signs, informed by a spiritual essence or *kynde;* they are not circumscribed, earthly things, but signs of the "inner word," the understanding, and the will "that shines within."

ᴄ꙳ʟ CHAPTER FOUR ᴊ꙳ꙮ

"Where Dowel [and] Dobet and Dobest ben in londe,
Here is Wille wolde ywyte, yif Witte [coude hym teche]."

Musing fruitlessly on the problem of Dowel, Will continues his wandering, and the efforts to correct his mistaken comprehension determine the structure of Passus VIII–X. There are two repeated refrains in Will's search for knowledge: his persistent question "What is Dowel?," and his equally persistent complaint, "I haue no kynde knowyng to conceyue [. . . þi] wordes." Dowel and *kynde* are the two key words which provide both the source of Will's mistake and its cure. While it is perfectly evident that Dowel presents a problem for Will, the problem of *kynde*, though less emphatically stated, is actually more basic. Indeed, it seems to me that Passus VIII–XII are concerned less with the nature of Dowel than they are with the meaning of *kynde*.

It is apparent from the outset that Will has mistaken the *kynde* of the word Dowel itself. His plaintive query, "What is Dowel?," cannot be answered to suit his understanding, because he has made a mistake about the function of the word in the pardon;[1] he has made the fundamental interpretive error of misreading the literal text. In the pardon, Dowel is an

---

1. David Mills, "The Rôle of the Dreamer in *Piers Plowman*," in *Piers Plowman: Critical Approaches,* ed. S. S. Hussey (London, 1969), has noted that Will treats Dowel like a noun (pp. 194–95). I am most indebted to Andrea Rosnick, of the University of Toronto, who analyzed the syntactic function of Dowel in the language of Will and his interlocuters in a paper which she has kindly made available to me, and who suggested the general outlines I have followed in discussing the epistemological consequences of Will's misuse of the term.

[81]

imperative verb: "Dowel, and haue wel, and god shal haue thi sowle." But as Will uses the word, it is a noun. Obviously, Will should have availed himself of the priest's offer to "construe eche clause." Instead of understanding the word as a command to action, a command to live in a spiritually meaningful way—as Piers does—Will understands Dowel as a substantive problem in theology.

It is for this reason that the problem of *kynde* is basic to the problem of Dowel. Will has mistaken the *kynde* of the word as it is given in the pardon; this leads him to his mistaken understanding of the quarrel between Piers and the priest. *Kynde* is a recurrent term in the early passus of the *Vita de Dowel*. It is the creator of Sir Dowel's castle, Caro, in Wit's fable of Passus IX, it appears directly to Will as the lord of creation in Passus XI, and it is the key term in Will's desire for "kynde knowyng." The word *kynde* means "nature," yet it always carries the idea of innate or inherent being, "essential character," "inherent qualities." [2] Thus, to understand *kyndely* would be to understand a thing in its essential being, its "quiddity," to use the clerkly term. Clerk that he is, especially in arguing with clerical faculties of Passus VIII–X, Will most often uses the word in this sense, to complain that his teachers have not taught him the quiddity of Dowel. But the phrase "kynde knowyng" also means to understand something according to one's own nature or essential being,[3] which in Will's case would be according to his nature as the will, the inquiring motivation of the poem. If Will understood his own *kynde,* and knew *kyndely* in this sense, he would understand that to do well is the essence of man's being and the essential expression of his will. He is created in God's image and thus is created innately good, with an innate disposition to do well. Thus the *kynde* of Dowel and Will's own *kynde* will are inextricably linked; yet one of the compelling ironies of his search is that he does not see until much later that the real *kynde* of Dowel lies within himself.

There is one other meaning of the word *kynde* which seems to me important in these passus, for it links the thematic concerns of the search for Dowel with their rhetorical and allegorical structure. *Kynde* is also used as a technical term in grammar, to refer to one of the aspects which must be satisfied in grammatical accord. It is used in this sense in the grammatical argument in C. IV:

---

2. *MED,* s.v. *kinde, passim,* but especially 1–8.
3. *Kinde,* in the sense of "the natural disposition or temperament of a person . . . inherent character"; *MED,* s.v. *kinde,* 2(a) and 2(c).

"Thus is relacion rect ryht as adiectif and substantif
A-cordeth in alle kyndes with his antecedent.
Indirect thyng ys as ho so coueited
Alle kynne kynde to knowe and to folwe,
With-oute case to cacche to and come to bothe numbres."

(C. IV. 363–67)

Although the *MED* suggests that *kynde* is synonymous with "gender," [4] I am not sure that Langland uses it consistently with so precise a meaning. More often, it seems to mean the essential grammatical nature of a word; there is also the implication that the word's meaning results from its being used in accordance with its true grammatical *kynde*. This meaning of *kynde* adds another ironic dimension to Will's complaint; indeed, he has no "kynde knowyng" of Dowel, for he consistently misuses the word, having no idea of its proper grammar. And until he can construct a sentence in which Dowel is used according to its *kynde*, he will never come to an understanding of it, or of himself.

Thus, the word *kynde* is a good focus for Will's search. Not only does it mean true or essential nature in all its many applications, but it has here a threefold level of reference: first, to language, the *littera*, as a term of grammar; secondly, to the essential, inner nature of man, his free will and understanding, rightly illuminated by in-dwelling Truth; and thirdly, to *kynde* the Creator, God Himself. This threefold meaning exactly corresponds to the threefold figural relationship between expression, right understanding, and the Word, which comprises the true nature of meaning. In searching for "kynde knowyng" of Dowel, Will is also seeking himself and seeking God —though the key to the proper understanding of the others lies within himself.

When confronted with Dowel, Will responds by treating the word as though it were the same kind of sign he had already encountered in the poem, the personification of a concept. This is clear from the syntactic role that Dowel plays in Will's sentences:

And demed that Dowel indulgences [passeþ]
. . . .
[. . .] Dowel at the day of dome is dignelich vnderfongen
[He] passeth al the pardoun of seynt Petres cherche.
. . . .

---

4. *MED,* s.v. *kinde,* 14(b).

Ac to trust [on] thise triennales trewly me thinketh,
[It] is nou3t so syker for the soule, certis, as is Dowel.
(VII. 169, 171–72, 179–80)

In none of these sentences does Dowel function according to its proper grammatical nature as an imperative. Indeed, it does not function as a verb at all, being used continually as though it were a nominative, like "indulgences" or "triennales." When he uses the term at the end of his meditative discourse, Will twice makes it the subject of an active verb:

> but if Dowel [þee] help,
> I sette 3oure patentes and 3owre [pardoun] at one pies hele!
> . . . .
> That after owre deth-day Dowel reherce
> At the day of dome we dede as he hi3te.
> (VII. 193–94, 199–200)

In both these cases, Dowel is fully personified, performing actions in the same way as Meed or Conscience, Sloth or Reason, and has become in Will's mind a noun like them rather than an imperative verb.

Will is still approaching the problem of the nature of meaning as the folk did in the *Visio*, by turning everything into personification allegories. The trouble with this approach is that it embodies language in things, the word in the personification, obscuring its nature (particularly when the word is a verb) as a sign of something other than itself. Will's erroneous sentence structure, making a noun of Dowel, is an expression of the error he has made about the *kynde* of Dowel—he thinks of Dowel as a person to guide him. Conscience has left the poem, Piers has disappeared—maybe this fellow Dowel can help him. The search for an exterior guide to Truth in the *Visio* expresses a fundamental misapprehension about the nature of Truth and of meaning, for Truth is not a "corseint," or an all-wise teacher, or a feudal lord, something external to one's self. Truth illuminates from within, as Augustine says; true understanding can only be gained by reference to the True Word which dwells in the soul. Will's understanding of the true nature of meaning must be corrected before he can possibly understand the nature of Dowel, or of Truth, or of anything at all.

The form of Will's search for Dowel in Passus VIII–X is determined by his understanding of what he is looking for. It is a search structured for defining a personified noun, but, unfortunately, he should not be looking for Dowel in these terms—and it takes him all of the *Vita de Dowel* to learn this. Will's quest for Dowel takes two basic forms in these passus. He regards Dowel as a problem of definition, which he pursues in the form of clerkly debate. And the form which his intellectual instructors adopt to teach him of Dowel is that of parable or fable. Both these structures are employed in Will's first attempt to discover Dowel, his meeting with the friars-masters in Passus VIII.

Will starts out in search of a personified Dowel:

> Thus yrobed in russet I romed aboute
> Al a somer sesoun for to seke Dowel,
> And frayned ful oft of folke that I mette,
> If ani wiȝte wiste where Dowel was at inne,
> And what man he miȝte be of many man I axed.
>
> (VIII. 1–5)

He then meets two friars, who do nothing to discourage his impression that Dowel is a particular man:

> "[Marie, quod þe maistres, amonges vs he dwelleþ],
> And euere hath, as I hope, and euere shal hereafter."
>
> (VIII. 18–19)

Will, however, is out to show up these egg-headed clerks for pretentious fools, and disputes them in the manner of a scholastic debate:

> "*Contra,*" quod I as a clerke and comsed to disputen,
> [. . .] "*sepcies in die cadit iustus;*
> Seuene sythes, seith the boke, synneth the riȝtful.
> [Ac] who-so synneth, I [seye certes] me thinketh,
> [That] Dowel and Do-yuel mow nouȝt dwelle togideres.
> Ergo, he nys nauȝt alway [at hoom] among ȝow freres;
> He is otherwhile ellis-where to wisse the people."
>
> (VIII. 20–26)

Will is prepared to marshall texts, argue from the logical order of propositions, and so forth. But the form of his argument, basically syllogistic, is designed to deal with definition, to distinguish a separate conceptual entity from other conceptual entities. It is clear that Will has no idea of the real nature of what he is asking about; his whole method of inquiry is based on the wrong premises for discovering the true nature of Dowel.

The friars try to correct Will's understanding, not by more debate but by means of a "forbisene," a parable or fable. A man is in a boat, buffeted by the winds and waves, but so long as he keeps hold of the tiller he will be safe, though he may be tossed about. The man is the soul, the boat the body, the waves temptation, but:

> Dowel hym [helpeþ]
> [. . .] That is Charite the champioun, chief help aʒein synne;
> For he strengtheth [þee] to stonde and stereth [þi] soule.
>   (VIII. 45–47)

In the literal narrative of this story, Dowel is a mysterious champion, an external character who somehow keeps the boat afloat. The internal, spiritual quality is objectified in a personification which acts upon the soul. This narrative form is the one most often used by Will's teachers to explain to him the nature of Dowel, and it proves to be disastrously wrong, given Will's initial misunderstanding of Dowel.

Thought, for example, tells Will that Dowel, Dobet, and Dobest are "three faire vertues and beth nauʒte fer to fynde." This is a most unfortunate form of statement for Thought to have chosen, since it means, to Will, that the one obscure person he has been seeking is now multiplied by three. Thought consistently uses Dowel as the subject of active verbs: Dowel "folweth" the man who is true of his tongue, Dobet "helpeth [þer nede is]," Dobest "bereth a bisshopes crosse." Each of these sentences is a little parable, in which Dowel and its multiples function as personified subjects performing a particular action.

The model for the use of parables to teach spiritual truth is, of course, Jesus. Jesus uses simple stories or examples drawn from common life—a sower, a mustard seed—which illustrate a more complex spiritual truth. This truth is concealed in the commonplace, and the story itself has no especial significance without its spiritual meaning; the real truth of the tale resides wholly on a level that is not explicit in the story itself. Structurally speaking, one can only derive the significance of the story from a prior knowledge of its spiritual meaning—the metaphor does not work in the opposite direction. Very little about a mustard seed *qua* mustard seed suggests the kingdom of heaven, any more than does a woman searching for a lost coin, or a merchant buying a priceless pearl, or a guest refusing an invitation to a marriage feast. As meaningful fictions the parables, taken singly or together, can make sense only by reference to a prior signifying truth. Thus the parable is more than a simple heuristic fable; it is a means of testing the spiritual receptivity of the hearer, the degree to which he perceives that its everyday surface conceals a hidden, "other" meaning.[5] The process involved in learning to read a parable is a paradigm of what the phrase *recte legendum* means. It cannot be rightly read without a spiritually illuminated understanding and will. In a parable, cognition is made conditional upon the spiritual state of the reader, right reason dependent on right will.

Jesus emphasizes the testing nature of his parables when he explains why he uses this method of teaching:

> And the disciples came, and said unto him, Why speakest thou unto them in parables? He answered and said unto them, Because it is given unto you to know the mysteries of the kingdom of heaven, but to them it is not given. For whosoever hath, to him shall be given, and he shall have more in abundance: but whosoever hath not, from him shall be taken away even that he hath. Therefore speak I to them in parables: because they seeing see not; and hearing they hear not, neither do they understand. . . . But blessed are your eyes, for they see: and your ears, for they hear.
>
> (Matt. 13:10–13, 16)

The ability to understand a parable is a test of one's faith, of one's understanding, and ultimately of one's will. "He who has ears to hear, let him hear," says Jesus after many of his parables. Parables make words into veiled signs. The language of parable is a spiritual language, requiring a special, spiritual understanding of the hearer. Yet the words used are the common words of speech; what the parable changes is their significance. Words are revealed by the parable within a spiritual context, in exactly the same way that the figural dimension of the historical Moses is revealed within the pattern of figural history. And the ability to perceive this changed significance depends upon the state of the listener's "ears," his will and heart. At this point in *Piers Plowman*, Will hasn't the ears to hear, nor the understanding of what he seeks to be able to conceive, what Thought and Wit try to teach him in their parables of Dowel; his will is not yet in order.

Yet Will's failure to understand is not entirely his fault. The parable form as used by Thought and Wit is peculiarly adapted to reinforce his misconception about the nature of Dowel. In each of the tales he is told,

---

5. This characteristic of the parable form was suggested to me by Andrea Rosnick.

Dowel is made the subject of actions predicated of it, a fact which makes of it a noun, or at best a verb in the infinitive, which cannot help to correct Will's misapprehension of its grammatical *kynde*. Wit's parable of Dowel, the most elaborate of the fables Will is told, is a case in point:

> "Sire Dowel dwelleth," quod Witte, "nouȝt a day hennes,
> In a castel that Kynde made of foure kynnes thinges;
> Of erthe and eyre [it is] made, medled togideres,
> With wynde and with water [wittily] enioyned.
> Kynde hath closed there-inne craftily with-alle
> A lemman that he loueth like to hym-selue,
> *Anima* she hatte, [to hire haþ enuye]
> A proude pryker of Fraunce, *prynceps huius mundi,*
> And wolde winne hir away with wyles, [if] he myȝte.
> Ac Kynde knoweth this wel and kepeth hir the bettere,
> And hath do hir with sire Dowel, [. . .] duke of this marches.
> Dobet is hir damoisele, sire Doweles douȝter,
> To serue this lady lelly bothe late and rathe.
> Dobest is aboue bothe a bisschopes pere;
> That he bit, mote be do, he [boldeþ] hem alle;
> [Bi his lerynge is ladde þat lady *Anima*]."
>
> (IX. 1–16)

There is nothing wrong with the doctrinal content of this fable; indeed, it is the most complete statement in the poem so far of the true nature of Kynde (something Will badly needs to know), of the relationship between body and soul, and of the role of "do well" in keeping the soul from harm. The trouble with it lies entirely in its form. Not only does its structure cast Dowel into a substantive role, thus violating its *kynde,* but it also distorts the real relationship of Dowel, Dobet, and Dobest. Grammatically, the comparative and superlative are aspects, degrees, of a single adverb. But Wit's fable divides these three degrees among three separate characters, very different in function. This suggests that they are substantively different, when in fact their proper grammatical *kynde* requires just the opposite analysis of their relationship.

Will's misunderstanding of the *kynde* of Dowel should have been apparent to Wit and Thought from the very form of his questions. He asks them both where Dowel lives, where "in londe" he may be found. Yet instead of correcting the form of Will's question to indicate to him that Dowel is not a substantive quality, both Thought and Wit use the question to lead into a parable in which Dowel retains a fully substantive nature. This suggests to me that both characters are demonstrating a limitation inherent in their natures as intellectual faculties. To them, the world is constructed primarily of nouns, objects of thought. It is instructive to compare their response to the term Dowel with that of Piers Plowman. Truth's pardon inspires Piers to an immediate obedience to its command to do well, while Thought and Wit both treat the word as something to be defined, the subject of a series of fables.

Furthermore, the fact that they adopt Will's own structures so readily in explaining to him about Dowel suggests further that Will himself is determining the forms which his search takes. While he perceives the cognitive challenge presented by the pardon, he immediately thinks of that puzzle as an intellectual one, a problem in definition, instead of seeing it primarily as an ontological one, concerning the nature of life itself. And considering it as a problem of doctrine, he turns the command into an object of thought: at once his intellectual faculties rise up to deal with it, in terms appropriate to the form in which he has conceived of the problem, intellectual and substantive.

Of course the whole poem does occur in Will's mind, in the manner of visions, but nowhere else in the poem is it so apparent that the characters Will meets are aspects of himself as in Passus VIII–X. In the first place, they look like him. Thought is "a moche man, as me thou3te, [. . .] lyke to my-selue" (VIII. 70); Wit is "longe and lene, liche to none other" (VIII. 115), as is Long Will himself; Dame Study is "lene . . . of [liche]" (X. 2). And they reflect the terms Will has set up for his inquiry as faithfully as they reflect him. The search for Dowel often seems to go around in circles in these passus, not because the content of the explanations Will is given is wrong, but because the form in which they are cast is wrong. One doesn't explain Dowel, one does well. The intellectual faculties to whom Will turns here are limited by the very form their understanding of the world takes, which is precisely the form Will's misunderstanding takes in the first place. Until the problem of Dowel can be cast in a different form, the intellectual circularities are bound to continue. And the only one who can recast the terms of the poem is Will himself, by learning to understand why the terms he has chosen are wrong.

The first character to see that Will cannot profit from intellectual argument is Dame Study:

> She was wonderly wroth that Witte [so] tau3te,
> And al starynte dame Studye sternelich seyde,
> "Wel artow wyse" [wit quod she], "any wysdomes to telle
> To flatereres or to folis that frantyk ben of wittes!"
>
> (X. 3–6)

She berates not Will but Wit—evidently perceiving that Wit's methods are wrong, since Will cannot possibly understand what Wit tries to tell him. Dame Study herself embodies the application of Wit to the world, so it is not surprising that she sides with her husband to the extent of berating Will as a fool and a sot. But her ensuing speech indicates that she both realizes the nature of Will's problem and understands that neither she nor Wit can deal with it. For her speech castigates those who concern themselves with problems of doctrine without having set their wills in order, those who have ears but hear not:

> Clerkes and [kete] men carpen of god faste,
> And haue hym moche in [hire] mouthe, ac mene men in herte.
> (X. 70–71)

Such men cannot know God in any way. As she concludes, in characteristically strong language:

> And tho that vseth this [hauylounes] [for] to blende mennes wittes,
> What is Dowel fro Dobet, now def mote he worthe,
> [For alle þat wilneþ to wite þhe [whyes] of god almyȝty
> I wolde his eiȝe were in his ers and his [hele] after]
> But [. . .] he lyue in the [leeste degree] that longeth to Dowel;
> [. . .] I dar ben his bolde borgh that Dobet wil he neuere,
> Theigh Dobest drawe on hym day after other.
> (X. 129–34)[6]

She seems to understand that for Will Dowel, Dobet, and Dobest are intellectual quibbles, as her final riddling use of the term suggests. And she most clearly articulates the ontological nature of Dowel: it is a way of life, a mode of being, requiring a basic change in the will, or the heart, rather than more questions, more "whys."

Yet Dame Study is also bound by the limits of her nature. She sends Will off to her cousin Clergy and his wife Scripture, who is "sybbe to the seuene artz" which Study embodies. She does not understand theology herself, as she says, but seems to believe that anyone who can will be able to help Will. For theology is the science of love:

---

6. Kane-Donaldson moves Skeat's lines 122–23 down to follow Skeat's line 130 and omits line 131 of Skeat's text. I have indicated the reordered lines in square brackets.

It is no science for sothe for to sotyle inne;
[Ne were þe loue þat liþ þereinne a wel lewed þyng it were]
Ac for it [leteþ] best by Loue I loue it the bettre;
For there that loue is leder ne [lackeþ] neuere grace.
Loke thow loue lelly ʒif the lyketh Dowel;
For Dobet and Dobest ben [drawen] of Loues [scole].

                                        (X. 183–88)

Her admonition to Will is interesting, for it displays both Study's perception of the problem and her inability to deal with it. Dowel is indeed of
Love's school, but when Study says this to Will in the particular form she
has chosen, she is inevitably reinforcing the same misconception about
Dowel that he has held since first hearing the word. Dowel is the subject of
the verb *lyketh* (or could, perhaps, be an infinitive verb), drawn from
Love's school. She has constructed another small parable for Will. Moreover, Will must learn of Dowel through the science of theology, the objects of whose study are different from those with which Dame Study is
concerned, but whose cognitive instruments are exactly the same. Study
set Clergy to school and wrote Scripture's books, as she says.

    For Study, like Wit and Thought, inhabits a world of substantives. This
is clearest in her directions to Will concerning the way to Clergy's house:

        "Axe the heighe waye," quod she, "hennes to Suffre-
        Bothe-wel-and-wo, ʒif that thow wolt lerne,
        And ryde forth by Ricchesse, ac rest thow nauʒt thereinne
        . . . .
        Tyl thow come to a courte Kepe-wel-thi-tonge-
        Fro-lesynges-and-lither-speche-and-likerous-drynkes."

                                        (X. 157–59, 163–64)

Like the allegorical map which Piers gives the pilgrims in Passus V, every
action necessary for Clergy is translated into a geographical place. The
imperative verbs become compounded nouns: Will is instructed to go to
a place called "Endure-both-good-and-ill." Thus the action is transformed
into a substantive object, the imperative into nouns, and the form in which
Will's search is conducted remains exactly the same as ever. An imperative
demands action, while a noun simply calls for more discussion, which is
exactly what Will proceeds to do with Clergy and Scripture.

    The form of Clergy's reply reveals that he indeed went to school at
Study. Clergy is far more direct than any of Will's previous teachers in

defining Dowel in terms of Will's personal life, but the three "Do's" are still cast in the old sentence structures. Dowel is "a comune lyf . . . on holycherche to bileue" (X. 230); Dobest is "to suffre for thi soules helth, / Al that the boke bit bi holycherche techyng" (X. 249–50); Dobest is "to be bolde to blame the gylty" (X. 256). And Clergy continues with a lengthy speech on the evils of the clergy, who do not practice what they preach, and who live lives of pride and riches without concern for learning. Learning, says Clergy, produces love and peace:

> For if heuene be on this erthe and ese to any soule,
> It is in cloistere or in scole, be many skilles I fynde;
> For in cloistre cometh no man to [carpe] ne to fiȝte,
> But alle is buxumnesse there and bokes to rede and to lerne.
> In scole there is scorne but if a clerke wil lerne,
> And grete loue and lykynge for eche [loweþ hym to] other.
>
> (X. 300–305)

Clearly, Dowel is a clerk. So Will promptly tries to demonstrate just how clerkly he can be, becoming much more academic in his discourse with Clergy and Scripture than he has been at any point since meeting the friars-masters in Passus VIII.

Clergy concludes his speech to Will with the prophecy that a king will come with his knights to beat down the abbot of Abingdon, and Cain shall awake but "Dowel shal dyngen hym adoune and destruyen his myȝte" (X. 330). So, says Will, drawing the evident conclusion, "Thanne is Dowel and Dobest . . . *dominus* and kniȝthode" (X. 331). Of course, this is the wrong conclusion, but it is one which Clergy invites. Will simply cannot understand Dowel in these intellectual terms, for the terms themselves translate the word into a form different from its proper *kynde,* the forms of personification allegory and fable. And when Scripture acidly comments on the conclusion he has drawn from Clergy's speech, Will continues to treat what she says as academic argument and disputes her exactly as he did the friars.

But when Scripture takes up the debate and shows signs of winning it, Will abruptly throws it all over:

> "This is a longe lessoun," quod I, "and litel am I the wyser:
> Where Dowel is, or Dobest, derkelich ȝe shewen;
> Many tales ȝe tellen that Theologye lerneth."
>
> (X. 372–74)

He disparages the value of learning as a means to salvation, arguing that simple faith is the best way to get into heaven. He falls back on his simple, anti-intellectual opposition of words to works. And then he quotes Augustine's *Confessiones: "Ecce ipsi idioti rapiunt celum, vbi nos sapientes in inferno mergimur,"* which Will says means:

> Aren none rather yrauysshed fro the riȝte byleue
> Than ar this [kete] clerkes that conne many bokes;
> Ne none sonner saued ne sadder of bileue,
> Than plowmen and pastoures and pore comune laborers.
>
> (X. 456–59)

His paraphrase is an outrageous distortion of Augustine's meaning, to be sure, and he deserves the sharp rebuke he promptly receives from Scripture. Yet in the long run, Will is acting rightly to reject the kind of instruction he has been receiving from the intellectual faculties he has encountered.

It is fully consistent with Wills *kynde* that he should be unable to understand what he hears in Passus VIII–X. For Will is not only the dreamer-narrator of the poem; he also personifies the will, the Will behind the whole poem.[7] And the will is not a rational faculty, but an appetitive one, to use the scholastic term. It is moved by veneration or disapprobation.[8] It is the source of love in man,[9] without which, as Paul says, any intellectual knowledge is dead. Thus, Will's effort to embody Dowel in a personification is in harmony with his own *kynde,* for he is trying to find an object of love.

Will can, however, be faulted for not really knowing his own *kynde.* He has misunderstood his nature by seeking an intellectual, doctrinal answer to the problem of Dowel. What he needs is not the "kynde knowyng" of Dowel that he has been seeking, but the "kynde knowyng" which "kenneth in thine herte / For to louye thi lorde leuer than thi-selue" (I. 140–41). Only by understanding his own *kynde* can he learn to understand the *kynde* of Dowel. Will cannot understand as the intellectual powers understand;

---

7. D. W. Robertson and B. F. Huppé, *Piers Plowman and Scriptural Tradition* (Princeton, N.J., 1951), have the most elaborate reading of Will's role as a personification of the will. They assert that "the dreamer is representative of the faculty will rather than of any individual person" (p. 34). They tend not to recognize Will's other functions, however—a failure which hampers their argument.

8. See St. Thomas Aquinas' discussion of the will, *ST* (trans. Fathers of the English Dominican Province) Iᵃ. Q. LXXXII and I–II, Q. IX.

9. See *ST* I–II. Q. XXVI, a. 1–3.

his only stupidity lies in thinking that he can. Scripture's scornful dismissal of him is exactly right: *"Multi multa sciunt, et seipsos nesciunt."*

To treat Will as a personification of the will is not to suggest that his larger function in the poem as the dreamer through whose eyes we see the visions is in any way limited. Indeed, the two functions are complementary. For the essence of man lies to a great extent in the freedom of his will, as the doctors from Paul to Augustine to Aquinas taught. Christ himself suggests that the purpose of knowing truth is to make one free, to give man that freedom of will which is primary to a loving being. The free will is the image of God implanted in man's soul, the stamp of his unique being, and the pivot of his relationship with his Creator. Thus, to regard Will as personifying the will is to make him quintessential man, Everyman in his primary aspect. And if we understand this about him, the progress of his understanding becomes even more crucial to the poem. Will's failure to understand his own nature is not the peculiar weakness of a doltish narrator. To appreciate his true function in the poem is to see that this failure of will is a failure of human nature itself.

When Scripture scorns him in her brutal fashion, Will weeps for wrath and woe and falls into an inner dream. This device occurs only twice in the poem, here and in Passus XVI, which deals with the vision of the Tree of Charity. In each case the inner dream marks the beginning of a radical change in Will's understanding. The nature of the change in Passus XI is indicated by the first actions that occur in the inner dream:

> A merueillouse meteles mette me thanne,
> [For] I was rauisshed riȝt there [. . .] Fortune me fette,
> And in-to the londe of Longynge [and loue] she me brouȝte,
> And in a myroure that hiȝt Mydlerd she mad me to biholde.
> (XI. 5–8)

Passus XI introduces a new allegorical structure into Will's quest for Dowel, that of the figural mirror, or *speculum*.[10] Paul's words—"Videmus nunc per speculum in aenigmate; tunc autem facie ad faciem"—lie behind all the imagery of mirrors and mirroring in this poem. Paul's text is the basis of figural allegory; thus, recognizing the *speculum* as a cognitive form is a prerequisite for figural understanding.

---

10. On the importance of the figural mirror in medieval thought, see H. Leisegang, "La Connaissance de Dieu au miroir de l'âme et de la nature," *Review d'histoire et des philosophies religieuses*, XVII (1937), 145–71, and E. Mâle, *The Gothic Image*, trans. D. Nussey (1913; rpt. New York, 1958).

The mirror of Middle Earth provides Will with a more complete, thus a more truthful, image of himself than he has met before. The personifications of Thought, Wit, and Study are only partial and fragmentary reflections, pieces of Will encountered as discrete entities. And, as the experience of the *Visio* shows, this kind of fragmentation is the mark of a fallen, misdirected understanding. The *speculum*, however, provides Will with a whole image of himself, in a context that is simultaneously human and spiritual. It is thus a mode of self-perception that is a radical alternative to the overly rational, piecemeal, and personified self-images that Will meets earlier in the *Vita de Dowel*. This change of perception on Will's part is vital to the poem's progress, for it must occur in order to enable the poem to break out of the deadening, self-limited circularity of the debates in Passus VIII–X and to prepare for the vision "face to face" of Passus XVIII. And the change in form of this vision, the mirror of Middle Earth, from personification to *speculum*, from debate to typological narrative, represents the first step in the process of changing the mode of Will's understanding that is finally completed by the end of the *Vita de Dowel*.

The main stumbling block to Will's instruction has been that both he and his instructors have treated Dowel in the same way, as a problem of doctrine, of differentiation via definition. For Will to proceed further, he must come to understand that Dowel is embodied in action; it is a whole way of life, the wholeness of charity. And what Will sees in Fortune's mirror is a life, his own, presented to him in the shape of a parable. Fortune's handmaidens, *Concupiscencia-carnis*, "coueytise-of-eyghes," and "Pryde-of-parfyte-lyuynge" promise to follow him all through his life. Age warns him against trusting Fortune, but Recchelessnesse tells him to do as he pleases. And Will takes the bad advice:

> Coueitise-of-eyghes conforted me anon after,
> And folwed me fourty wynter and a fyfte more,
> That of Dowel ne Dobet no deyntee me [. . .] thou3te;
> I had no lykynge, leue me [. . .] the leste of hem [. . .] to knowe.
>
> (XI. 45–48)

The three ladies of Will's retinue are the worldly pursuits mentioned in I John 2:16. Exegetical tradition had made figural images of these terms.[11]

---

11. See the discussion of the traditional understanding of these three terms in Donald R. Howard, *The Three Temptations: Medieval Man in Search of the World* (Princeton, N.J., 1966), especially pp. 43–75.

Thus, they are not simple personifications of ordinary words, but are weighed heavily with figural significance drawn from the context of I John. This epistle is one of the most succinct statements in the New Testament of the Christian life which is the life of Dowel, the life of love and good works. Love is the informing quality of Christianity: "God is love; and he that dwelleth in love dwelleth in God, and God in him" (I John 4:16). The Christian is known by the life he leads: "Love not the world, neither the things that are in the world. If any man love the world, love for the Father is not in him" (I John 2:15). The sole criterion for distinguishing the true Christian from false prophets and the followers of Antichrist is their contrasting ways of life: "My little children, let us not love in word, neither in tongue; but in deed and in truth" (I John 3:18). Doing well means charity, expressed in good works and truthful words. And because of I John's emphasis on deed and truth as the proper expressions of charity, it seems to me most significant that Langland draws on this particular epistle to supply the narrative situation of Will's self-vision in Passus XI.

The life that Will sees himself (or, more exactly, his mirror image) leading in this visionary parable is one of "do-evil," of falseness and worldliness. It is a life which is fundamentally "unkynde," as the author of I John would perceive it. Will is invited to see his own nature in the mirror of Middle Earth and to understand what a false, unnatural life he has led, *if* he is perceptive enough to read the allegory. And it seems that he has too much pride-of-perfect-living to be able to do so. At the end of his vision, Will finds himself deserted in his impecunious old age by the friars. He harshly castigates them for abandoning him because of his "lele" desire to be buried in his own parish churchyard rather than in their convent. The lesson he draws from the parable he has witnessed is "Never trust a friar," rather than the one that is more evident: that he, Will, has led a bad life.

Lewte, who catches him glowering over what he has just seen in the mirror, tries to suggest to him that it is not his place to rebuke the friars, lest he fall into the sin of presumption. He quotes Paul: *"Non oderis fratrem,"* a sentiment echoed with a significant twist in I John:

> We know that we have passed from death unto life, because we love the brethren. . . . Whosoever hateth his brother is a murderer: and ye know that no murderer hath eternal life abiding in him.
> (I John 3:14–15)

By chastizing the friars while he himself remains in sin, Will fails the test of the Christian posed by John, and demonstrates again that he is unable to read the parable properly. He seems to regard the image in the mirror as something apart from himself, as mere image instead of as true *speculum*, with a level of meaning that applies directly to him. His ears are dulled, even though Lewte provides him with the interpretive key to the parable. Scripture then sets him Christ's parable of the hesitant wedding guests:

> *"Multi* to a maungerye and to the mete were sompned,
> And whan the peple was plenere comen, the porter vnpynned the
> ȝate,
> And plukked in *pauci* priueliche and lete the remenaunt go rowme!"
> (XI. 107–9)

This parable puts Will in great anxiety, for it suggests to him that he has fundamentally misunderstood the vision he has just seen. His worry takes the specific form of concern over whether he is one of the chosen or not, but I think that this particular worry is a manifestation of his larger misapprehension of the nature of Dowel and of Truth. Will has slipped into a comfortable assurance that because he has the name of a Christian, given him in baptism, he can do as he pleases. Once again, he has placed too much emphasis on a name, a noun, a form, mistaking the thing for what it signifies. But the pardon of Dowel implies that the name is nothing without the deed, just as the outward sign is nothing without the inner spirit which gives it significance.

Trajan breaks in on Will's quandary with his rude "ȝee! baw for bokes!" His appearance at this juncture in the poem is most significant. Trajan's example directly challenges Will's hope that Christianity and salvation are synonymous. For Trajan was in name a heathen, though he was saved because of the truthful deeds of his life. What brought him from hell was "loue and leute and my lawful domes." The contrast he makes to Will's reliance on having been "lele" to the laws of the Church is very similar to that between Piers's immediate comprehension of the pardon as applying to his own life and the priest's formal objections to it. It is a contrast between interior meaning and external form, analogous to the distinction between *kynde* and accidental quality. The emergence of Trajan once again brings into focus the difference between name and commandment inherent in Will's grammatical misperception of Dowel. Trajan is a mirror of the life of Dowel, intruding roughly into Will's vision in order to clear away the misunderstandings engendered by an overly intellectual approach to the problem. Thus, Trajan also suggests an alternative mode in which to understand *kyndely* the nature of Dowel, from the perspective of deed and truth.

There follows in the B-Text a speech of about one hundred and fifty lines which develops the seminal idea from I John implicit in the rest of Passus XI—that one can only know the true Christian by his life: *"Qui non diligit, manet in morte"* (XI. 170). In the B-Text this speech is unattributed.[12] It concentrates on the life of Dowel as exemplified by Christ; he is seen by the speaker as a poor wanderer who, by his works of loyal love, tests each man in order to prove his *kynde:*

> For oure ioye and owre [Iuel] Iesu Cryst of heuene,
> In a pore mannes apparaille pursueth vs euere,
> And loketh on vs in her liknesse and that with louely chere,
> To knowen vs by owre kynde herte and castyng of owre eyen,
> Whether we loue the lordes here byfor [þe] lorde of blisse.
>   (XI. 179–83)

Christ is known through his works:

> Soi bi his werkes thei wisten that he was Iesus;
> Ac by clothyng thei knewe hym nouȝte [so caitifliche he yede]
> . . . .
> And in apparaille of a pore man and pilgrymes lyknesse
> Many tyme god hath ben mette amonge nedy peple.
>   (XI. 230–31, 235–36)

I do not think that this speech argues for a life of patient poverty so much as it urges the test of action as the only way to know the *kynde* of a Christian. Certainly, a life of poverty is better than a life of luxury, and being heedless of the world is following the commandment of Jesus to love God above all else. But I do not think the poem means to settle on one pattern of life as the only goal to which it strives, whether this be the life of contemplation, perfection, patient poverty, or whatever, though it does see Dowel in all these lives. The speech addresses itself primarily to a cognitive problem: what does Dowel mean in this wicked world, and wherein lies a reliable test for knowing it *kyndely*. This is precisely the problem Will has been having all along; but now the cognitive solution is

---

12. The C-Text (XIV. 129) attributes this speech to Recchelessnesse, explained by Donaldson as the heedless unworldliness which is the essence of patient poverty (*Piers Plowman: The C-Text and Its Poet* [New Haven, Conn., 1949], p. 172).

presented: that Dowel is known in works of loyal love, and that charity is typified in the Christ-like deeds which express the *kynde herte* of his true followers.

The problem of the attribution of this speech in the B-Text is probably insoluble. The speech has been given to Lewte (by Skeat), to Will (by Chambers), to Scripture (by Robertson and Huppé), to Trajan (by Frank).[13] This takes care of all the available characters on the scene, but none of the choices is particularly satisfactory. The evidence for Lewte is slight, as Frank has noted,[14] and the evidence for Scripture desperate. Nor does it seem likely that the speaker is Will, simply because at the end of the speech Will says that "one" has been disputing him (XI. 311). An obvious choice is Trajan, but even this possibility is not without its difficulties, as it would involve a sudden shift in mid-speech at line 148 from the first to the third person. The authority of the delivery as well as its content are in keeping with Trajan's exalted position, and he is certainly an important enough character to be given more exposure than he is by Skeat's punctuation of the text. Yet it is perhaps best that the speaker remain anonymous. For, as the speech now stands, we have only the speaker's truthful words by which to recognize in him one of the purest types of charity in the poem. And, as the poem moves toward a figural mode of allegory in the later passus of the *Vita de Dowel,* the most fitting attribution of the speech is the one it is given—to "one," an unknown precursor of later figures of Dowel like Patience, habited as a poor hermit, at Conscience' gate.

Will is next granted a vision of Kynde from the mountain of Middle Earth, a vision of the *speculum naturae.* This is the most difficult *speculum* Will has yet encountered in the poem, though, of the two great *specula* of nature and of history, it is the easier to comprehend. When St. Thomas Aquinas sets out to demonstrate the nature of God to the Gentiles (the Moors of Spain), he turns to the *speculum naturae.* And in this mirror, if he will, Will can learn not only of Kynde in its most comprehensive aspect, but also of the two specific *kyndes* he has most diligently sought— the *kynde* of Dowel and the *kynde* of himself. Indeed, the whole of Passus

---

13. In Skeat's Oxford edition, note on C. XIII. 88; R. W. Chambers, *Man's Unconquerable Mind* (London, 1939), p. 136 (see also Donaldson, *Piers Plowman: The C-Text and Its Poet,* p. 173); Robertson and Huppé, *Piers Plowman and Scriptural Tradition,* pp. 134–41; R. W. Frank, Jr., *Piers Plowman and the Scheme of Salvation* (New Haven, Conn., 1949), p. 60, n. 1.

14. Frank, *Piers Plowman and the Scheme of Salvation,* p. 60, n. 1.

XI can be seen as an unfolding vision of the meaning of *kynde*. Will beholds his own *kynde* in the mirror of Middle Earth, then the *kynde* of Dowel in the figure of Trajan, and lastly the *kynde* of created Nature itself, reflecting the *kynde* of its Creator:

> I was fette forth, by [forbisenes] to knowe,
> Thorugh eche a creature [. . .] Kynde my creatoure to louye.
>
> (XI. 316–17)

Unfortunately, Will is no more receptive to this vision than he was to his two earlier ones. The birds and beasts demonstrate their proper *kynde* in response to the instincts given them by Kynde and Reason. Will is moved by what he sees to remark that man alone is out of place in the harmonious scheme of nature, that man alone does not enjoy the rule of Reason. But instead of realizing that man is to blame for this disharmony, this "unkyndeness," he rebukes Reason. This is characteristic of Will. The lesson he should draw from this vision is that there is a contrast between the orderly life of nature and the unnaturalness of his own life; the fact that both the mirror he looks into and the mountain from which he sees the vision of Kynde are called Middle Earth invites this comparison. Instead, Will faults Reason for not making man behave more reasonably.

This is the most unreasonable charge Will has made so far, and it earns him a stern rebuke:

> "recche the neuere,
> Whi I suffre or nou3t suffre thi-self hast nou3t to done;
> Amende thow it, if thow my3te, for my tyme is to abyde."
>
> (XI. 367–69)

Will is shamed by this rebuke and wakens from the inner dream sorry he has not seen more. The attack of shame is most important here. For it marks the first time that we are given any indication of self-awareness in Will. A person cannot feel genuine shame without an awareness of self, however dim that awareness may be. And at this moment of dawning self-perception, Imaginatyf appears to Will, and commends his shame:

> Shal neuere chalangynge ne chydynge chaste a man so sone,
> As shal Shame, and shenden hym and shape hym to amende.
>
> (XI. 415–16)

Of all the faculties of his soul that Will has yet met, Imaginatyf is the one most closely identified with him:

"I haue folwed the in feith this fyue and fourty wyntre,
And many tymes haue moeued the to [mynne] on thine ende,
And how fele fernȝeres are faren and so fewe to come,
And of thi wylde wantounesse [whiles] thow ȝonge were,
To amende it in thi myddel age, lest miȝte the [faylle]
In thyne olde elde, that yuel can suffre
Pouerte or penaunce or preyeres bidde."

(XII. 3–9)

As the agent who recalls to Will his past life, Imaginatyf is a kind of talking version of the mirror Will looks into at the beginning of Passus XI; yet it is clear that his role encompasses more than this. The problem of exactly what Imaginatyf or *vis imaginativa* is within this poem has not been resolved. A recent article translates it as "recollection," an aspect of memory.[15] In its root meaning, Imaginatyf is the faculty that records sensory images and presents them to the intellect.[16] It is also capable of recalling images no longer present to the senses—this makes it almost synonymous with memory.[17] It is clear that Imaginatyf plays a pivotal role in the poem, for he sets Will up for the dinner that Conscience gives for Clergy in Passus XIII, wherein the nature of the allegory changes sharply. He appears just as Will discovers a new self-awareness, and his function is to provide Will with a clearer understanding of himself, of his own *kynde*. Why this function should be given to the memory, the faculty which recalls to Will his past life and moves him to think on his future, becomes clearer from the rest of his speech.

Imaginatyf does not simply recall Will to himself. Most of his speech, in fact, is taken up with defining to Will what knowledge is—the difference between Clergy and Kynde Wit, and the importance of Clergy in the scheme of salvation. He tells Will that he is foolish to say that ignorant men are saved sooner than learned ones, for Clergy teaches a man what sin is and helps him to avoid it:

---

15. Barbara Raw, "Piers and the Image of God in Man," in *Piers Plowman: Critical Approaches,* ed. S. S. Hussey (London, 1969), p. 147.

16. *MED,* s.v. *imaginatif.* Compare s.v. *imaginacioun* and *imagienen.*

17. See Morton W. Bloomfield, *Piers Plowman as a Fourteenth-Century Apocalypse* (New Brunswick, N.J., 1961), pp. 171–72. See also Aquinas' discussion of the relationships of memory and imagination, *ST* I^a. Q. LXXVIII. a. 4. Aquinas states that the imagination, as the power of fantasy, is unique in man, while memory is shared with the animals.

For-thi I conseille the for Cristes sake Clergye that thow louye,
For Kynde Witte is of his kyn and neighe cosynes bothe
To owre lorde, leue me; for-thi loue hem, I rede;
For bothe ben as miroures to amenden [by] defautes,
And lederes for lewed men and for lettred bothe.

(XII. 94–98)

Kynde Wit is knowledge based on this world—"of *quod vidimus* cometh kynde witte, of siȝte of dyuerse peple" (XII. 69). Imaginatyf is concerned with presenting sensory images, past and present, to Kynde Wit. But he also understands Kynde Wit's limits:

Namore kan a kynde-witted man, but clerkes hym teche,
Come for al his kynde witte to Crystendome and be saued.

(XII. 109–10)

Clergy makes the wisdom of Kynde Wit seem a trifle in comparison—"the wisdom of this world is foolishness with God" (cf. XII. 140). Thus, Imaginatyf demonstrates that by reproving both Clergy and Wit, Will has been guilty of the highest presumption.

Will has abused his own wit, by desiring to know extraneous and meaningless lore. He is one who seeks "after the whyes," (XII. 217) and all the "whyes," as Dame Study had warned, are distracting him from the main purpose for which he has been given reason: to know wherein his salvation lies, to know Dowel and himself. In the *Confessiones*, Augustine considers this kind of meaningless curiosity to be an intellectual manifestation of "Covetise-of-eyes," the lady who promised to follow Will in his vision of the mirror:

There is also present in the soul . . . a kind of empty longing and curiosity which aims not at taking pleasure in the flesh but at acquiring experience through the flesh, and this empty curiosity is dignified by the names of learning and science. Since this is in the appetite for knowing, and since the eyes are the chief of our senses for acquiring knowledge, it is called in divine language *the lust of the eyes*.[18]

Will has been guilty, in his search for more knowledge, of indulging his eye and his mind without taking proper heed of the function of his wit. He treats Dowel as though it were an intellectual problem on the order

---

18. Augustine *Confessiones* (trans. Rex Warner) X. 35.

of why birds build their nests as they do, instead of bringing his wit to bear meaningfully on the problem of his own nature.

He has also abused his *vis imaginativa* by seeking to store it with merely curious images. He begins the poem as an idle wanderer, watching the earthly round, storing up information. Thus, it is only Imaginatyf, the faculty Will has most directly abused, who can set him on the right track. He accuses Will of using his experience only as grist for the mill of his poetry, instead of as a way of learning more about himself:

> And thow medlest the with makynges, and my3test go sey thi sauter,
> And bidde for hem that 3iueth the bred; for there ar bokes ynowe,
> To telle men what Dowel is, Dobet, and [Dobest] bothe,
> And prechoures to preue what it is of many a peyre freres.
>
> (XII. 16–19)

The proper function of Imaginatyf, as the image-making faculty, is not to make idle poems or to provide the materials for idle speculation: it is to teach one oneself, to know one's own *kynde* and one's own end.

Indeed, Imaginatyf seems to perform very much the same function that Augustine assigns to the memory in the *Confessiones:*

> I come to the fields and spacious palaces of memory, where lie the treasures of innumerable images of all kinds of things that have been brought in by the senses. . . . There I have by me the sky, the earth, the sea, and all things in them which I have been able to perceive. . . . There too I encounter myself, I recall myself— what I have done, when and where I did it, and in what state of mind I was at the time.[19]

Memory is the basis for any sort of knowledge, of this world, of oneself, and of God. Likewise, Imaginatyf is the source of knowledge, the only character Will has met who is capable of distinguishing the various kinds of knowledge possible for man, and who has a clear idea of their relations and limitations. In short, in meeting Imaginatyf, Will is meeting the source of his own knowledge.

As Bloomfield has pointed out, he is also meeting the source of his visions.[20] The imagination is the source of dreams, and thus can best teach

---

19. *Ibid.* X. 8.
20. Bloomfield, *Piers Plowman as a Fourteenth-Century Apocalypse,* pp. 173–74.

Will the real nature of what he is seeing. Most importantly, Imaginatyf, as the keeper of images, is the key to figural understanding: as recollection is the storehouse of the past, it is the key to man's perception of history, and of the figural pattern unfolding through time.[21] Imaginatyf is at great pains to correct Will's anti-intellectual bias, and his misperception of the nature of words and works. And he redirects Will's understanding along figural lines. Both Clergy and Kynde Wit are mirrors, *specula*, whose purpose is spiritual, "to amenden [by] defautes." Wisdom of all kinds is made meaningful only in relation to "the clergye of Cryst," which is love:

> For the heihe holigoste heuene shal to-cleue,
> And loue shal lepe out after in-to this lowe erthe,
> And clennesse shal cacchen it, and clerkes shullen it fynde.
>
> (XII. 141–43)

The concept of the figural mirror underlies all of Imaginatyf's correction of Will's understanding. He also reads the *speculum naturae* for Will. For example, the peacock, beautiful but foul of flesh and slow of flight, is a type of rich men, while the lark, like poor men, is small but much sweeter of voice and swifter of wing. Thus, right reading, which has been Will's problem throughout the *Vita de Dowel*, depends upon the ability rightly to understand the nature of the *speculum* as a true, if partial, mirror of the spiritual reality which gives it significance. This, of course, is why Will is presented with so many mirrors, especially in Passus XI. But only Imaginatyf truly understands the nature of images and can read them rightly for Will.

Imaginatyf thus deserves the importance he is given. He is the source of all Will knows, in his waking life and in his visions, and, as the keeper of his past, he encompasses all that Will is as well. In meeting Imaginatyf, Will is meeting the means he has for understanding himself, and for understanding Dowel—the only true means he has for "kynde knowynge." Finally, Imaginatyf completes Will's spiritual *kynde,* the trinity of memory, understanding, and will, which is God's image or *speculum* in the soul.

Imaginatyf both places in proper perspective the characters Will has met in Passus VIII–X, and sets Will straight on what his intellectual abuses have been. Yet Imaginatyf himself suffers from being bound by some of the same intellectual formulations as Will. "Dowel," he says, is "Feith,

---

21. On the necessity of the memory to man's perception of time past and anticipation of time to come, see Augustine, *Confessiones* XI.

hope, and charitee"; it is obedience to the laws of one's station in life, one's self. And when challenged by Will, Imaginatyf responds in exactly the way Will has before, with a clerkly *Contra*. This, too, is inevitable. For the function of all the characters in Passus VIII–XII is to surround Will with mirrors of himself, in order that he may know himself. They provide him, if only by leading him to a self-imposed dead end, with the kind of "kynde knowynge" he needs in order to continue his cognitive search. Thought, Wit and Study, Clergy and Scripture, the mirror of Middle Earth and the mountain of Middle Earth, and Imaginatyf himself are all "as miroures to amenden [by] defautes." Imaginatyf teaches Will the nature of the mirrors to be encountered, so that by recognizing their truthfulness and their partialness, their "defautes," Will may gain a new perspective on himself and on his search that he has not had before.

The shape of this new perspective is figural. At the end of his speech, Imaginatyf invokes the figure of Trajan and repeats for Will the verse from Psalms that Piers used when he renounced his plow for Dowel, *"si ambulavero in medio vmbre mortis."* Piers and Trajan are the two figures of Dowel Will has met so far in the poem. And, after evoking them, Imaginatyf suddenly vanishes. He has cleared up one form of Will's cognitive problem, only to leave him with a more mysterious one. The terms in which Will's search is recast by Imaginatyf are not the misleading abstractions of Dowel, Dobet, and Dobest, but the living figures of Trajan and Piers the Plowman. This shift of mode signals the next major development in the cognitive structure of the poem, which occurs in Passus XIII.

ᕙ CHAPTER FIVE ᕗ

Clerkis kenne me that Cryst is in alle places;
Ac I seygh hym neuere sothly but as my-self in a miroure,
[Hic] *in enigmate, tunc facie ad faciem.*

hen Conscience bids farewell to Clergy at the conclusion of his
dinner, in order to go on pilgrimage with Patience, the poem
decisively rejects the adequacy of the cognitive forms it used in
Passus VIII–XII for another mode of understanding.[1] This mode expresses
meaning through figurally significant action. Essentially, Patience introduces
a figural reordering of the poem's narrative, which has been invoked before
in the pardon of Dowel, but which Will's cognitive tools have not been
able to realize, until Imaginatyf makes him understand the relationship between the image and its creator that is embodied in the *speculum.*

The true life of the Christian, as the thirteenth chapter of Paul's first
letter to the Corinthians implies, is predicated upon an understanding of
the *figura:* the man of God must be a mirror of charity, for charity is the
only quality which ensures the truthfulness of what he says and does—

---

1. I have avoided the term "level" in my discussion of the poem's allegorical language. Whether the "levels" work for other medieval allegories or not
I am not prepared to say, but the whole concept seems to me deeply misleading
for *Piers Plowman.* The change in allegorical mode from personification to
figural allegory is not a matter of adding (or subtracting) "levels"; it is a
matter of a whole new kind of narrative mode, which in turn signals a different
way of giving meaning to that narrative, and a different type of understanding
of the world. Cognitive problems in *Piers Plowman* are problems in language;
they are reflected in different structural and narrative forms in the poem.
"Level" seems to imply a basic sameness in the narrative structure; the concept
is thus too limited and too static to be of any real use in this poem.

since the understanding produced by words and prophecies is only "in part," *"in enigmate."* Charity is Christ, and to embody charity is to mirror Christ. Thus, the man of Christ proves his truth by being a living *figura* of Christ and of his saints, as Augustine shows himself to be in the *Confessions;* he mirrors God's charity and shows himself to be part of his redemptive pattern for man in all that he does, by deliberately invoking the figural meaning of his life and conversion. Erich Auerbach has demonstrated how St. Francis of Assisi patterned his own life on that of Christ, consciously making his actions into a figural parable. For example, Auerbach draws attention to the following anecdote recounted by Thomas of Celano:

> It happened one Easter Day that the brothers at the hermitage of Grecchio set the table more lavishly than usual with linen and glassware. When the father comes down from his cell to go to the table, he sees it with its vain decoration. But the pleasing table in no way pleases him. Furtively and quietly he retraces his steps, puts on his head the hat of a pauper who happened to be there, takes his staff in his hand, and leaves the house. Outside he waits until the brothers begin, for they were accustomed not to wait for him when he did not come at the signal. When they begin their meal, this true pauper calls out at the door: For the love of God, give this poor sick pilgrim an alms. The brothers answer: Come in, man, for the love of Him whom you have invoked. So he quickly enters and appears before the diners. But what surprise do you think seized the household at the sight of this stranger? At his request he is given a bowl, and alone he sits down on the floor and sets his plate in the ashes. "Now," he says, "I am seated like a Minorite." [2]

Francis' action is dependent for its impact on its deliberate evocation of a specific incident in the life of Christ, in which he gives the injunction to seat oneself at the very lowest place when invited to a feast, for "he that humbleth himself shall be exalted" (Luke 14:11). Indeed, Francis' action cannot be understood except by reference to the pattern provided in Christ's life; considered simply by itself, it becomes theatrical and mean-spirited, not to say ludicrous. Only when seen in the light of Christ does it become significant: Francis' action is a figural action, pure and simple.

---

2. Erich Auerbach, *Mimesis,* trans. W. Trask (New York, 1957), pp. 147–48. See also his essay, "St. Francis of Assisi in Dante's 'Commedia,'" in *Scenes from the Drama of European Literature* (New York, 1959).

From the first, Patience' actions are figural in their significance. Will arrives at Conscience' dinner:

> And there I [mette] a maistre, what man he was I neste,
> That lowe louted and loueliche to Scripture.
> Conscience knewe hym wel and welcomed hym faire;
> Thei wesshen and wypeden and wenten to the dyner.
> Ac Pacience in the paleis stode in pilgrymes clothes,
> And preyde mete [pur charite] for a pore heremyte.
>
> (XIII. 25–30)

The narrative begins with literal, earthly actions—the greeting of the friar by Scripture and Conscience, washing before dinner. There is nothing in these actions which suggests another dimension or places them in an unstated context larger than the immediate scene described. But Patience' action is of a different sort. Standing in the yard, dressed as a pilgrim, begging meat for charity, he is a figure from Christ's parables, from the lives of the apostles and saints, a character whose actions figure the life of patient poverty. And these figures are evoked deliberately in Patience' dress and speech. In modern terms, Patience is performing a bit of guerrilla theater for the benefit of the company, particularly the doctor, since one of the figures Patience is recalling is St. Francis, the founder of the friars. Patience' actions encompass a larger meaning than that invoked by the personification itself, for they make Patience into a type of one aspect of the life of charity, by deliberately relating his actions to those of Christ, St. Francis, and others who embody that virtue.

The spiritual change which Patience brings to the narrative of the poem is emphasized by the deliberate contrast within the dinner scene between the kind of food eaten by Patience (and—significantly—Will) and that eaten by the doctor. First, the doctor is served:

> Ac this maister [of þise men] no manere flesshe [eet],
> Ac [he eet] mete of more coste, mortrewes and potages;
> Of that men mys-wonne thei made hem wel at ese.
>
> (XIII. 40–42)

Patience' dinner is clearly different:

> He sette a soure lof to-for vs and seyde, "agite penitenciam";
> And sith he drough vs drynke, diu-perseverans.
> . . . .

[And he brou3te vs of *Beati-quorum*, of *Beatus-virres* makynge,
And thanne he brou3t vs forth a mees of other mete, of
Miserere-mei-deus;]
Et-quorum-tecta-sunt-peccata
[In a disshe] of derne shrifte, *Dixi* and *confitebor tibi!*
(XIII. 48–49, 52–55)

The difference between these two dinners points up the literal understanding of the doctor and the figural understanding of Patience.[3] The
doctor eats earthly dishes, stews, soups, meats of more cost. Patience and
Will also eat, but the food they consume is spiritual and penitential. Since
the object of the verb denotes spiritual "food" like *Miserere-mei-deus*, the
literal action of eating is made metaphorical, in a quasi-sacramental way;
it refers to the spiritual act of penance in the material form of the act of
eating. The earthly realm is thus brought into a figural relationship with
the spiritual, which fully significates it.

Furthermore, the metaphorical significance of food and of eating in
the Bible, particularly in Jesus' parables, is evoked in these lines, through
their use of Biblical quotations and their reference to Penance, without
which salvation is impossible. The implicit setting of Patience' feast within
the whole context of traditional Christian feast imagery—from the Old
Testament Passover to the Last Supper, the linking of feasting with the
kingdom of heaven in Christ's parables, the Eucharist, and the eternal
Feast of the Lamb—makes Patience' action genuinely figural. It is an action
which takes place within a threefold temporal moment, including past,
present, and future in terms of the divine historical pattern. And to set
an action in such a figural scheme is to infuse it with a fullness of meaning
which no purely earthly and momentary individual action can have. The
feast of Patience is made fully significant as the feast of the doctor can
never be. And it seems to me that Patience' chief function in the poem is
to provide the understanding which can make possible this kind of full
signification.

A figural dimension informs all that Patience does in the rest of the
scene and, by virtue of his presence, all that the others do (or don't do) as
well. The whole dinner scene recalls a parable—Christ's parable of the
wedding feast to which "many are called and few are chosen" in Matthew
22 and (in a somewhat different version) Luke 14. Patience' presence at the

---

3. I am once again indebted to Andrea Rosnick, who discussed the syntactic
and cognitive values of these two passages in a paper she made available to me.

feast and the figurally significant actions which he performs make clear the parable that lies behind this whole scene (and behind the Haukyn episode as well). The seating of the guests at the feast, for example, recalls Christ's advice about the first and the last.

> This maistre was made sitte as for the moste worthy,
> And thanne Clergye and Conscience and Pacience cam after.
> Pacience and I [prestly] were put to be [mettes],
> And seten by owre selue at a syde-borde.
>
> (XIII. 33–36)

The parable of the wedding feast is a parable of salvation, of the true nature of the kingdom of heaven, and, like all of Christ's parables, it poses the test of true understanding for those who hear it. This parable has been introduced in the poem before—by Scripture when she challenges Will to interpret the events of his inner dream, thus throwing him into confusion. The reintroduction of the parable in dramatic form in Passus XIII seems to me designed to show the progress of Will's understanding. This change is most clearly evident when Patience undertakes to answer the persistent question of the *Vita*—what is Dowel? Will, as usual, is the first to bring up the question, in an attempt to bait the doctor. The friar responds by defining Dowel negatively: Dowel is to do no evil. But, says Will acidly, the doctor has done evil to him by eating up all the pudding at dinner. At this point Conscience intervenes, and, true to his knightly, "conscientious" nature, asks the doctor "curteisliche" to define Dowel. This time, the friar responds with a set of definitions:

> "Dowel," quod this doctour, "do as clerkes techeth,
> [That trauailleþ to teche oþere I holde it for a dobet]
> And Dobest doth hym-self so as he seith and precheth."
>
> (XIII. 115–17)

These definitions are exactly the sort the poem has presented before in the words of Thought, Wit, Study, Clergy, and Scripture. Their effect is to circumscribe and limit the nature of Dowel to a particular kind or quality of action, and to make it a thing which can be conceptually defined. But the inadequacy of such an approach to the meaning of Dowel has already been amply displayed.

Conscience then asks the same question of Clergy. Clergy responds with an allegorical fable whose form is reminiscent of Wit's fable in Passus IX: he has seven sons who serve in a castle with the lord of life, but they are not in accord about the meaning of Dowel. And Piers the Plowman has impugned all sciences save love:

> And no tixte ne taketh to meyntene his cause,
> But *dilige deum* and *dominus, quis habitabit, etc.*
> And [demeþ] that Dowel and Dobet are two infinites,
> Whiche infinites, with a feith, fynden oute Dobest,
> Which shal saue mannes soule, thus seith Piers the Ploughman.
>
> (XIII. 125–29)

Clergy is clearly puzzled by Piers's explanation of Dowel. There is scholarly disapproval in his remark that Piers has so few texts to support what he says. Piers's definition is in fact no definition at all—Dowel is an "infinite." And an infinite is precisely something that cannot be defined, that has no limits.[4] It has recently been pointed out, moreover, that as a grammatical term, *infinite* refers to a class of nouns which are indefinite in character.[5] The *kynde*, both cognitive and grammatical, of an *infinite* is thus insusceptible to any definition-oriented mode of understanding, such as that embodied by Clergy and his intellectual relatives. Indeed, Piers's words are the final statement in the form of a definition of the *kynde* of Dowel—and what Piers's definition states is that Dowel cannot be defined, except "with a feith." Yet faith is another "infinite," something without finite boundaries, "the substance of things hoped for, the evidence of things not seen" (Heb. 11:1).

At this point Patience, with Conscience' urging, comes forward to explain what Piers means. And, as he does so, he changes the context in which Dowel must be understood, from a false analysis of the word as a definable substantive to a truer analysis of the term as a figure, whose meaning is locked in the pattern of divine love expressed in history through the lives of God's servants, those who have lived by charity. Dowel is *dilige*—this is the ultimate meaning of Patience' speeches.

Patience begins with a threefold explication of Dowel:

> "*Disce . . . doce, dilige inimicos.*
> *Disce* and Dowel; *doce,* and Dobet; [*Dilige* and Dobest
> Thus lerede] me ones a lemman [. . .], Loue was hir name."
>
> (XIII. 136–39)

---

4. *MED,* s.v. *infinite.*
5. P. M. Kean, "Justice, Kingship, and the Good Life in the Second Part of *Piers Plowman,*" in *Piers Plowman: Critical Approaches,* ed. S. S. Hussey (London, 1969), p. 92.

This is the first full set of definitions of these terms in which the defining term is an imperative, having the same grammatical structure that Dowel has in the pardon. *Disce, doce, dilige* are commandments; so, as Patience uses them, are Dowel, Dobet, and Dobest. They are demands for action, directed toward each one who hears them. This is the crucial step in logic which Will must make, the step that can open to him the true *kynde* of Dowel. How the figure (the expression of divine Love) makes significant the imperative Dowel is a problem Will pursues in the rest of the *Vita;* at this point, it is enough that Patience finally corrects his understanding of the term and joins it with its proper significator.

The true teacher of Dowel is love. The identity between Dowel and Love is made by Patience in the "riddle" he poses to the company. And the form of logic which the riddle employs is figural; it can only be understood by a mind which comprehends figurally, and a will which responds lovingly to the love it figures. The riddle is a "signe" of Dowel; as such, it provides true understanding of the term:

> "I bere there inne a [boste] fast ybounde Dowel,
> In a signe of the Saterday that sette firste the kalendare,
> And al the witte of the Wednesday of the nexte wyke after;
> The myddel of the mone is the miȝte of bothe.
> And here-with am I welcome there I haue it with me."
>
> (XIII. 152–56)

Dowel is personified in Patience' speech—it is even bound fast in a box. But that enclosed word is then placed within a figural context which reveals its nature, as the sign of God's boundless love. Dowel is thus bounded and boundless, tangible yet ineffable, a true mirror of the incarnate Word. Two studies have argued persuasively that the "riddle" refers to the events of the Creation, the Passion, and the Resurrection, the whole development of history bounded by two of the major events in the divine redemptive pattern, the Fall and the Resurrection.[6] This is the sign of the true *kynde* of Dowel—the pattern, figurally manifested, of God's plan. But the significance of the riddle does not end here, for the events veiled in its language are themselves a sign, or figure, of the true *kynde* of the God who willed them. They are a parable of divine love expressed in the temporal actions of human history.

---

6. R. E. Kaske, " '*Ex vi transicionis*' and Its Passage in *Piers Plowman,*" *JEGP,* LXII (1963), 32–60, and Ben H. Smith, *Traditional Imagery of Charity in Piers Plowman* (The Hague, 1966), pp. 41–55.

The riddle poses a test, of exactly the sort that Christ's parables pose. And the responses to it of the other three major characters in the scene exactly reveal the limitations of their understanding. The doctor is totally ignorant—all he sees in the riddle is a lying tale, which he does not care to understand. Clergy seems able to gloss the Scriptural allusions in the riddle, but he is impatient with Patience' ability to make a really difficult problem in exegesis. He accuses Conscience of running to read riddles when he, Clergy, can gloss the most difficult passages of Scripture:

> I shal brynge 30w a bible, a boke of the olde lawe,
> And lere 30w, if 30w lyke, the leest poynte to knowe,
> That Pacience the pilgryme perfitly knewe neuere.
> (XIII. 185–87)

This, it seems to me, is pure professional jealousy on Clergy's part. And, in dismissing the difficulty of the riddle, Clergy reveals his lack of understanding. For he is not aware that the answer to the "riddle" is itself a figure, or "signe," of charity. Conscience, however, does understand the real nature of Patience' figure, and he reveals it in an action which has a repeated, cumulative significance within the poem; renouncing Clergy's way of understanding, he goes on a pilgrimage with Patience "til I haue proued more." This action recalls the pilgrimage of Piers in Passus VI and prefigures the final pilgrimage of Conscience at the poem's end; each journey signifies a major change in the cognitive mode of the poem.

Will is also in a changed state in this passus. Though his function in the dinner scene is more that of observer than actor, he has clearly experienced a considerable change in the course of his previous vision, which is indicated by the new way in which he understands this one. He is Patience' companion from the start of the dinner, and he accompanies Patience and Conscience on their pilgrimage. This change in Will is signaled at the beginning of Passus XIII by an abrupt disruption of his relationship with the waking world:

> And I awaked there-with, witles nerehande,
> And as a freke that [feye] were forth gan I walke,
> In manere of a mendynaunt many a 3ere after,
> And of this metyng many tyme moche thou3t I hadde.
> (XIII. 1–4)

It is true that Will has never been on the best of terms with the everyday world, but after he awakens from the vision of Passus VIII–XII he is completely estranged from ordinary life. He is witless and "feye," like a doomed man, dead to the waking world, concentrating completely on his visions. It is notable, too, that the visions he muses on when he awakens are those of Passus XI and XII, of the inner dream and Imaginatyf. He does not mention his conversations with Thought, Wit, or Clergy; near-hand witless, he has moved beyond the intellectual modes of understanding, which have heretofore blocked his comprehension of Dowel, into a different sort of intellection. Will's witlessness is ironically the best preparation for his attendance at Conscience' dinner.

Just as Patience' riddle of Dowel and charity is the test of comprehension for Clergy and Conscience, so Will's test is Haukyn. Haukyn is the fullest mirror image that Will encounters in the poem; thus, to understand Haukyn is to understand *kyndelich* Will's own deficiencies and faults. The self-images Will has met before, like Thought, have been particular faculties, split off from the complete individual soul. Haukyn is a complete self; it is crucial for Will to perceive him wholly. During their encounter continual stress is placed on Will's *seeing* Haukyn closely and yet more closely:

> I toke [greet] kepe, by Cryst and Conscience bothe,
> Of Haukyn the actyf man and how he was y-clothed.
> . . . .
> And he torned hym as [tyd] and thanne toke I hede,
> It was fouler by felefolde than it firste semed.
> . . . .
> I wayted wisloker, and thanne was it soiled
> With lykyng of Lecherye, as by lokyng of his eye.
> (XIII. 272–73, 319–20, 343–44)

In seeing Haukyn, Will should be able to see much of himself, and it is therefore essential that he perceive him clearly.

The likenesses between Will and Haukyn have been noted before but should be repeated here briefly. Like Will, Haukyn is a minstrel and a rather unsuccessful one at that. Like Will, he is quick to condemn the clergy for their faults while living comfortably with every manner of sin in himself. And, like Will, he believes himself to be "singular" and is consequently disobedient:

> Was none suche as hym-self ne none so pope-holy.
> Y-habited as an hermyte, an ordre by hym-selue,
> Religioun sanz reule and resonable obedience;

Lakkyng lettred men and lewed men bothe,
In lykyng of lele lyf, and a lyer in soule;
. . . .
And entermeten hym ouer-al ther he hath nou3t to done,
Wilnyng that men wende his witte were the best,
Or for his crafty kunnynge or of clerkes the wisest.

                                        (XIII. 284–88, 291–93)

This description of Haukyn easily fits the character of Will as we have
come to know it in the poem.

There is one other important trait which Haukyn shares with Will.
His confession to Patience climaxes in shame, the mark of self-awareness and
self-knowledge which Haukyn gradually achieves. It is a moment which
closely parallels Will's earlier shame, when Imaginatyf rebukes him for
his presumption. And Haukyn's shame, like Will's, results from a self-
knowledge gained through a mirroring process. Thus Will can perceive
that Haukyn is undergoing a process quite similar to his own earlier
experience with Imaginatyf. And as Will's whole perception of himself is
changed by that experience, so is Haukyn's—to the point where he re-
nounces his filthy old garment, accepting no covering but shame, as he

> Swowed and sobbed and syked ful ofte,
> That euer he hadde londe or lordship, lasse other more,
> Or maystrye ouer any man, mo than of hym-self.
> "I were nou3t worthy, wote god," quod Haukyn, "to were any
>   clothes,
> Ne noyther sherte ne shone, saue for shame one,
> To keure my caroigne," quod he, and cryde mercye faste.
>
>   (XIV. 326–31)

The chief function of the mirror images in *Piers Plowman* is defined
by Imaginatyf in Passus XII—"to amenden [by] defautes." The cognitive
value of the image resides in two disparate activities undertaken simultaneously by the perceiver. First of all, he must recognize himself in the
mirror. But the mirror image is not an exact copy; like all mirrors, it distorts, rearranges, changes the perspective upon the object it reflects. The
perceiver recognizes his likeness, but his self-knowledge is extended and
refined by means of the image's dissimilarity to himself (or to the self-
image he is accustomed to perceiving). Haukyn is not simply a mirror
image which corroborates Will's previous experience in the poem. Through
the agency of Patience and Conscience, Haukyn provides a cognitive test

[116]

for Will, a test of his abilities to understand in the changed terms of the poem which Patience has announced. For Haukyn, too, is a figure of Dowel, albeit an oblique one, and the process of resignification of Dowel which Patience begins in the dinner scene is continued in the Haukyn episode. Haukyn becomes a true *speculum*, as his activities are resignified in a figural way by Patience.

Haukyn's name is *Actiua-vita*, activity for profit (as a waferer) and for pleasure (as a minstrel):

> Alle ydel ich hatye for of actyf is my name.
> A wafrere, wil ʒe wite, and serue many lordes,
> [Ac] fewe robes I fonge or furred gounes.
> . . . .
> Beggeres and bidderes of my bred crauen,
> Faitoures and freres and folke with brode crounes,
> I fynde payne for the pope and prouendre for his palfrey,
> And I hadde neuere of hym, have god my treuthe,
> Noither prouendre ne parsonage ʒut of the popis ʒifte,
> Saue a pardoun with a peys of led and two pollis amydde!
> (XIII. 225–27, 241–46)

Haukyn works hard for all, to feed both body and spirit, though with earthly food and earthly pleasures. And his bread is good even if his minstreling isn't:

> Alle Londoun I leue liketh wel my wafres,
> And lowren whan thei lakken hem—
> (XIII. 264–65)

"Give us this day our daily bread": its provision, by Haukyn's lights, is not God's doing but his own, the sweat of his brow on cold mornings:

> For ar I haue bred of mele ofte mote I swete.
> And ar the comune haue corne ynough many a colde mornynge;
> So, ar my wafres ben ywrouʒt moche wo I tholye.
> (XIII. 261–63)

Haukyn *does*. This is surely the most evident and important thing about him. The other characters in the *Vita* may think all they please, but Haukyn acts. His whole life is taken up in constant activity for his own welfare and that of the whole community, from the papal palfrey to the Pope himself.

Thus, as he is first presented, Haukyn is perhaps the most completely mundane creature in the poem. He is cheerful, well-liked, and useful to all. Yet, for all that he does, he does not do well. This becomes clear on Will's closer inspection of Haukyn's garments, which reveal the result of his earthly activities, the Seven Deadly Sins which have stained his soul. As Will looks at Haukyn, his mode of perceiving him gradually changes. This is an important shift. Haukyn is resignified before Will's very eyes, seen first as a wholly earthly character and then in a manner more and more spiritual in its reference. Haukyn's resignification recapitulates that of the poem, from literal character to personification to *speculum* and figural type. The person who guides this process is Patience, but the eyes through which we perceive the change are Will's. And the process is carried out through the allegory of Haukyn's coat.

Will first notices the coat when he looks more closely at Haukyn, just after Haukyn has explained his many activities:

> He hadde a cote of Crystendome as holykirke bileueth.
> Ac it was moled in many places with many sondri plottes,
> Of Pruyde here a plotte, and there a plotte of vnboxome speche.
>
> (XIII. 274–76)

This is no ordinary coat. It is "of Crystendome," the Christianity which Haukyn professes, spotted with the stains left by Haukyn's sinful activities. Evidently, the coat should be seen as an allegory of Haukyn's soul, for of course it is not an ordinary earthly coat but the soul, blackened by sin, Pride, and disobedient speech.

Yet Haukyn does not perceive the coat as an allegorical sign of his spiritual state. To him, it is simply a dirty garment:

> "Bi Criste," quod Conscience tho, "thi best cote, Haukyn,
> Hath many moles and spottes; it moste ben ywasshe."
> "ȝe, who so toke hede," quod Haukyn, "byhynde and bifore,
> What on bakke and what on bodyhalf and by the two sydes,
> Men sholde fynde many frounces and many foule plottes."
>
> (XIII. 314–18)

Conscience gives no hint that he sees the coat to be anything more than a simple coat. Haukyn merely regrets its filthiness. As he describes it, it is clear that he perceives it as an earthly garment, with a front and a back and two sides. But when Will looks at it again, after Haukyn turns himself about, he sees even more clearly that the spots on the coat are Haukyn's sins:

And he turned hym as [tyd], and thanne toke I hede,
It was fouler by felefolde than it firste semed,
It was bidropped with Wratthe and wikked wille,
With Enuye and yuel speche . . .

(XIII. 319–22)

Not only is it blotched with sin, but the spots on it begin to speak. One presumes, of course, that it is Haukyn's sinful words which are actually recorded, but the sentence structure of the passage does not make it clear that this is so; rather, as they are described on the coat, the sins start to confess in the first person. For example,

It was bidropped with Wratthe and wikked wille
. . . .
Lyinge and [lakkynge] and leue tonge to chyde;
Al that he wist wykked by any wiȝte, tellen it,

. . . .
And made of frendes foes thorugh a false tonge,
"Or with myȝte of mouthe or thorugh mannes strengthe
Auenge me fele tymes, other frete my-selue [wiþInne]
As a [shepsteres] shere [ysherewed myn euencristen]."

(XIII. 321, 323–24, 328–31)

The "he" of the third line must refer back to Wratthe as the subject of the sentence; it is also the only possible subject of the verb "made." Yet, the clause in direct discourse is a continuation of the sentence containing the verb "made," and so the speaker of this speech must be the subject of the verb "made," which, as I have already argued, can only be Wratthe. This identification is made clear by the fact that the self-biting, literally fretting figure depicted here is a standard iconographic representation of Wrath. Thus, the drop of wrath Will first saw quickly changes itself into a lively picture of the sinful act itself. To take another example,

I wayted wisloker and thanne was it soiled
With lykyng of Lecherye, as by lokyng of his eye.
For vche a mayde that he mette he made hir a signe
Semynge to-synne-ward and some [. . .] he gan taste
Aboute the mouth, or bynethe bygynneth to grope,
Tyl eytheres wille waxeth kene and to the werke ȝeden.

(XIII. 343–48)

Haukyn's coat has become a personification of his spiritual state, bearing the fruits of his wicked will, which is seen in action in these narrative vignettes of his sins.

[119]

At this point, Conscience steps in to show Haukyn the true significance of his garments:

> "And I shal kenne the," quod Conscience, "of contricioun to make,
> That shal clawe thi cote of alkynnes filthe,
> . . . .
> Shal neuere [myx] bimolen it ne moth after biten it,
> Ne fende ne false man defoulen it in thi lyue;
> Shall none heraude ne harpoure haue a fairere garnement
> Than Haukyn the actyf man, and thou do by my techyng."
>
> (XIV. 16–17, 22–25)

Conscience resignifies Haukyn's coat, by recognizing it as an allegorical figure of a sinful soul which cannot be washed with water or brushed with a comb but can only be cleansed by contrition. That Conscience resignifies Haukyn's coat in figural terms, of the sort introduced by Patience in the dinner scene, reveals perhaps better than anything else Conscience' full understanding of what Patience meant.

Patience carries the resignification of Haukyn a step further. While Conscience sees the spiritual allegory in Haukyn's coat, Patience sees it in Haukyn's life:

> "And I shal purueye the [paast]," quod Pacyence, "though no plow erie,
> And floure to fede folke with as best be for the soule,
> Though neuere greyne growed ne grape vppon vyne."
> . . . .
> But I [listened and] lokede what liflode it was
> [That] pacience so preisede [and of his poke hente]
> [. . .] A pece of þe *Pater-noster* [and profered vs alle]
> [And þanne was it] *fiat voluntas tua* [sholde fynde vs alle]
> "Haue, Haukyn!" quod Pacyence, "and ete this whan the hungreth,
> Or when thow clomsest for colde or clyngest for drye."
>
> (XIV. 28–30, 47–50)

Haukyn has been a waferer of the body; Patience now tells him to be a waferer of the soul. The food with which he must learn to feed himself and others is spiritual food, the will of God. Understanding his activities in their spiritual significance makes Haukyn the doer into Haukyn the welldoer. And his contrition, the sign of his own right understanding of his actions, thus becomes a figure of the *kynde* of Dowel for Will. As Patience explains, "contricioun, feith, and conscience is kyndelich Dowel." Like Conscience' faith, which was demonstrated earlier when he left with Patience, Haukyn's contrition embodies Dowel through a figural action like Piers's renunciation of his plow.

Haukyn is made completely figural and is given the anagogical significance in terms of divine history, which is the mark of all true *figurae*. At the beginning of Passus XIV, he explains to Patience and Conscience:

> "I haue but one hool hatere . . . I am the lasse to blame
> Though it be soiled and selde clene; I slepe there-inne on niȝtes;
> And also I haue an houswyf, hewen and children—
> *Vxorem duxy, et ideo non possum venire*—
> That wolen bymolen it many tyme, maugre my chekes!"
> (XIV. 1–4)

His quotation of Luke 14:20 puts him among the worldly guests at the Lord's marriage feast.[7] And the attention paid to his coat is the clue to his figural significance, in its similarity to the parable as recounted in Matthew:

> And when the king came in to see the guests he saw there a man which had not on a wedding-garment. And he saith unto him, Friend, how camest thou in hither not having a wedding-garment? And he was speechless. Then said the king to the servants, Bind him hand and foot, and take him away, and cast him into outer darkness; there shall be weeping and gnashing of teeth. For many are called, but few are chosen.
> (Matt. 22:11–14)

Haukyn in his stained coat is the man without a proper wedding garment. It is not clear, as we leave him at the end of Passus XIV weeping for his sins, whether he has succeeded in cleansing his coat or whether he is doomed to suffer the fate of the man in the parable. Nor do I think that this question is particularly important to the significance the parable has for our (and Will's) understanding of Haukyn. Of far greater importance is the implicit linking, as intersignifying figures, of Haukyn, the man in

---

7. Pointed out by D. W. Robertson and B. F. Huppé, *Piers Plowman and Scriptural Tradition* (Princeton, N.J., 1951), p. 169.

Christ's parable, and Will, made through the last verse of the parable—
"Many are called, but few are chosen." This is the verse with which
Scripture scorns Will during his inner dream in Passus XI, the verse which
brings about Will's first major step forward in understanding. And the
fact that again this verse is implicitly invoked, together with the full context of the parable from which it is taken, suggests, I believe, the way in
which the parable clarifies the entire significance of the *Vita de Dowel*.

The exegetical tradition of the parable of the marriage feast considers
it to be concerned with teaching the meaning of charity. Augustine's sermon
on the text in Matthew pays special attention to the guest who lacks a wed-
ding-garment.[8] Noting that the invited guests were a haphazardly chosen lot,
he asks how one could distinguish between the good and the evil men. By
their garments, he replies. Arguing first that the garment has a spiritual
meaning, he then defines the significance of the proper wedding garment:

> Vestis quippe illa in corde, non in carne inspiciebatur. . . . Quae
> est ergo vestis illa nuptialis? Haec est vestis nuptialis: *Finis autem
> praecepti est*, Apostolus dicit, *charitas de corde puro, et conscientia
> bona, et fide non ficta* (I Tim. 1:5). Haec est vestis nuptialis.[9]

And later, he urges, "Ergo habete fidem cum dilectione. Ista est vestis
nuptialis."[10] This tradition simply reinforces what is already evident in
the text of *Piers Plowman*. To see Haukyn as the man without a proper
garment, as the man who must wash his coat and become clothed with
the garment of contrition, and of faith with love, is not only to see him
as a figuration of this parable, but also to understand Haukyn as the most
complex figure of Dowel Will has yet encountered. Haukyn justly
climaxes the *Vita de Dowel*. And it is surely significant that Haukyn is
also the most complete and evident mirror image of Will in the poem.

---

8. In reference to another context, Robertson and Huppé draw attention
to Augustine's commentary on this parable, *ibid.*, p. 134.

9. Augustine *Sermo* XC (Migne, *PL* XXXVIII. 561–62). [Wherefore the
garment is seen to be those things in the heart, not in the flesh. . . . What is
the wedding garment? This is the wedding garment: 'The end of the commandment is,' the Apostle says, 'charity out of a pure heart, and of a good
conscience, and of faith unfeigned' (I Tim. 1:5). This is the wedding garment."]

10. *Ibid.*, 564. ["Therefore have faith with love. This is the wedding
garment."]

As a mirror to Will of his own *kynde,* he provides him with the fullest *kynde knowynge* he gains in the poem. Moreover, as *speculum,* he provides Will with an understanding of the *kynde* of Dowel and of Kynde, which is charity. Haukyn thus integrates all the chief concerns of the *Vita de Dowel* in a relationship which is finally figural.

When Will awakens from his meeting with Haukyn, he finds himself even more estranged from the normal, waking world than at the beginning of Passus XIII:

> Ac after my wakyng it was wonder longe,
> Ar I couth kyndely knowe what was Dowel.
> And so my witte wex and wanyed til I a fole were,
> And somme lakked my lyf, allowed it fewe,
> And leten me for a lorel, and loth to reuerencen
> Lordes or ladyes or any lyf elles,
> As persones in pellure with pendauntes of syluer;
> . . . .
> That folke helden me a fole, and in that folye I raued,
> Tyl Resoun hadde reuthe on me and rokked me aslepe,
> Tyl I seigh, as it a sorcerye were, a sotyl thinge with-al,
> One with-outen tonge and teeth tolde me whyder I shulde,
> And wher-of I cam and of what kynde; . . .
>
> (XV. 1–7, 10–14)

It is evident from these lines that the terms of the dream vision have become completely removed from their ordinary associations. What was wisdom is now folly, what is "Resoun" is that which is strangest and most uncommon, in earthly terms. Reason comes to rock Will to sleep, and the dream Reason gives to him is of the strangest, most unnatural creature Will has yet encountered—Anima. The waking world is the least real and the most estranged from truth; the visions are real and reasonable and truthful. One can trace, from Passus XIII on, an increasing estrangement between the two worlds of waking and sleep, the everyday and the visionary; it is articulated most sharply here at the beginning of Passus XV, but it carries through to the beginning of Passus XVIII, where Will, "wolleward and wete-shoed" wanders wearily until he can sleep again.

This sharp divergence of the two worlds serves to give the visions of Passus XV–XVIII (the *Vita de Dobet*) a self-contained quality which is not found in any other parts of the poem. The world of these visions is definitely not the world to which we (and Will) are accustomed; its logic, its imagery, its structure are based on principles which are not those of everyday reality. The change in the poem's terms that was initiated by Patience in Passus XIII is fully evident in these passus; the very nature of the allegory, the kinds of figures who appear, the temporal and spatial relationships within the dream visions are all emphatically different from those which governed the earlier parts of the poem. For one thing, there are no characters from contemporary life in these passus. Piers Plowman, appearing for the first time since Passus VII, loses those characteristics which made him a contemporary plowman and is seen in an atemporal aspect. And the "Resoun" who gives Will this sequence of visions is distinctly not the same Reason who counseled the king along with Kind Wit in Passus IV. Then, Reason reasoned in accordance with the principles of natural law and common sense; here, the visions he inspires are figural and symbolic, governed by a logic which appears to be mere raving to a world unaccustomed to such a mode of understanding.

Will's introduction to this new world is Anima, the creature without tongue or teeth who nonetheless speaks. From Anima's first appearance it is clear that even a semblance of naturalistic representation has been suspended in this vision. Yet, for all his strangeness, Anima has some very familiar faces:

> "The whiles I quykke the corps," quod he, "called am I *Anima;*
> And whan I wilne and wolde *Animus* ich hatte;
> And for that I can and knowe called am I *Mens;*
> And whan I make mone to god *Memoria* is my name;
> And whan I deme domes and do as treuthe techeth
> Thanne is *Racio* my riȝt name, Resoun on Englisshe;
> And whan I fele that folke telleth, my firste name is *Sensus,*
> And that is wytte and wisdome, the welle of alle craftes;
> And whan I chalange or chalange nouȝte, chepe or refuse,
> Thanne am I Conscience ycalde, goddis clerke and his notarie;
> And whan I loue lelly owre lorde and alle other,
> Thanne is lele Loue my name, and in Latyn *Amor;*
> And whan I [flee] fro the flesshe and forsake the caroigne,
> Thanne am I spirit specheles and *Spiritus* thanne ich hatte."
>
> (XV. 23–36)

Anima is Thought, Wit and Clergy (as Mens), Reason, Conscience, Lewte and Patience both (as aspects of Lele Love or Amor), Will (as Animus), and Imaginatyf (as Memoria). He is thus all the major characters of the preceding passus, appearing here in a different form. And the form is not merely different and strange; it is also the root form of the various functions it embodies, which appeared as distinct characters earlier in the poem but which are seen here in their essential, integrative relationship as the different manifestations of a single being, the soul. These two characteristics of Anima extend to the whole structure of this vision and the next (Passus XVIII). In them, the concerns of the earlier part of the poem are reconsidered, but in a wholly different way. The *Vita de Dobet* acts as a mirror of the *Vita de Dowel,* one which reflects its concerns in their essential aspect, *sub specie eternitatis.*

This new world puzzles Will. The first thing that concerns him is how Anima fits together, with all his different names (after all, Will has encountered them before as discrete characters). Yet Anima rebukes him:

> "Thou woldest knowe and kunne the cause of alle her names,
> And of myne, if thow my3test, me thinketh by thi speche!"
> "3e, syre," I seyde, "by so no man were greued,
> Alle the sciences vnder sonne and alle the sotyle craftes
> I wolde I knewe and couth kyndely in myne herte!"
> "Thanne artow inparfit," quod he, "and one of Prydes kny3tes";
> . . . .
> "It were a3eynes kynde," quod he, "and alkynnes resoun,
> That any creature shulde kunne al, excepte Cryste one."
> (XV. 45–50, 52–53)

Will wants to know the causes of all things, to know all sciences. He is still thinking of the world as amenable to Reason and Wit. Of course, he has been chastized before for his overpresumptive desire for knowledge, but Anima is the first of his teachers to explain to him that full understanding, as he conceives of it, is not only presumptuous but "a3eynes kynde," against nature. For the true nature of the world cannot be grasped in terms of the causal logic of earthly knowledge:

> Coueytise to kunne and to knowe science
> [Adam and Eve putte out of Paradys]
> *Sciencie appetitus hominem immortalitatis gloria spoliauit.*
> (XV. 61–62)

It is most important to understand that what Anima criticizes in Will is not just the desire to know but the desire to know in a particular and inadequate way. "Science" is the epistemological realm of Dame Study, Wit, Clergy, and Scripture, whose many books Dame Study wrote (X. 168–69). But the way of "science" cannot produce a true, *kynde* understanding of the world. Will must learn a new epistemology, constructed in terms of a figural logic, whose key is Christ, and whose expression is charity. Without this mode of cognition, Will's understanding of the world can only be aȝeynes kynde."

Most of Anima's discourse is devoted to cataloguing the ways in which the world has fallen on evil times. It would be hard to find a gloomier prophet in the poem than he. Many of his examples are variations on the familiar *topos* of "the world-upside-down," a depiction of the chaotic topsy-turviness which, in the figural scheme of history, is one sign of the end of time.[11] And most of his wrath is directed against those priests who have neglected their proper duties for money and worldly position. As Anima analyzes their fault, the clergy are deficient in charity, and because they lack charity they also lack understanding of their proper function and behave in ways which are contrary to their proper *kynde*.

The link between lack of charity and misunderstanding of *kynde* is quite clear in Anima's speech. He begins, in response to Will's question, with reflections on the nature of charity and its absence in the life of contemporary Christians. This leads him to conclude:

> For-thi I conseille alle Cristene to confourmen hem to charite;
> For charite with-oute chalengynge vnchargeth the soule.
>
> (XV. 337–38)

He continues with what would appear to be an odd *non sequitur:*

> Ac there is a defaute in the folke that the faith kepeth;
> Wherefore folke is the feblere and nouȝt ferme of bilieue.
> As in Lussheborwes is a lyther alay and ȝet loketh he lyke a sterlynge.
>
> (XV. 340–42)

Some mysterious "fault" is abroad, weakening and coarsening the folk. And, what is worse, things are no longer what they seem; they are like the poor-quality lushburg which appears to be sterling but is not. The world is out of joint—even natural signs are no longer trustworthy:

> For thorw werre and wykked werkes and wederes [vnsesonable],
> Wederwise shipmen and witti clerkes also

---

11. E. R. Curtius, *European Literature and the Latin Middle Ages,* trans. W. R. Trask (New York, 1963), pp. 94–98.

Han no bileue to the lifte ne to the [lodesterre],
Astrymyanes alday in her arte faillen,
That whilum warned bifore what shulde falle after.
. . . .
Tilieres that tiled the erthe tolden her maistres,
By the sede that thei sewe what thei selle miȝte,
. . . .
Now failleth the folke of the flode and of the londe bothe,
Shepherdes and shipmen and so do this tilieres;
Noither thei kunneth ne knoweth one cours bi-for another.
Astrymyanes also aren at her wittes ende;
Of that was calculed of the element the contrarie thei fynde.
(XV. 349–53, 357–58, 360–64)

Earthly wisdom, whether it be that of the pragmatic, weather-wise shipmen and plowmen or that of wise clerks steeped in astronomical lore, is no longer adequate for discerning the truth of things. Even grammar, "the grounde of al, bigyleth now children." The traditional cognitive disciplines, based upon nature and natural logic, fail because the signs in nature are now no longer trustworthy. The world, having lost charity, has also lost its proper *kynde*, and is given over to misunderstanding and misbelief. Charity, which comprehends divine understanding, must replace science, which comprehends only natural logic, as the epistemological basis for the poem. This is the basic thrust of Anima's speech, the logical turn he announces which is also mirrored in the changed structure of the poem.

Anima's method of teaching Will differs from that of his other instructors. He shows the nature of charity to Will in a series of figural mirrors, who embody the life of charity—Edmund, Edward, St. Francis, the early hermits, and St. Thomas Becket, "a briȝt myroure" in which bishops may learn the true nature of their calling. Charity, emblematically shown as a launderer hard at work in his penitential laundry, washes out the stains on all the coats of Christendom, including (I believe) that of Haukyn.[12] Seeing the world as a series of *specula* or emblems, partial embodiments of a prior truth, is a distinctive feature of the figural view of things; it is

---

12. This traditional representation of Charity, as Robertson and Huppé note (*Piers Plowman and Scriptural Tradition*, p. 181), is derived from Ps. 7:6. I have reserved the term "emblem" for this kind of iconographic image, which is, however, figural in its structure, having specific Scriptural antecedents and reverberations, including Christ washing the feet of the apostles, and Magdalene washing the feet of Christ.

exactly in accord with the way in which God reveals himself to man in time through the figural pattern of history. The tangible manifestations of the *figurae* are mirrors of an unseen and intangible reality, just as charity, which is "a fre liberal wille," manifests itself in the mirror of charitable works and words. Yet, what is important is not the charitable work but the right will which it reveals. This is why, Anima explains, Will can never see the person of Charity without the help of Piers Plowman:

> "Clerkes haue no knowyng," quod he, "but by werkes and bi wordes.
> Ac Piers the Plowman parceyueth more depper
> What is the wille and wherfore that many wyȝte suffreth,
> *Et vidit deus cogitaciones eorum.*"
>
> (XV. 192–94)

Thus, Anima has completed the shift of the poem's guiding term from Dowel, the manifested action, to charity, the unseen spiritual essence which informs the doing. Dowel mirrors charity; the will manifests itself in the action. This is the truth which Piers understood on receipt of Truth's pardon, and that is the reason he is chosen by Anima as the only being in the poem who can truly perceive charity.

The "logic" of the mirror, of the figure, is most important in this passus. Not only does Anima use it, but Will himself makes a cryptic remark when he first asks Anima, "What is Charity?"

> Clerkis kenne me that Cryst is in alle places;
> Ac I seygh hym neuere sothly but as my-self in a miroure,
> [*Hic*] *in enigmate, tunc facie ad faciem.*
>
> (XV. 156–57)

The text which Will cites is the basis of all Christian figural interpretation. Here men see *"in enigmate"*; there men will see face to face. The vision of Christ, true knowledge of the Savior, comes only through the mirror of charity in the deeds of his servants. And this vision is difficult to come by— Will has seen Christ only "as my-self in a miroure." The rest of Anima's speech to him is designed in part to give him a whole set of other mirrors of charity.

Now, while the mirror is the only way in which knowledge of invisible things can be gained in this world, the fact is that it is a partial, fragmentary, dark sign of truth, subject to "defautes," the errors of human vision and the fact that the mirror is earthly. For the material sign of a spiritual reality must always be incomplete and in some measure distorting. This seems to be Will's complaint in these lines, if complaint it be. The best mirror he has met of the action of charity upon the soul is his own closest mirror image, Haukyn. But the figure of charity which Haukyn ultimately presents is elliptical and unclear, perceived through the muddiness of its earthly forms. Haukyn, like the other figures in the poem, does not present charity *"facie ad faciem."*

It is the face-to-face vision of charity which Will desires. Anima has told him that "with-outen helpe of Piers Plowman . . . his persone seestow neuere" (XV. 190). When Will, after thanking Anima for his lessons "for Haukynnes loue the actyf man," complains that he is still "in a were what charite is to mene," Anima gives him the vision he seeks of the "persone" of Charity, a vision guided by Piers Plowman. And it is surely no accident that this direct vision comes in the form of the most elaborately prepared and executed figure which the poem contains—the Tree of Charity.[13]

The Tree of Charity is first introduced by Anima at the end of his conversation with Will. It is carefully prepared for by several references which Anima makes to allegorical trees, most notably in XV. 93–100 and in the quotation from the commentary on Matt. 21:18–22 by "Johannes Crysostomus" which follows it (XV. 115 ff). The traditional exegesis of Matt. 21:18–22, Jesus' curse on the barren fig tree, saw in this incident a rebuke of the wicked and unprofitable clergy, who were failing in proper charity. It is with this interpretation in mind that Anima uses the tree image at the beginning of Passus XV. The fruitfulness of the tree is a sign of charity—from here it is a very easy transition to make of the tree a full-fledged allegory of Charity. But the fig tree is also used by Christ as an eschatological sign:

> Now learn a parable of the fig tree; When his branch is yet tender, and putteth forth leaves, ye know that summer is nigh; So likewise ye, when ye shall see all these things, know that it is near, even at the very doors.
>
> (Matt. 24:32–33)

---

13. For a discussion of the sources of the Tree of Charity emblem, see Smith, *Traditional Imagery of Charity in Piers Plowman*, pp. 56–73, and Morton W. Bloomfield, *"Piers Plowman* and the Three Grades of Chastity," *Anglia,* LXXVI (1958), 225–53. Two good critical analyses of the structure and function of the emblem in the poem are E. T. Donaldson, *Piers Plowman: The C-Text and Its Poet* (New Haven, Conn., 1949), pp. 183–88, and E. Salter, *Piers Plowman: An Introduction* (Cambridge, Mass., 1962), pp. 73–76.

And in Revelation, when the sixth seal is opened:

> the stars of heaven fell unto the earth, even as a fig-tree casteth
> her untimely figs, when she is shaken of a mighty wind.
>
> (Rev. 6:13)

Both these associations, much reinforced by the eschatological tenor of the latter part of Anima's speech,[14] carry over into the fully developed image of the tree in Passus XVI.

The Tree of Charity is thus set in the context not only of moral absolutes but of temporal and anagogical ones as well; it contains the figural, moral, and theological truths which shape all that Will has seen before in the poem. Because it is a vision of charity, it is a vision of God, who is Love; because it is a vision of God, it is a vision of history, through which God reveals himself to man; because it is a vision of history, it is a vision of time and change as well as of eternity and stasis, conceived figurally and centered in the person of Piers the Plowman, who is both the guide and occasion for the vision.[15] Considered together with the whole progression of events which it initiates through Passus XVIII, the Tree of Charity is thus the cognitive heart of the poem, the first moment at which its allegorical strands come together in one illuminative image.

Anima presents the tree to Will in terms of a static allegory, like those we have encountered earlier in Piers's map to Truth or in the landscape Will sees at the very beginning of his visions:

> "Mercy is the more ther-of, the myddel stokke is Reuthe.
> The leues ben Lele-Wordes, the lawe of Holycherche,
> The blosmes beth Boxome-Speche and Benygne-Lokynge;
> Pacience hatte the pure tre and pore symple of herte,
> And so, thorw god and [. . .] good men groweth the frute Charite."
>
> (XVI. 5–9)

---

14. Bloomfield has noted the "apocalyptic picture of the times" in Anima's speech: *Piers Plowman as a Fourteenth-Century Apocalypse* (New Brunswick, N.J., 1961), pp. 121–22.

15. The mystical nature of this vision is indicated by Will's swoon (XVI. 19) at the mention of Piers's name. This is the only time Will swoons in the poem, and in this state of "death to the world," including the ordinary world of his visions, he sees the Tree of Charity. The swoon is akin to the mystic's state of *raptus,* and also serves to differentiate and isolate the vision of Dobet from all the others in the poem.

This is an image which incorporates many of the values developed earlier in the poem, either through personifications or through their chief concerns —Repentance, Loyalty, Obedience, Patience. Like Anima himself, this image puts together earlier characters in the poem in a new way, one which shows their relationships and demonstrates their essential unity as parts of the organically related tree.

At this point, the tree exists only as an emblematic pattern, nonliving and static. Yet, as a figure, it implies a temporal context. In Christian history, the tree is a major emblem—the tree of the Fall, the tree on which Christ was crucified, the eschatological tree, the tree of life in the garden of the New Jerusalem, the tree of virtues or of vices which grows in all men's hearts. As a symbol, the tree links all of time, from the beginning through the present to the end. And since this tree is the Tree of Charity, it expresses also in emblematic form the basic meaning of all Christian life and history.

When Anima first signifies the tree for Will, all these associations within time are only potential, for the Tree of Charity remains static in Anima's hands, expressing, as it were, only the nonchanging, eternal, timeless pattern itself. When Piers takes over as Will's guide in the inner dream, however, the complete *figura,* within and without time, gradually takes form. The tree ceases to be an absolute, atemporal emblem and is brought fully into relationship with historical time. And it is surely significant that the agent for this is Piers Plowman, a contemporary, fourteenth-century figure, who, although created in this particular poem, figures forth other persons in history (like Moses, Peter, Christ) as well as the ideal life of charity. He thus combines history and eternity, change and stasis, serving as the perfect vehicle for moving the poem to its final and proper form.

In contrast to the static emblem described by Anima, the tree as Piers shows it to Will is continually moving, so much so that it needs three sturdy props to keep it from falling down altogether. Covetise creeps among the leaves and gnaws the fruit, the Flesh blows fiercely through it, the worms of sin eat up the blossoms, the Devil shakes it from the roots and throws unkind neighbors at the fruit or takes a ladder made of lies in order to fetch away the blossoms. Piers puts the tree into a natural, temporal context of blossom time and fruit time, of winds and worms and fruit-stealers. This tree is living and growing, unlike the atemporal tree Anima describes. As such it is a far more satisfactory vehicle for understanding the nature of Dowel or the life of charity, for action and living presuppose a context of time, of change and movement.

And when Will asks Piers to describe its fruit, Piers does so in terms not of absolute virtues but of states of life, matrimony, widowhood, and virginity. It is certainly true that these states are associated with certain virtues and degrees of perfection,[16] but the important difference between the nature of Piers's fruit and that described by Anima is that Piers speaks of ways of living in a historical, temporal world. Thus, the Tree of Charity effects a union between the realm of eternal truth and the world of time and action, that union which Will has been seeking to understand for so long.[17] It is as though Will were getting a God's-eye view of things in this passus, a vision of the eternal pattern itself, gathering all things in time into itself with the inessentials pared away. Piers himself shares in the essential and yet temporal nature of this vision. When we saw him before, it was as the enigmatic guide of a disparate bunch of fourteenth-century folk trying to plow a half-acre; he appears here in a far more evident figural aspect. He, too, is an aspect of the pattern of charity itself, seeing all earthly action in its proper form, that of the Tree of Charity and its plowman.

Eternity visibly and audibly enters time when Will asks Piers to knock an apple down for him so that he can try its flavor. This Eve-like request touches off the whole chain of history:

> And Pieres caste to the croppe and thanne comsed it to crye,
> And wagged Wydwehode and it wepte after.
> And whan [he] meued Matrimoigne it made a foule noyse,
> That I had reuth whan Piers rogged, it gradde so reufulliche.
> For euere as thei dropped adown the deuel was redy,
> And gadred hem alle togideres bothe grete and smale,
> Adam and Abraham and Ysay the prophete,
> Sampson and Samuel and seynt Iohan the baptiste;
> Bar hem forth boldely, no body hym letted,
> And made of holy men his horde in *lymbo inferni,*
> There is derkenesse and drede and the deuel maister.
> And Pieres for pure tene that o pile he lau3te,
> And hitte after hym, happe how it my3te,
> *Filius,* bi the Fader wille and frenesse of *Spiritus Sancti,*
> To go robbe that raggeman and reue the fruit fro hym.
>
> (XVI. 75–89)

---

16. See Bloomfield, *"Piers Plowman* and the Three Grades of Chastity."

17. The mutual and fully significant union of temporal and eternal is demonstrated by Erich Auerbach to be the essential figural vision: *"Figura,"* in *Scenes from the Drama of European Literature* (New York, 1959), especially pp. 58–60, 72. Bloomfield has also noted the historical significance given to the Tree of Charity, which he associates with an apocalyptic, Joachite view of time: *Piers Plowman as a Fourteenth-Century Apocalypse,* p. 123.

As the apple falls from the tree it also falls into time, from the extrahistorical image of the Tree of Charity to the historical moment when Adam and Eve fell. Postlapsarian history is then condensed into the image of the devil gathering up all the fallen apples, Adam, Samson, Samuel, into his infernal horde. Immediately following these lines, the poem proceeds into a naturalistic description, perceived without the veil of imagery, of the moment when Gabriel announces to Mary the Incarnation of the Son—the moment which also most fully incorporates and reveals the divine pattern.

The episode of the Tree of Charity reveals the figural pattern of divine charity informing history far less ambiguously than anything else in the poem. Will actually sees the pattern enter time and shape history, as Piers reveals the tree to him. And as the tree is brought into relationship with the events which it informs, it becomes less and less schematic and static; it moves, it initiates the moment, still perceived through the tree image, which begins human history, and then passes fully into history at the moment of Gabriel's announcement to Mary of the Advent of Christ. At this point, the tree as an emblem passes out of the poem, and Will witnesses the life of Christ, the perfect expression in time of the life of charity, which the tree has expressed as an extrahistorical emblem.

As allegory, the Tree of Charity is surely the most complex and satisfactory image in the poem. It presents the world as pure *figura,* uniting the individual moments of history from Fall to Redemption, uniting history with the poem through the figure of Piers Plowman, and uniting all these things with the image of charity which grows in the hearts of all men. As the tree enters time it loses its emblematic structure; yet the understanding of the nature of charity which Will first perceives through it remains, as the pattern informing the rest of Passus XVI and all of Passus XVII and XVIII. Thus, the vision of the tree is evidently the vision of the *kynde* of charity which Will has desired; yet, it is important to realize that he receives it not as a direct vision of God but as a *figura* revealed in history, as the emblematic tree enters time.[18]

When Will wakes up from his inner dream, he does not waken into the time scheme of the earlier part of his main dream (the conversation

---

18. It is interesting to compare the movement of Dante's *Paradiso* in conjunction with this, in which the pilgrim moves through an increasingly complete vision of time to the final direct vision. The process in *Piers Plowman* is almost the reverse, both here and in Passus XVIII, resulting in a much less confident and triumphal vision of divinity than Dante records in *The Divine Comedy.*

with Anima); rather, the time of the inner dream has become that of the main dream as well. This, of course, is as it should be, for the vision of the inner dream is now the informing vision of the poem. Will looks for Piers Plowman, his guide and the revealer of the truth he has seen, the key to the figure. But the person he encounters is Abraham:

> And thanne I mette with a man a Mydlenten Sondaye,
> As hore as an hawethorne and Abraham he hi3te.
> I frayned hym first fram whennes he come,
> And of whennes he were and whider that he thou3te.
> "I am Feith," quod that freke, "it falleth nou3te to lye,
> And of Abrahames hous [as] an heraud of armes.
> I seke after a segge that I seigh ones,
> A ful bolde bacheler, I knewe hym by his blasen."
>
> (XVI. 172–79)

The figure of Abraham is introduced in a significant way. First, Will says that he met a man called ("hi3te") Abraham, of whom he asks all the questions one would ordinarily ask of a mortal man—who he is, where he comes from, where he is going. He is asking, in short, for a temporal and earthly context in which to place the man called Abraham. But the man answers, "I am Faith." In other words, he regards his earthly qualities, like name and place of birth, as inessential. He *is* Faith. Abraham has become his own figural meaning here, a type of faith, seen under his permanent, eternal aspect.

And he is a herald of arms of Abraham's house, seeking a bachelor knight.[19] This statement makes no sense at all in earthly terms. But in figural terms it is accurate. The house of Abraham is not only the Hebrew nation founded by the man Abraham; it is figurally the Church, the community of the faithful throughout history. As the figure of Faith, Abraham becomes figurally the herald of the faithful—not Abraham, but Faith, herald of Abraham's house. Abraham is a character who is both a historical person, telling of the visit paid to him by God "as I satte in my porche," and an emblematic type of Faith.

---

19. The bachelor knight whom Faith seeks bears a blazon of three persons in one body, all of equal length—*Pater, Filius,* and Holy Ghost. This device is remarkably similar to the three props, "alle . . . aliche longe," which sustain the Tree of Charity. I believe that the similarity is a deliberate device to link this figure with the tree, as a clear extension of the same figural structure encountered there.

The emblematic type is finally more important than the historical personage. Will exclaims at the end of this passus on the oddity of "Faith" as he looks more closely at him:

> For in his bosome he bar a thyng that he blissed euere.
> And I loked on his lappe, a lazar lay there-inne
> Amonges patriarkes and profetes, pleyande togyderes.
>
> (XVI. 254–56)

This image is pure emblem, as much so as the Tree of Charity itself. It must be figurally understood, and it seems to me a mark of Will's progress in understanding that he does not hesitate over it at all: " 'lorde, mercy!' I seide, / 'This is a present of moche prys' " (XVI. 259–60). The emblem insists that the world be understood in terms of an extrahistorical divine pattern, the pattern which informs all of the vision of Dobet. The epistemology of the *figura* reverses the terms of ordinary human logic, as Anima showed Will long before. Beginning with a knowledge of the divine pattern, it then interprets history, the process so perfectly demonstrated by the evolution of the Tree of Charity, rather than vice versa. Faith, represented by the bosom of Abraham, makes significant the man Abraham; Abraham may be his name, but he is Faith.

This figural quality informs the conception of all the succeeding characters Will meets. When the next rider comes up, he asks him the same questions he had asked Abraham: "what he hiȝte and whider he wolde" (XVI. 275). And the reply is exactly of the same nature as that of Abraham: "I am *Spes* . . . and spire after a knyȝte" (XVII. 1). We never do learn his name; he is consistently referred to as Spes, and it is only because he carries letters on "a pece of an harde roche" (XVII. 10) that we know him to be Moses. Moreover, the law Spes carries is not the law of the Covenant but the New Law: *"Dilige deum et proximum tuum . . . In hijs duobus mandatis tota lex pendit et [prophete]."* As with Abraham, who can be said to be of the house of Abraham only when the term is figurally understood in the light of Christ's redemption, Moses can carry the New Law only because the Old figured forth the New. The character of Spes, like that of Abraham, makes sense only in figural terms, insisting that history has reality only in light of the essential divine pattern.

The Samaritan's presence makes evident the new, figurally structured reality of the poem. For he is a character without the historical reality of Moses and Abraham, a fictional character out of one of Jesus' parables, yet one who, as a type of Charity, has equal figural reality with Abraham and

Moses, the types of Faith and Hope. With the advent of the Samaritan, in fact, Will enters a world whose reality is wholly the figural pattern. He takes part in a parable:

> And as we wenten thus in the weye wordyng togyderes,
> Thanne seye we a Samaritan sittende on a mule,
> Rydynge ful rapely the riȝt weye we ȝeden,
> Comynge fro a cuntre that men called Ierico;
> To a Iustes in Iherusalem he [Iaced] awey faste.
> Bothe the heraud and Hope and he mette at ones
> Where a man was wounded and with theues taken.
>
> (XVII. 47–53)

Yet even the parable is not given in the exact form in which Jesus tells it. As I said earlier, a parable takes an incident from ordinary life and gives it meaning in divine terms. In these lines, however, the incident is not from ordinary life. The Samaritan, riding on a mule to joust at Jerusalem, is more than the character in Jesus' story—he is seen to be identical with Christ himself.[20] The logic behind this dovetailing of identities is purely figural, for as a type of charity he is unified with Christ. And the two persons who pass by are not Pharisees but Faith and Hope, Abraham and Moses as types of the Old Law. The beaten man is the human soul, whose wounds must be cured by "the blode of a barn borne of a mayde."

Thus, the historical pattern of events set in motion by the Tree of Charity is translated completely into a *figura* by Passus XVII. The incidents and characters Will meets are solely figural, their historical specificity blurred by the perspective of eternity. In fact, the only events which are presented as actual history in these passus are those of the life of Christ, because his life is in itself the full realization of the divine pattern. Christ is charity; his life, unlike the lives of the Patriarchs, is not one which depends upon a larger figural pattern for its comprehension, for it contains that pattern in itself.

The Samaritan's instruction of Will is couched in the same figural terms which inform the rest of these passus. In two of the strangest passages in the poem, he explains the nature of the Trinity to Will, first in terms of a human hand, and then in terms of a candle or torch. In both of these dis-

---

20. The figural exegesis of this parable is discussed by Smith, *Traditional Imagery of Charity in Piers Plowman*, pp. 75–78.

courses, the natural objects described are distorted in order to fit their supernatural tenors to such an extent that they cease to resemble commonplace objects. For example:

> The fader was fyrst, as a fyst, with o fynger foldynge,
> Tyl hym [likede] and lest to vnlosen his fynger,
> And [profred] it forth as with a paume to what place it sholde.
> The paume is [þe piþ of] the hande and profreth forth the fyngres
> To mynystre and to make, that my3te of hande knoweth,
> And bitokneth trewly, telle who so liketh,
> The holygost of heuene; he is as the paume.
> The fyngres that fre ben to folde and to serue,
> Bitokneth sothly the sone that sent was til erthe,
> That toched and tasted atte techynge of the paume
> Seynt Marie a mayde, and mankynde lau3te.
>
> (XVII. 138–48)

The anatomy of the human hand imagined here is forced from its natural conformity in order to fit the Samaritan's allegory. The palm-Holy Ghost "teaches" the fingers-Son to "touch and taste" the Virgin, an almost ludicrous, unnatural image, since the palm does not in fact teach the fingers to do anything. The spiritual significance of the figure does not grow naturally from it, as do the apples on the Tree of Charity. Similarly, the Samaritan says that the fist is a "ful honde" (l. 166), the fingers are a "ful hande" (l. 169), and the palm is "pureliche the hande" (l. 173). Yet, the ordinary English word *hand* refers to all three parts—no single one is in fact a complete hand. Obviously, the Samaritan says that the fist, fingers, and palm are each the full hand in order to symbolize the true nature of the three persons of the Trinity, but in order to do so he must stretch the natural configurations of his image and the ordinary meaning of these words almost beyond recognition. Thus, a tension is initiated in the Samaritan's speech between the earthly language he employs and the divine significance he is seeking to give it, a tension which persists throughout the rest of the poem.

At the end of Passus XVII, the Samaritan departs with a suddenness reminiscent of Imaginatyf's leave-taking in Passus XII. This fact suggests some similarity in the roles of these two figures, if only in terms of their function in moving the poem forward. Like Imaginatyf, the Samaritan puts together for Will much of what he has seen in the poem. Imaginatyf sees Will's desire for understanding in terms of his need for self-knowledge:

Will must learn how what he seeks is relevant to himself. The Samaritan reveals a divine pattern in terms of which all things, including Will, must be understood. For, by the time he has finished speaking, that process of re-understanding this world as a figure of a divine reality, a process which was begun by Patience back in Passus XIII, has been fully completed. From now on, through Passus XVIII, the temporal world in its normal aspect has only minimal significance for the poem. This is an important and troubling division, since it bears within it the seeds of an irresolvable tension between the divine and the earthly, rather than the harmony of the two which the integrative vision of figuralism should provide. Indeed, from this point on in the poem, Will expresses an increasing rejection of, and estrangement from, the world in his waking moments.

When Will awakens at the beginning of Passus XVIII, his break with the ordinary world is complete:

> Wolleward and wete-shoed went I forth after,
> As a reccheles renke that [reccheth of no wo]
> And ȝede forth lyke a lorel al my lyf-tyme,
> Tyl I wex wery of the worlde and wylned eft to slepe,
> And lened me to a lenten and longe tyme I slepte;
> [Reste me there, and rutte faste tyl *ramis-palmarum*.
> Of gerlis and of *gloria laus* gretly me dremed,
> And how *osanna* by orgonye olde folke songen,
> And of Crystes passioun and penaunce the peple that of-rauȝte.]
>
> (XVIII. 1–9)

The details of his waking life now have figural significance. He is "wolle-ward," dressed as a penitent in a hair shirt, wandering heedless of woe or discomfort. This image is one of patient poverty as well as of penance. The "reccheles" state Will describes is that which Christ enjoined on his disciples—"*ne soliciti sitis.*" Will is world-weary, gaunt from fasting, and during Lent he falls asleep again until Palm Sunday. Yet it seems probable that the times Will mentions refer not to discrete dates in the temporal world, but rather to times which have significance for the dreamworld. He met Abraham on Midlent Sunday, and the Palm Sunday he speaks of is not a fourteenth-century date but the first Palm Sunday, which he proceeds to witness in his dream. The reality of the dreamworld is clearly taking over the reality of Will's waking life, translating it into terms appropriate to itself. And, curiously, the result of this is less of a sharply drawn opposition between waking and sleeping than the contrast at the beginning of

Passus XV; here, in XVIII, the waking world seems to be on the verge of losing its distinctiveness from the dreamworld altogether.

Four separate allegories are conflated in Passus XVIII—the Christ-knight figure, the Debate of the Four Daughters, the testimony of Book, and the narrative of the Harrowing of Hell. These allegories are set within a frame of the waking world, as Will is depicted falling asleep at the beginning of XVIII and waking up again at its end. These features give Passus XVIII one of the most complex and interesting structures of the poem. Nowhere else is the allegory as richly developed, as variously pursued, and as clear to follow as here. Langland's success is not due to the fact that he is using traditional imagery; he has used common imagery throughout the poem, as practically every study of *Piers Plowman* has shown. The success of XVIII lies rather in Will's newly found ability to perceive the world figurally, an understanding signaled by his perception of the waking world at the beginning of this passus.

The allegories of Passus XVIII not only illuminate each other successfully but also bring together the chief thematic and imagistic strands of the rest of the poem. The first character Will sees is the figure of Christ as a knight:

> One semblable to the Samaritan and some-del to Piers the Plowman,
> Barfote on an asse bakke botelees cam prykye,
> Wyth-oute spores other spere spakliche he loked,
> As is the kynde of a kny3te that cometh to be dubbed,
> To geten hem gylte spores [and] galoches ycouped.
>
> (XVIII. 10–14)

In Passus XVII, the Samaritan is identified with the figure of Christ, riding to a joust in Jerusalem on his horse "that hatte *Caro* (of mankynde I toke it)" (XVII. 107). Similarly, Anima identified Piers with Christ—"*Petrus, id est, Christus*" (XV. 206). Before this vision, Will has perceived Christ in terms of the derivative figures of the Samaritan or Piers; here, however, the vision of Christ is granted to him directly. Will is seeing face to face in Passus XVIII to a much greater extent than was possible for him before. And what he sees is Christ as the figure who informs all the other figural characters he has encountered. Christ is seen here as a kind of composite character, "semblable to the Samaritan and some-del to Piers the Plowman," a person Will recognizes by means of the figures of him he has already met, yet one who makes the relationship of these figures to himself clear.

Jesus will joust in Piers's arms, says Faith.[21] This is the first time in the poem that Piers has acquired any armor, or anything resembling knightly status. Yet, the image serves, I think, to clarify exactly that aspect of Christ with which Piers is identified. For the arms of Piers the Plowman must be a plowman's arms—the garments of a poor, humble peasant, just as the mark of Christ's humility is his assumption of a mortal body, *"humana natura."* Piers figures the humility of Christ, his patient poverty. And in this way, through Piers, the Christ-knight assumes the characteristics of all the other humble characters within the poem, most notably Patience, another Christ-like figure who here receives his full comprehension. Furthermore, as a knight, the Christ-knight figure incorporates the other knights of the poem, from those true knights of whom Lady Holy Church spoke, and the knight who serves to protect Piers in Passus V, to the chief knight of the poem— Conscience.

The joust which Jesus undertakes is not against any mortal foe, but against those absolute opponents of which the false Jews and scribes are only figures—"the [. . .] fende and Fals-dome." Christ has promised to bind the fiend and retrieve "Piers fruite the Plowman." This mention of fruit links the passage immediately with the Tree of Charity, that emblem of the divine historical pattern which Christ's Passion and Resurrection fully reveals.

Christ's false joust with the blind Longinus seems to me to show most clearly the figural pattern which this passus extends to the whole poem. The false joust is a reversed image of the true joust Christ is undertaking, and his blood, which falls to unspear the blind knight's eyes, also marks the final unspearing of Will's eyes as he journeys outside of time to witness the divine events at the gates of Hell. Longinus' cry, "Haue on me reuth, ri3tful Iesu!," echoes the much earlier cry of Robert the Robber in Passus V— "Cryst, that on Caluarye vppon the crosse deydest / . . . [. . .] Dampne me nou3te at domesday for that I did so ille" (V. 472, 478). But where Will says that he knew not what happened to Robert, what happens to

---

21. Wilbur Gaffney, "The Allegory of the Christ-Knight in *Piers Plowman*," *PMLA*, XLVI (1931), 155–68, traces some literary analogues to the Christ-knight figure, and suggests that Christ's jousting in Piers's arms is a use of the romance motif of the knight riding in disguise (p. 156). While Piers's arms can be taken only to mean Christ's human nature, it seems to me that a clothing metaphor is also suggested by the word. The traditional depiction of this scene in medieval art shows Christ, dressed in ragged garments, surrounded by richly clad knights.

Longinus is quite apparent. The difference between the two episodes measures in part the development of Will's understanding.

Thus, the humble Christ-knight figure provides the informing pattern not only for history but for the poem as well. And this dual function of the figure helps to present a solution to the chief problem posed by the poem, the problem of discovering a common set of terms, a "rhetoric," to give meaning not only to Will's life but to society as a whole. Dowel is not only an individual problem for Will, it is also a social and historical one; and the clarity of Passus XVIII resides in part in the fact that the Christ-knight provides Will with a means to link the significant terms of his own search with those of the divine historical process. Society, history, the individual, and the poem all meet in the *figura*, which is perceived as informing them all, as the revealer not only of history but also, more importantly in this context, of the pattern within the disparate strands of *Piers Plowman* itself.

The symbolic unspearing of the poem's eyes, along with those of Longinus, by the Christ-knight ushers in the next allegory of Passus XVIII, the Debate of the Four Daughters of God. Faith (Abraham) pronounces a formal curse on the false Jews, setting their actions within an apocalyptic context. At this point, an interesting thing happens to Will:

> I drowe me in that derkenesse to *descendit ad inferna.*
> And there I sawe sothely *secundum scripturas.*
> (XVIII. 111–12)

These familiar echoes of the Creed not only signal the divine event which is about to occur but also associate Will with Christ in a figural relationship. This honor marks the highest point of Will's comprehension in the poem and completes the assimilative, unifying process which the Christ-knight brings about. At this point, every major figure in the poem has been deliberately associated with him.

The chief allegory of Passus XVIII is the Harrowing of Hell, a narrative which continues the historical events depicted in the earlier part of the passus. This account is introduced by the speech of Book, an anomalous figure within the poem, whose presence in this passus has never been adequately explained. Book is the Bible, of course. His speech records the proofs in nature of the divinity of Christ at all points during his life, from Nativity to Passion. But Book records the witness not only of nature but of history, from earliest times, to the divine shaping pattern. The truth of this pattern, and of the Book recording it, is authenticated only by Christ, by the revelation of God to man which is perfected in Christ. This is surely the meaning of the statement, "And I, Boke, wil be brent but Iesus rise to lyue" (XVIII. 252).[22] Only as Christ reveals his divinity in his Resurrection does Book's historical witness become validated. Book represents the world of nature, of time, of history which must be made significant by Christ or be discarded as meaningless.

The Harrowing of Hell is an extramondial event which catches up within itself all of the history recorded in Book. As the speeches of Christ and the devils make clear, it is an event which both looks backward in time to redress the disjunction of man and God caused by the Fall, and looks forward to the end of time in the Last Judgment, when Christ will "come as a kynge crouned with angeles / And han out of helle alle mennes soules" (XVIII. 369–70). It satisfies the demands of the Old Law:

> "Membre for membre [was amendes by þe olde lawe],
> And lyf for lyf also and by that lawe I clayme [. . .]
> Adam and al his issue at my wille her-after."
>
> (XVIII. 340–42)

Yet it reveals the New Law:

> "For I, that am lorde of lyf, loue is my drynke,
> And for that drynke to-day I deyde vpon erthe."
>
> (XVIII. 363–64)

And it also perfects the law of *kynde:*

> "For blode may suffre blode bothe hungry and akale,
> Ac blode may nouȝte se blode blede, but hym rewe."
>
> (XVIII. 392–93)

Thus, the episode of the Harrowing of Hell completes in one informing *figura* all of history and all of the progressive revelation of the law, from natural law to the law of Moses to the New Law of charity. This historical

---

22. The controversy over this speech has been conclusively settled, I believe: *but* means *unless.* See R. E. Kaske, "The Speech of 'Book' in *Piers Plowman," Anglia,* LXXVII (1959), 117–44, and the reply of R. L. Hoffman, "The Burning of 'Boke' in *Piers Plowman," MLQ,* XXV (1964), 57–65; and of E. T. Donaldson to both earlier essays, "The Grammar of Book's Speech in *Piers Plowman," Studies in Language and Literature in Honour of Margaret Schlauch,* ed. M. Brahmer et al. (Warsaw, 1966), pp. 103–9.

dimension of the episode cannot be overstressed: it is the event which completes the process of resignification begun by the Tree of Charity. And it resignifies the language and the narrative of the poem as well. It seems to me that this episode represents for the poem a restatement in openly figural terms of the hidden figures of Passus VI–VII, the plowing of the half-acre and the pardon of Piers Plowman. Christ pardons the righteous souls bound in hell under the Old Law through his grace—that is exactly the pardon of Dowel granted to Piers at the beginning of Passus VII. Only there it is couched in hidden terms which Piers alone can understand; here, it is revealed fully to Will in the divine event itself. Thus, the redemptive task of Passus XVIII does not simply extend to the righteous souls in hell. It redeems history through its revelation of the figural pattern, it redeems history through its revelation of the figural pattern, it redeems language by redefining it through the Word, it redeems the structural process of *Piers Plowman*, it redeems Will, and it provides the most complete means in the poem of linking these various aspects to each other as parts of one single process. By the end of the passus all the various worlds of the poem are united. Will wakens to the bells of Easter, the event which justifies history in the waking world as well as in that of the dream, as Book has testified. For Easter commemorates the manifestation in time of the event Will has already witnessed in his extramondial vision—the divine love made flesh in the Word, which is Christ. One would expect that the vision of harmony achieved in Passus XVIII would extend to the temporal, earthly world of the field of folk; yet as the events of the end of the poem suggest, this is not the case. And the reason for the inability of Passus XVIII to finally inform the whole of the poem lies in the nature of its redemption of language.

With the Four Daughters, the poem returns to personification allegory for the first time since Passus XIV. (Anima, I think, is too inclusive and multifaceted in meaning to be considered the personification of a concept.) Personification allegory is associated with the earlier stages of Will's knowledge, with his struggle to find full significance within the limited terms of human language. The figural allegory which takes over in Passus XVI seeks to go beyond the limitations of ordinary conceptual language to present divine truth in emblematic terms, to see Truth itself revealed finally in the informing figure of Christ. The personification allegory of Passus XVIII depends upon Christ to inform it exactly as the figural allegory does. The Four Daughters are deliberately antithetical terms— righteousness, mercy, truth, peace—which can be harmonized only by the divine reconciliation of Christ. The demands of justice, based upon reason, and of mercy, based upon love, are not reconcilable when argued in the ways in which those terms are understood among men. To Righteousness, the claims of Peace are drunken ravings. Only when the words "righteousness" and "peace" are resignified by Christ, the primal Word, can they be understood in their redeemed meaning.

The argument between the claims of reason and love is not limited to this passus, for it has been a major stumbling block throughout the poem. The king's attempts to establish a peaceful kingdom based upon Reason, Pier's attempts to deal with the recalcitrant folk through Kind Wit and Hunger, Clergy's conflict with Patience are all aspects of this fundamental conflict. The debate of the Four Daughters, in fact, raises in a concise form most of the important debates of the poem. And in Christ, who redeems not only man but also his language, the true significance of those four words is revealed, a significance which requires a radical redefinition of their ordinary meaning in human language. It seems to me that one of the major accomplishments of this passus is precisely to redeem language and its chief vehicle within the poem, personification allegory, through the medium of figural allegory in which it is placed. The one must give significance to the other. This is clear from their structural placing, in which the actions of the figure of Christ surround the whole debate and bring about the accord of language at the end.

The redemption of language is brought about in a manner most significant for the poem as a whole. There is a great deal of oxymoron and paradox in the expression of the chief personifications in this passus, as there is in the speech of Christ. The yoking together of opposite meanings is a basic technique of the argument. For instance, just before Christ appears, Peace says:

> "And I shal preue . . . her peyne mote haue ende,
> And wo in-to wel mowe wende atte laste;
> For had thei wist of no wo wel had thei nouȝte knowen.
> For no wiȝte wote what wel is that neuere wo suffred,
> Ne what is hote hunger that had neuere defaute.
> If no nyȝte ne were, no man, as I leue,
> Shulde wite witterly what day is to mene;
> . . . .
> So it shal fare bi this folke; her foly and her synne
> Shall lere hem what langour is and lisse with-outen ende."
>
> (XVIII. 201–7, 224–25)

What Peace is saying is that the true meaning of something can only be derived from its opposite. In saying this, Peace has in effect suspended the integrity of words as truthful, knowable signs in human language. For in ordinary speech, opposite terms are real opposites—they cannot yield real knowledge of a contrary term. To know woe is only to know woe—that is, what bliss is not. Knowing woe cannot teach what bliss is. Yet Peace says that woe does teach bliss. This implies that the two terms are only apparent opposites—that when properly understood they are perfectly reconcilable aspects of the same thing. This, of course, is also the logic behind the debate of the Four Daughters; opposites are seen to be reconcilable as aspects of the single, divine Word.

Christ carries through the full implications of this attitude toward human language in his final speech to Satan:

> "So leue it nou3te, Lucifer, a3eine the lawe I fecche hem,
> But bi ri3t and by resoun raunceoun here my lyges;
> *Non veni soluere legem, sed adimplere*
> Thow fettest myne in my place [maugree] al resoun,
> Falseliche and felounelich; gode faith me it tau3te,
> To recoure hem thorw raunceoun and bi no resoun elles,
> So that [þoru3] gyle thow gete, thorw grace it is ywone.
> Thow, Lucyfer, in lyknesse of a luther addere,
> Getest by gyle tho that god loued;
> And I, in lyknesse of a leode that lorde am of heuene,
> Graciousliche thi gyle haue quytte; go gyle a3eine gyle!
> And as Adam and alle thorw a tre deyden,
> Adam and alle thorwe a tree shal torne [. . .] to lyue;
> And gyle is bigyled and in his gyle fallen:
> *Et cedidit in foueam quam fecit.*
> Now bygynneth thi gyle ageyne the to tourne,
> And my grace to growe ay gretter and wyder.
> [. . . . .]
> That art doctour of deth, drynke that thow madest!
> For I, that am lorde of lyf, loue is my drynke,
> And for that drynke to-day I deyde vpon erthe."
>
> (XVIII. 346–64)

In the course of this speech, numerous terms are redefined in such a way that they come to mean the contrary of what they commonly mean among men. The most interesting example is the word *gyle*. The *gyle* by which Lucifer damned man has become the *gyle* by which Christ saves man; the guile which marks Satan's damnation is the guile which reveals Christ's divinity. The morally negative term is turned into a morally positive one. And the same radical reevaluation takes place with such words as *lawe*, *riȝte, resoun, deth, lyf,* and with the image of the tree, which killed and now gives life. These terms are not merely expanded in meaning; their ordinary connotative range is cut out from under them and replaced by one entirely contrary. In this way, justice becomes mercy, righteousness love, death life, reason pity, and law grace.

Passus XVIII ends in a vision of complete harmony, as Peace restates the theme of the union of opposites, which seems to me the keynote of this passus:

> "After sharpe shoures," quod Pees, "moste shene is the sonne;
> Is no weder warmer than after watery cloudes.
> Ne no loue leuere ne leuer frendes,
> Than after werre and wo whan Loue and Pees be maistres.
> Was neuere werre in this worlde ne wykkednesse so kene,
> That [. . .] Loue, and hym luste, to laughynge ne brouȝte,
> And Pees thorw pacience alle perilles [stoppeþ]."
>
> (XVIII. 409–15)

And just as the common oppositions of all experience are swept away, so the very world they define is swept away. The poem passes beyond language at this point, into the expressive dance of the Four Daughters.

The passing beyond language, however, is a necessary result of the attempt to encompass divine truth in the terms of human language. Indeed, the radical inversion of everyday meaning in order to express the inexpressible is a commonplace of mystical and visionary writing. Because the ineffable is just that, language is forced to distort itself in order to try to comprehend, and finally it must give way altogether.[23] Will expresses this thought when, toward the end of Christ's speech, he echoes Paul: *"Audiui archana verba, que non licet homini loqui"* (II Cor. 12:4). The common words of human speech have become *arcana verba*, hidden words, which are not permitted to be spoken among men—not because of an arbitrary divine decree, but because they are literally inexpressible, meaningless in human terms, since they have been so completely redefined.

When Will returns to the waking world, he can communicate his newly found knowledge only by pointing to the Cross and urging his family to

---

23. Compare the moment at the end of the *Paradiso*, where Dante's vision of God proves too much for his representational powers: "All'alta fantasia qui mancó possa" (Canto XXXIII, 142), *Dante's Paradiso*, ed. J. D. Sinclair (Oxford, 1946). One significant difference between this poem and *Piers Plowman* is that Dante's vision stops at this supreme moment.

participate in the wordless ritual of "creeping to the Cross," a ceremony corresponding to the wordless dance of the Four Daughters in heaven:

> "Ariseth and reuerenceth goddes resurrexioun,
> And crepeth to the crosse on knees and kisseth it for a Iuwel!
> For goddes blissed body it bar for owre bote,
> And it afereth the fende, for suche is the my3te,
> May no grysly gost glyde there it shadweth!"
>
> (XVIII. 427–31)

The Cross is one of the *arcana verba,* the tree of shame which is really the tree of glory. It is the final manifestation of the Tree of Charity in the poem, occurring significantly enough in the waking world. Yet as Will perceives it, the Cross is not a sign of something else; it is the thing in itself. It is an agent of divine power directly manifesting itself in redemptive ways against the power of the devil. It is extralinguistic, even extrasignatory; because of this, it serves to underscore the complete inadequacy of human language as a medium for knowing and communicating truth.

Passus XVIII provides Will with a redeemed language, but not an expressible one. Will is given the vision of Truth he has desired, but he is not given a rhetoric. For to show that human language is meaningless in divine terms—so much so that it must be redefined in terms of its very opposites— is to show equally that divine language is meaningless in human terms. The Word is *arcanum verbum, "que non licet homini loqui."* Thus, the all-embracing pattern of reconciliation and resignification which runs through Passus XVIII also makes the problem of finding an adequate language for the poem more difficult. As I have said before, the primary problem for the poem is to discover a redeemed rhetoric which will make divine truth meaningful in comprehensible human language. But the solution posed to this problem by Passus XVIII does not in fact work to reconcile divine truth with human language. On the contrary, it makes the gulf between the two more apparent; the two realities are literally meaningless in each other's terms—they are *arcana verba,* each to each. And this realization leads directly to the apocalyptic breakdown of the poem in Passus XX. What we witness in Passus XIX and XX is the inability of redeemed speaking to inform the field of folk—to become a true rhetoric, in short. Yet, the reasons for that inability are implicit in the linguistic structures in which the vision of Passus XVIII is cast, for, the poem suggests, they demand such a radical reordering of experience that only "a new heaven and a new earth" could comprehend them.

✑ CHAPTER SIX ✑

Antecryst cam thanne, and al the croppe of treuthe,
Torned [tid] vp so doune, and ouertilte the rote.

B eginning the vision of Passus XIX, the risen Christ enters, icono-graphically perceived, appearing before the "comune peple." This figure strikes the keynote of the vision: it is redemptive, it is figural, and, most importantly, it occurs once again amid the field of folk, a location which the poem has not revisited since the end of the *Visio*. The human community is of paramount importance in the last two passus of the poem. It provides the test for the figural mode of knowledge evolved in the earlier *Vita*.

Will returns to earth from the gates of hell with a renewed sense of community, apparent in the domestic close of Passus XVIII, and emphasized in his waking hours at the beginning of XIX:

> Thus I awaked and wrote what I had dremed,
> And diȝte me derely and dede me to cherche,
> To here holy the masse and to be houseled after,
> In myddes of the masse, tho men ȝede to offrynge,
> I fel eftsones a-slepe . . .
>
> (XIX. 1–5)

An evident change has occurred in Will's attitude toward the waking world. No longer wandering like a ragged "lorel," he dresses himself "derely" to go to Church and receive the Host, an act of community not only with God but with all his Christian brethren. At the moment of Communion, he falls asleep again to dream of the Redemption, that event which makes the community of Christians meaningful and which extends the communion of

[149]

saints throughout time into eternity. The sense of harmony and union achieved in Passus XVIII is thus continued into the populous world of XIX.

The continuation of allegorical mode and tone from Passus XVIII to XIX is also apparent in language. When Will sees the figure of Christ, he asks Conscience to explain to him what he has seen—whether it is Piers, or Christ, or Jesus. Conscience follows with a lengthy exposition of the names of Jesus, during the course of which he recapitulates the chief events of Christ's ministry and Passion. This section is one of the more tedious in the poem, and, since it reviews what Will has just witnessed in the flesh, it would seem to be an excrescence. I think, however, that it should be understood as a careful exercise in redeemed speaking. The language is deliberately nontensive and nondramatic. Unfortunately, such language makes for dull poetry. Yet it also seems to me that a cognitive problem is manifested in this clash of judgmental values. Earthly experience is by nature tensive and dramatic, *in enigmate,* but redeemed rhetoric cannot include these values, since it is precisely in the tension, the approximateness, of earthly speech to truth that falseness lurks. Redeemed speech purges the limitations and distortions of earthly language by redefining all words in the Word. This very exclusion, however, proves finally to be its undoing on the field of folk.

The whole attitude toward language displayed by both Will and Conscience clearly assumes that names—particularly divinely appointed names—are truly significant. Will wants to know how Jesus can have more than one name, especially since

> "Patriarkes and prophets propheceyed bifore,
> That alkyn creatures shulden knelen and bowen,
> Anon as men nempned the name of god Iesu.
> *Ergo* is no name to the name of Iesus.
> . . . .
> And 3e callen hym Cryst—for what cause, telleth me?"
> (XIX. 16–19, 23)

Will's difficulty here is reminiscent of his problem with Anima's multitudinous names, and Conscience answers Will in the same way that Anima did. The names of Jesus have reference to the phases of his activity, and to the progressive revelation which his life affords. Conscience begins his exposition with a common analogy:

> "Thow knowest wel, . . . and thow konne resoun,
> That kny3te, kynge, conqueroure may be o persone."
> (XIX. 26–27)

As Conscience develops his theme, he draws in more and more terms which have had significance in other parts of the poem, until at the end he has linked them all together in a relationship of true, mutual signification in the Word. As a knight, his name is Jesus. This was his birth name, the name under which the Magi kneeled to him, in prefiguration of his role as a conqueror. The name corresponds to his early life, when he was learning his task while concealed among the humble:

> "owre lorde prynce Iesus
> Was neyther kynge ne conquerour til he [comsed] to wexe
> In the manere of a man, and that by moche sleight;
> As it bicometh a conquerour to konne many sleightes,
> And many wyles and witte, that wil ben a leder."
>
> (XIX. 92–96)

He revealed a glimpse of his true nature at the marriage feast in Cana, where he turned the water to wine. At this point also, he first began Dowel:

> "And tho was he cleped and called nou3t [oonly] Cryst, but Iesu
> A faunt fyn, ful of witte, *filius Marie."*
>
> (XIX. 113–14)

The revelation of Dowel is also the revelation of the New Law:

> "For wyn is lykned to lawe and [lyf holynesse];
> And lawe lakked tho, for men loued nou3t her enemys."
>
> (XIX. 107–8)

As he begins his ministry, he adds the name Iesu. The new name marks a new period of activity:

> "Thus he conforted carful, and cau3te a gretter name,
> The whiche was Dobet where that he went.
> For defe thorw his doynges [. . .] and dombe speke [and herde],
> And alle he heled and halp that hym of grace asked.
> And tho was he called in contre of the comune peple,
> For the dedes that he did *fili David, Iesus!"*
>
> (XIX. 124–29)

He has now revealed himself more fully, as a king as well as a knight, as Dobet as well as Dowel, as *fili David* as well as *filius Marie* (a change of epithet which suggests that he is not only man, but man in history, part of God's progressively revealed plan).

In his Passion and Resurrection the revelation is completed:

> "Ac Marie Magdeleyne mette hym bi the wey,
> Goynge toward Galile in godhed and manhed,
> And lyues and lokynge, and she aloude cryde,
> In eche a compaignye there she cam, *'Christus resurgens!'* "
>
> (XIX. 152–55)

Jesus is Christ, conqueror, and son of God. The complete revelation of his own true nature marks also the full revelation of his new covenant based on love. He grants a pardon to all mankind through Piers the Plowman, as a token of Dobest:

> "And whan this dede was done Dobest he [þouȝte],
> And ȝaf Pieres [pardoun and power] he graunted [hym]
> [Myȝte men to assoille of alle manere synnes,
> To alle manere men, mercy and forȝfynes,]
> In couenant that thei come and knowleche to paye,
> To Pieres pardon the Plowman, *redde quod debes.*"
>
> (XIX. 177–82)

Knight, king, conqueror; *filius Marie, fili David, filius Dei;* Jesus, Jesu, Christ; lawlessness, law, pardon; Dowel, Dobet, Dobest—all these terms become linked as Conscience works out their significance in reference to Christ. Such is the nature of redeemed language—like figuralism itself, a system of interdependent signs, each a partial truth, but together revealing the divine truth concealed within them all. But there is also another dimension. Conscience adds the very lexicon of the poem to the levels of meaning contained in Christ's names. Evidently, the revelation of Christ is intended also to be a revelation of *Piers Plowman* itself.

The intended revelation of the poem is made explicit, I believe, by the restatement of the pardon sent to Piers, "*redde quod debes.*" This action links Passus XIX to Passus VII. The action of the latter passus is figural, a figure it has taken Will all of the *Vita* to learn how to read. Will's advance in knowledge is apparent in the different nature of the images in the later part of the poem; whereas the figural dimensions of the actions of Passus VII are dark to all but Piers, in Passus XIX their significance is revealed. The narrative of Passus XIX is closely modeled, in its earlier stages, upon that of the later part of the *Visio* (from the Confession of the Seven Deadly Sins to the end of Passus VII). Many of these parallel actions have been noted before.[1] Yet, it is not true to say that the world of Passus XIX is the same as that of VII; certain radical differences in conception and understanding characterize the two, differences which are the most tangible evidence of Will's increased understanding. To define the quality of these differences, it may be helpful to note some of the more important parallels. These fall into three main groupings: the pardon, the establishment of a society under a spiritual leader, and the agricultural motif centering around the character of Piers Plowman.

In the first place, the pardon in Passus XIX is granted before the society is established. This is a complete reversal of the sequence of action in Passus V–VII. Moreover, the pardon is granted by Christ, and the circumstances of its granting are fully described. In Passus VII, the pardon comes from Truth, and its nature is described in an obscure allegory which Piers alone can comprehend. Two things are clear from this. First, Passus XIX does indeed reveal the full significance of the pardon in Passus VII. It is now given its full meaning, both in terms of what Christ has achieved for man by his sacrifice, and what man's responsibility is before the Final Judgment, when Christ will "demen hem at domes daye, bothe quikke and ded" (XIX. 191). Secondly, the reversal of order in XIX is significant. The society of V–VII is preredemptive, when figurally understood, but its allegorical nature is obscure in the *Visio*. Passus XIX manifests the historical *figura* of VII by describing a postredemptive society, one established after the granting of the pardon to Piers.

After Conscience tells Will of Piers's pardon, the action of XIX continues with the folk of the field witnessing the advent of the Redeemer.

---

1. A general parallel between the latter part of the *Visio* and the *Vita de Dobest* was first analyzed as a structural feature of the poem by Henry W. Wells, "The Construction of *Piers Plowman*," *PMLA*, XLIV (1929). This feature, which has since become a commonplace of *Piers Plowman* criticism, was restated and developed most fully by John Lawlor, *Piers Plowman: An Essay in Criticism* (London, 1962), pp. 171–85. Two recent articles have noted specific parallels between the two parts of the poem: P. M. Kean, "Justice, Kingship, and the Good Life in the Second Part of *Piers Plowman*," in *Piers Plowman: Critical Approaches*, ed. S. S. Hussey (London, 1969), p. 108, and Barbara Raw, "Piers and the Image of God in Man," in Hussey, *Critical Approaches*, pp. 178–79. See also Ruth M. Ames, *The Fulfillment of the Scriptures: Abraham, Moses, and Piers* (Evanston, Ill., 1970), especially pp. 188–92.

Grace, *spiritus paraclitus,* descends on Piers and his fellows, and Conscience commands Will to kneel and sing *veni, creator spiritus:*

> Thanne songe I that songe and so did many hundreth,
> And cryden with Conscience, "help vs, [crist] of grace!"
>
> (XIX. 206–7)

This action parallels that in Passus V, when the folk cry for help to "Cryst and to his clene moder / To haue grace to go with hem [god leue that they moten]" (V. 518–19). Their prayers go unheeded until Piers pops into the poem and offers himself as their leader, though his leadership is largely ineffectual until he is given Truth's pardon. Once again, Passus XIX reveals the full meaning of the earlier scene within a redemptive context. Grace comes to Piers and with him helps the folk:

> "For I wil dele to-day and dyuyde grace,
> To alkynnes creatures that kan [hise] fyue wittes,
> Tresore to lyue by to her lyues ende,
> And wepne to fy3te with that wil neure faille."
>
> (XIX. 210–13)

Grace then establishes a society based not on Kind Wit and Reason, but upon love and grace: "Loke that none lakke other but loueth [. . .] as brethren" (XIX. 249).

The society which Grace establishes is an agricultural one, like the one Piers set up to plow his half-acre. Once again, however, while the plowing of the half-acre in Passus VI is described in earthly terms, its allegorical significance apparent only obscurely, Passus XIX makes the allegorical dimension explicit and clear. Piers is Grace's plowman, set to till truth with a team of spiritual oxen:

> That on was Luke, a large beste and a lowe-chered,
> And Marke, and Mathew the thrydde, myghty bestes bothe,
> And Ioigned to hem one Iohan, most gentil of alle,
> The prys nete of Piers plow, passyng alle other.
>
> (XIX. 258–61)

The ground is harrowed after the plowing by four bullocks—Augustine, Ambrose, Gregory, and Jerome—with the two harrows of the Old and New Testaments. In addition, Grace gives Piers four seeds to plant, *spiritus prudencie, temperancie, fortitudinis,* and *iusticie,* the four cardinal virtues.

The Gospels revealed the figural nature of the Old Testament in their account of the life of Christ; the harrow which the later clerks used in order to cultivate the truth in Scripture was figural exegesis. Nothing could make more emphatic the importance of figural understanding within the poem; it is that which Grace gives Piers in order to till the seeds of virtue:

> Thise foure sedes Pieres sewe and sitthe he did hem harwe
> Wyth olde lawe and newe lawe, that loue myȝte wexe
> Amonge the foure vertues and vices destroye.
>
> (XIX. 306–8)

These parallels suggest to me that these scenes from Passus XIX, the culmination of the *Vita,* are intended to reveal the meaning of Passus VI–VII, the culmination of the *Visio,* through a relationship which binds the two parts of the poem in an explicitly figural way. Passus XIX redeems Passus VII, as the life of Christ redeems that of the men of the Old Law. It produces a fullness of understanding brought about through a figural perception of the disparate parts of the poem, the cognitive perception which Will has so painstakingly learned through the *Vita.* It is a redemption not only of mankind and human society, but of the poem's allegory and of its language.

Yet it is not able to stand.

The *arcana verba* Will has learned in Passus XVIII, which at first seem communicable to the folk on the field in XIX, prove to be incomprehensible even to the defenders of Unity-Holychurch, and as the edifice of Piers's barn collapses so does that of the poem itself. This collapse is brought about through a destructive parody of the very processes by which the poem builds up its comprehension—but now the uses of language and the exploration of verbal meaning, especially in personification, are turned to negative ends. The first indication of this wholesale destruction comes in a prophecy of Grace:

> "For Antecryst and his al the worlde shal greue,
> And acombre the, Conscience, but if Cryst the helpe.
> And fals prophetes fele, flatereres and glosers
> Shullen come, and be curatoures ouer kynges and erlis,
> And Pryde shal be pope, prynce of holycherche,
> Coueytyse and Vnkyndenesse cardinales hym to lede."
>
> (XIX. 214–19)

The moment Holychurch is established, Pride sets out to gather a great host against it, sending his lieutenants to threaten Conscience:

"ȝowre carte the Byleue
Shal be coloured so queyntly and keuered vnder owre sophistrie,
That Conscience shal nouȝte knowe [. . .] who is Cristene or
hethen."

(XIX. 342–45)

The establishment of Unity and its entrusting to Conscience is itself another reenactment of events in the *Visio*. Piers's aids in the *Visio* were Conscience and Kind Wit; here Conscience is again Piers's lieutenant. As the guardian of Piers's barn, he holds a position similar to that of Piers in Passus VI: he is the leader of a community of folk, now spiritually united. Conscience is one of the most acute perceivers of truth within the poem, and he has learned a great deal during its course. He was the one to see through Lady Meed, and the one who first perceived Patience' meaning in Passus XIII. When Piers leaves Holychurch in Conscience' hands, he is entrusting it to an educated and perceptive conscience, one worthy to lead the Holy Spirit into men's hearts.[2] As a human faculty, Conscience occupies the same position of wise leadership that Piers has with respect to the folk in Passus VI. Unfortunately, his fate is much the same.

At first, when Pride threatens, he tries to organize a defense of Unity-Holychurch, only to be subverted by the wasters among the folk. In response, he calls to the true Christians to come and satisfy their hunger after their labors:

"Here is bred yblessed and goddes body ther-vnder.
Grace thorw goddes worde gaue Pieres power,
[. . . Myȝte] to maken it and men to ete it after,
In helpe of her hele onys in a moneth,
Or as ofte as they hadde nede—tho that hadde ypayed
To Pieres pardoun the Plowman, *redde quod debes*."
(XIX. 383–88)

Once again, this scene would appear to be a redeemed fulfillment of the earlier scenes in the *Visio*. The folk in XIX are engaged in a spiritual venture, the defense of Unity-Holychurch, just as the folk of the *Visio* were engaged in the plowing and defense of the half-acre. And, like Hunger

---

2. According to the conception of the role of conscience in monastic theology. See Morton W. Bloomfield, *Piers Plowman as a Fourteenth-Century Apocalypse* (New Brunswick, N.J., 1961), pp. 168–69, and my article on "The Character of Conscience in *Piers Plowman*," *SP*, LXVII (1970), 13–30.

coming to aid Piers against the wastrels, Conscience offers to satisfy the hunger of his workmen, only with spiritual rather than physical food. Such parallels are entirely in keeping with the nature of the earlier parallels between Passus XIX and the *Visio*.

But the folk rebel. They want no part of *redde quod debes;* and the cruel irony, in light of the poem's real advance in understanding, is that their rebellion is in exactly the spirit of the wastrels of Passus VI:

> "ȝe, bawe!" quod a brewere, "I wil nouȝt be reuled,
> Bi Iesu! for al ȝowre Ianglynge with *spiritus iusticie,*
> Ne after Conscience, by Cryste, whil I can selle
> Bothe dregges and draffe and drawe it at on hole,
> Thikke ale and thinne ale, for that is my kynde,
> And nouȝte hakke after holynesse; holde thi tonge, Conscience!"
>
> (XIX. 394–99)

The intention of the brewer to sell the dregs of the beer sounds very much like Avarice' confession of false marketing practices in Passus V. But his complaint to Conscience is not couched in confessional terms; rather, he appeals to the fact of his own unchangeable nature and mocks Conscience' use of obscure Latin phrases, like *spiritus iusticie*. He does not understand Conscience, in short, for the language Conscience speaks means something entirely different to him, as the "lewed vycory" proceeds to explain.

The assault of Pride and his associated lieutenants is a verbal one, directed toward the disintegration of meaning. This fact is crucial to realize, for it strikes at the very heart of the poem. Conscience knows what he is up against, at least at first, for he has been in this situation many times before and realizes how vulnerable his position is. His knowledge was equal to the puzzle presented by Lady Meed, but it almost broke down before the sophistries of the drunken doctor at Clergy's feast. Had it not been for Patience, Conscience would have faltered then. It is no wonder that he views with misgiving the far more subtle and difficult challenge of Pride and his "grete oest" (XIX. 332), a challenge which threatens to color over the meaning of Conscience himself. For the attack of Pride threatens everything: " 'To wasten . . . / Al the worlde in a while thorw owre witte' " (XIX. 350–51). Pride's lieutenants deliver a cataclysmic ultimatum directed against the poem's whole structure of meaning.

Language is almost totally subverted and negated in the last two passus. As Conscience' discourse earlier in Passus XIX is a fine attempt through redeemed speaking to overcome the limits of human speech by reference to the redeeming Word, so the speeches of the folk at the end of XIX are pure sophistry, the distortion and emptying of language. The process by which disintegration of meaning is achieved is through the negative parody of earlier processes in the poem. In Passus XVIII, redeemed language is characterized by its stretching of the ordinary connotations of human words, often to change them into their very opposite meanings; death is seen to be life, shame victory, and so on. The lieutenants of Antichrist also subvert language by depriving words of their ordinary meaning. But where redeemed language substitutes another meaning for the humanly limited one by showing that a word's redeemed meaning is actually a reconciling fulfillment of its literal, more limited one (exactly as the successive *figurae* through history reveal each other more fully), the false parody of Antichrist dilutes meaning until a word is rendered totally negative and meaningless. Words are made to betray themselves by their weakest or most literal meanings. For example, when Conscience warns that only the "cardynale vertues" can save the folk, the vicar replies that while his parishoners know nothing of cardinal virtues they understand that

"The contre is the curseder that cardynales come inne;
And there they ligge and lenge moste lecherye there regneth."
(XIX. 415–16)

The pun destroys spiritual meaning by substituting for it a weaker, more specific, earthbound one. Moreover, it recalls the pun on "cardinal" made in the Prologue, and suggests that the anarchy of the poem's beginning is about to be unleashed again.

The disintegrative process is particularly apparent in the sophistical redefinition given to the cardinal virtues by the adherents of Pride. Of course, some of them are more vulnerable to this process than others. *Spiritus prudencie,* as Grace earlier defined it (XIX. 271–75), is perhaps most vulnerable of all, for it teaches a man to follow his common sense and native prudence. This virtue is easily corrupted to practical advantage. As the vicar tells Conscience, the people use the cardinal virtues only

"But [it soune] as by sy3te somwhat to wynnynge;
Of gyle ne of gabbynge gyue thei neuere tale.
For *spiritus prudencie* amonge the peple is gyle,
And alle tho faire vertues as vyces thei semeth."
(XIX. 450–53)

More boldly, *fortitudo* is understood in its basic meaning as "force," at least by the lord who boasts that his reeves take all they can get by *spiritus fortitudinis.*

This distortion of meaning is even more evident in the case of justice. Grace tells Piers:

> "*Spiritus iusticie* spareth nouȝte to spille [þe gilty],
> And [to] correcte [þe kyng if þe kyng falle in gilt]."
>
> (XIX. 298–300)

The king uses this virtue for his own advantage in a most sophistical manner:

> "I am kynge with croune the comune to reule,
> And holykirke and clergye fro cursed men to defende.
> And if me lakketh to lyue, by the lawe wil I take it,
> There I may hastlokest it haue for I am hed of lawe;
> . . . .
> And what I take of ȝow two, I take it atte techynge
> Of *spiritus iusticie* for I iugge ȝow alle."
>
> (XIX. 463–66, 470–71)

This argument reflects one of the major practical dilemmas of medieval political theory, for the king is quite right that he is "hed of lawe," and keeper of *spiritus iusticie* for his people. On the other hand, Grace is also right in saying that even the king is subject to justice. The difficulty is that no man can implement the law or serve justice on his king, and thus, practically, the implementation of justice depends on the king's own virtue. The fault of this system is evident in Conscience' reply:

> "In condicioun . . . that thow [þe comune] defende
> And rule thi rewme in resoun [as] riȝt [wol] and [treuth],
> [Haue] thow may [þyn askyng] as thi lawe asketh."
>
> (XIX. 474–76)

As long as the king is governed by reason, which here seems synonymous with temperance or *mesure*, things will be all right.

Indeed, what is lacking so far in this discussion of the cardinal virtues is the virtue of temperance. Temperance corrects all the other virtues:[3] it saves prudence from becoming mere self-interest; it saves justice from be-

---

3. For a discussion of the "unusual" role of temperance in Langland's ethics, see Bloomfield, *Piers Plowman as a Fourteenth-Century Apocalypse*, pp. 136–37.

coming tyranny; it saves fortitude from becoming a simple show of brute strength. And temperance is absent from the list of virtues invoked by the corrupted folk at the end of Passus XIX. *Spiritus prudencie, spiritus fortitudinis, spiritus iusticie* are all there, but something called *spiritus intellectus* is substituted for temperance.[4] This omission is significant, for temperance is the idea of *mesure*, the foundation of the society which Piers establishes in the *Visio*. It is the touchstone which leads to the exposure of Lady Meed, and it is the beginning of virtue and wisdom for Will. "Mesure is medcyne" (I. 35), as Lady Holy Church tells him. Thus, it is no wonder that Conscience appeals to it as the corrective medicine for the folk's distorted ideas of what the various virtues mean. The only trouble is that the medicine itself has been altered.

Will awakens after Conscience' speech, and wanders about the now totally dreamlike landscape of his waking world:

> Heuy-chered I 3ede and elynge in herte;
> I ne wiste where to ete, ne at what place.
>
> (XX. 2–3)

At the noon hour he meets Need, who insults him and calls him a "faitour" for not doing something about his hunger. Need's argument is most important, for it indicates the direction of the action in Passus XX. He says to Will:

> "Coudestow nou3te excuse the as dede the kynge and other,
> That thow toke to thi bylyf to clothes and to sustenance,
> [Was] by techynge and by tellynge of *spiritus temperancie,*
> And thow nome namore than Nede the tau3te,
> And Nede ne hath no lawe, ne neure shal falle in dette?"
>
> (XX. 6–10)

Considering what the king and the rest have done with the virtues to which they appealed, this introduction should serve as a warning for what follows. Need's argument, baldly stated, is a justification for stealing.[5]

The argument he uses is parallel to a well-known teaching of the

---

4. This seems to be synonymous with intellect, and, in the speech of the boastful lord, with a shrewd business "intellect."

5. R. W. Frank, Jr., has noted the insidiousness of Need's arguments, especially their radical distortion of the concept of patient poverty, *Piers Plowman and the Scheme of Salvation* (New Haven, Conn., 1957), pp. 113–14.

scholastics, that in cases of extreme need a man may steal in order to keep himself alive. Now this is a dangerous argument, as St. Thomas Aquinas realized, and his discussion of it is fenced with stringent conditions. The doctrine applies only in a case of need so extreme that the act of theft is in effect lifted out of the moral sphere altogether:

> Nevertheless, if the need be so manifest and urgent, that it is evident that the present need must be remedied by whatever means at hand (for instance, when a person is in some imminent danger, and there is no other possible remedy), then it is lawful for a man to succor his own need by means of another's property, by taking it either openly or secretly: nor is this properly speaking theft or robbery.[6]

St. Thomas clearly argues that such a case is most extraordinary—"when a person is in some imminent danger, and *there is no other possible remedy*" (italics mine). Thus, it is a case which falls outside the normal ethical sphere; extreme need is essentially a nonmoral condition.[7] Moreover, a man can only take enough to satisfy need; anything more becomes simple theft. Temperance and *mesure,* questions of more or less, do not apply to the unusual situation of extreme need.

Need distorts this argument by mixing up the moral and nonmoral categories. He places himself entirely outside the moral law, outside the governance of Conscience and the cardinal virtues:

> "So Nede, at grete nede, may nymen as for his owne,
> Wyth-oute conseille of Conscience or cardynale vertues,
> So that he suwe and saue *spiritus temperancie."*
> (XX. 20–22)

But, by his appeal to temperance, he is using a moral concept to justify a nonmoral necessity. If temperance applies in this case, so must theft; if

---

6. St. Thomas Aquinas, *ST* (trans. Fathers of the English Dominican Province) II–I. Q. LXVI. a. 7. See also II–I. Q. XXXII. a. 7, ad. 3.

7. Thus, Bloomfield's argument that need is the foundation for the virtue of temperance, an admirable character and temperance' true spokesman, seems to me exceedingly shaky (*Piers Plowman as a Fourteenth-Century Apocalypse,* pp. 135–36); the same point has been made by D. W. Robertson and B. F. Huppé, *Piers Plowman and Scriptural Tradition* (Princeton, N.J., 1951), p. 228, and by Willi Erzgräber, *William Langlands "Piers Plowman"* (Heidelberg, 1957), p. 217.

theft does not apply, then neither can temperance. But having gotten this foot in the door, Need goes on to the most outrageous and insidious part of his argument, and makes what he says sound like the doctrine of *ne solliciti siti*, the basis of Dowel. "[Philosophres]," says Need:

". . . forsoke wele for they wolde be nedy,
And woneden [wel elengely] and wolde nou3te be riche.
And god al his grete Ioye gostliche he left,
And cam and toke mankynde and bycam nedy."

(XX. 37–40)

The ideal of patient poverty itself is here pressed into the service of something which must be, in moral terms, petty thievery.

The worst aspect of all this is not that it bathes criminal acts in the odor of sanctity, but that it lifts moral ideas out of their relevant contexts entirely. From one point of view, Need's argument is not vicious; it is merely the argument of Need. But his confusion of moral and nonmoral concepts, which is challenged neither by Will nor Conscience, radically alters the understanding of the poem. Need forces moral concepts to function in a realm of meaning to which they do not apply. This process is worse than distortion, for it deprives these concepts of their proper references and hence of their meaning. Thus, the process of the disintegration of meaning, the overturning of Grace's gifts to man, enters an acutely dangerous stage with this speech of Need. Conscience' authority has been directly, and successfully, challenged, and the walls of Unity-Holychurch become even less steady.

After the speech of Need, Will falls asleep and dreams that Antichrist comes:

. . . and al the croppe of treuthe
Torned [tid] vp so doune and ouertilte the rote,
And made fals sprynge and sprede and spede mennes nedes;
In eche a contre there he cam he cutte awey treuthe,
And gert gyle growe there as he a god were.

(XX. 52–56)

Meaning has been completely destroyed here, "torned [tid] vp so doune." Everything is topsy-turvy; the confusion indicated in the speeches of Need and the folk has become general. Antichrist's use of False to speed men's needs seems, in fact, to be a direct comment on Need's argument. All the folk, with friars and the religious in the lead, come forth to welcome

Antichrist, "saue onlich folis" (XX. 60), one of whom is undoubtedly the "frantik" Will himself, and another the "lewed" vicar of XIX. Fools are the only wise men. In the chaotic, inside-out world which Pride and Antichrist create with their sophistical "coloures and queyntise" (XIX. 348), every word has its opposite meaning. Conscience says with bitter emphasis:

> "cometh with me, ȝe foles,
> In-to Vnyte holy-cherche, and holde we vs there,
> And crye we to Kynde that he come and defende vs,
> Foles, fro this fendes lymes for Piers loue the Plowman."
>
> (XX. 73–76)

Passus XX presents the apocalypse prophecied since the earliest stages of the poem.[8] Yet, where most apocalypses, even those foretold in *Piers Plowman*, are directed toward visions of a millennial order following upon the destruction of the old, the apocalypse of Passus XX is almost entirely destructive in its vision of collapse and decay. The action of the evil forces in XX is another parallel to the earlier parts of the poem, to the vision of False and Lady Meed. In the *Visio*, language is so corrupted and distorted by False that a completely new structure of meaning is needed for the poem. Here, the corrupter is not False but Antichrist, a figure out of the apocalypse, a character who is himself part of figural history. Thus, though the results are similar, the scale of action in XIX–XX includes not just the earthly sphere, but the divinely appointed scheme as well. This fact serves to emphasize the greater comprehensiveness of the action of Passus XIX–XX as compared to the *Visio*, and also suggests that the end of the *Vita*, like the end of the *Visio*, dramatizes the need for a new structure to replace the exhausted remnants of the old. Yet, the mood of the two parallel scenes is entirely different. The corrupted language of the *Visio*, expressed in personification, can be redeemed by the alternative structure of figural signification. Now, the figuralism of the *Vita*, instead of closing with the triumphal vision of the risen Christ, has produced Antichrist as its end product—a bleak conclusion indeed. The world is in reversal, rushing to its negation with the forces of Antichrist.

Most of the poem's chief characters, themes, and concerns are brought into play in Passus XX, only to be negated—the good vitiated or with-

---

8. The apocalyptic nature of the poem and the context in which this quality should be understood have been fully discussed by Bloomfield, *Piers Plowman as a Fourteenth-Century Apocalypse*.

drawn from power, the evil grown infinitely strong. Those domesticated foibles, the Seven Deadly Sins, who have appeared before in common human apparel, are manifested here as terrible sins, the seven great giants who lead the siege against Unity. Covetise and False rear themselves again, with all the rout of miscreant priests, dishonest tradesmen, and wastrels from the Prologue. One group leads all the rest—the friars, here become as numerous and pestiferous as the apocalyptic plagues described in Revelation.

Even forces which might be presumed friendly to Unity's cause have a destructive effect. Conscience calls for aid from Kynde, last seen in company with Reason, guiding Will's vision of harmonious nature in Passus XI. In Passus XX, Kynde has lost his benevolent aspect; he dispenses pestilence with complete disregard for the station or virtue of those whom he attacks. Conscience' call to him is reminiscent of Piers's call to Hunger in Passus VI, but Hunger, however terrible he seemed at first, proved an adversary easily tamed by the folk. The same thing is not true of Kynde. With his lieutenants, Elde and Death, Kynde rides forth indiscriminately over all, like the terrible riders in Revelation who are the first heralds of the impending end, and in grim parody of the three riders of Passus XVII, Faith, Hope, and Charity, who herald the redeeming Christ.

Among those whom they hurt mortally is Will, who has been standing in the middle of the battlefield observing the action and finds himself in the path of Elde. Elde rides right over his head, leaving him bald—a liberty which Will takes greatly amiss:

> "Sire euel-ytau3te Elde," quod I, "vnhende go with the!
> Sith whanne was the way ouer mennes hedes?
> Haddestow be hende," quod I, "thow woldest haue asked leue!"
> (XX. 185–87)

Elde's response to this complaint is to lay on Will even harder, making him deaf, toothless, and sexually impotent. Amusing as this incident is, especially in so dark a vision, I believe it has serious implications. For Elde robs Will not only of his physical strength but of his intellectual curiosity as well. After this, Will loses control over himself and over his visions; he departs from the scene a querulous old man, crying on Kynde to avenge him for Elde's rudeness. Will's physical impotence mirrors the vitiated state of his soul; weakened in body and spirit, the end of his long quest is to seek a dubious refuge in the doomed house of Unity. And with this anticlimactic final appearance of Will, the poem loses its chief motivating force, its will —a serious loss indeed.

CHAPTER SIX

Will's loss of his intellectual equipment, including all that he has learned, is most apparent in the brief interchange he has with Kynde. For the question he asks—"What crafte is best to lerne?"—is the same question he asked of Lady Holy Church at the poem's very beginning. And the reply Kynde gives him—"Lerne to loue . . . and leue of alle other"—is exactly what Holy Church had told Will then. One cannot help feeling a futility in this familiar catechism, despite its doctrinal worth. What can the poem have accomplished, if Will is still asking the same old question and getting the same old answer? The ironic recollection of the scene in Passus I has even more negative implications, since the lovely lady in white linen is now the weakened, defenseless Holychurch of Passus XX, and Will's teacher is no longer the kind benefactress who supported him all through his life but is instead the terrible avenger, Kynde, whose kinship to the love he counsels is difficult to perceive.[9]

But the overthrow of Unity-Holychurch does not come from outside, despite the strength of Sloth's bow and the assaults of the priests of Ireland. It comes from within, initially from the friars who come to help Conscience defend the castle. The friars are the "false prophets" whom Jesus speaks of as the forerunners of Antichrist. To understand their significance in these scenes, it is necessary to recall the doctrine of *ne solliciti sitis,* as represented particularly by Patience and Piers Plowman. *Ne solliciti sitis,* the manifestation of reason and law, is the chief virtue of the *Visio.* This doctrine and the associated doctrine of *mesure* both make their reappearance in Passus XX. They are embodied, falsely, in two associated figures—Need and the friars. Need's speeches center primarily on the virtue of *mesure* or *spiritus temperancie.* His advice to Conscience concerning the friars is based upon an application of *mesure.* As I have shown, however, Need's use of this doctrine serves only to distort and rob it of its true meaning. Thus, Need is a false manifestation of *mesure,* whose speeches both to Will and to Conscience destructively parody this doctrine. In similar fashion, the friars manifest a destructive parody of patient poverty, *ne solliciti sitis.* And it is an ominous turn for the poem when Conscience' second cry for help is answered first by the friars and then by Need.

The *mesure* Need advocates to Conscience is peculiarly mundane, much like the advice of Hunger to let the wastrels starve while honest men enjoy the fruits of their toil. The friars are poor, says Need, because they have

---

9. It should, of course, be noted that because of the apocalyptic character of the last two passus, all things appear in their most terrible, least forgiving, aspect.

[165]

no patrimony, and therefore they deserve to eat angels' food (XX. 233–40). The implication of his logic is that the friars should be rich so that they would not have to beg food from hard-working men. This is an analysis that shows no understanding at all of patient poverty or *ne solliciti sitis;* it is wordly advice in the fullest sense, entirely in keeping with the wordly corruption that all the poem's virtues suffer in Passus XX.

Conscience laughs at Need's advice, but not, I think, with approval. Instead of rejecting the friars outright, he invites them into Unity, on the condition that they live after their rule. Conscience has a very good perception of the nature of these false friars. Not only do they parody virtue, but they also display all the other marks of Antichrist's nature—lawlessness, formlessness, and sophistry. Indeed, they are literal Antichrists, false imitators of Christ's poverty. In order to correct them, Conscience advocates *mesure,* rule and order. In doing this, Conscience is proceeding on sound doctrinal grounds, explored within the poem. *Mesure* is the prologue and basis for *ne solliciti sitis* just as law is the basis for charity (and just as the *Visio* is the basis for the *Vita*). The mark of God's nature is harmonious rule; the mark of Christ's is charity. Conscience tells the friars to learn

> That in mesure god made alle manere thynges,
> And sette [it] at a certeyne and at a syker noumbre,
> And nempned [hem] names [. . .] and noumbred the sterres;
> . . . .
> Heuene hath euene noumbre and helle is with-out noumbre.
> (XX. 253–55, 268)

This speech of Conscience' seems to me a last-ditch effort to correct not only the friars,[10] but also the lawlessness that has undermined the language of the poem. God not only numbered the universe, he also named it, and the names he gave to things are a sign coequal with the number that is derived from him. Name and number together make order, harmony, and union with God—the characteristics of the redeemed language of Passus XVIII. What Conscience expresses in this speech is the ideal of Christian rhetoric as well as the ideal of Christian living, as the two are interlinking aspects of truth.

Unfortunately, the language of Passus XX, like everything else in it, does not exhibit number and rule. The workers of false signs, the followers of Antichrist, have undermined all the basic terms which lie at the heart

---

10. See Bloomfield's comments on this passage, *Piers Plowman as a Four-teenth-Century Apocalypse,* pp. 145–46.

of the poem. Even Conscience is not free from taint. For not only the friars betray Unity. It is betrayed by one part of the nature of Conscience himself, his weakest meaning as "tenderness of heart," "conscientiousness," his courtliness and courtesy. Knowing full well the nature of the friars, Conscience lets them into Unity:

> Conscience of this conseille tho comsed forto laughe,
> And curteislich conforted hem and called in alle freres,
> And seide, "sires, sothly, welcome be 3e alle
> To Vnite and holicherche . . . "
>
> (XX. 241–44)

His courtesy is a distinctive handicap to him in his dealings with these friars, just as it has been a weakness in his character throughout the poem.[11] When the friars do not behave themselves, but continue to learn sophistry and to neglect their rule, Conscience does not throw them out. Friar Flattery comes from within the "sege" of Holychurch (XX. 311); the fact that he is so readily available is entirely Conscience' fault.

Now, there is nothing inherently wrong with being polite even to rascals, except when politeness blinds judgment and becomes the unwitting aid of treachery. It is no accident that the figure who admits Friar Flattery to Unity, over the vigorous protests of Peace, is called Hende-speech (gracious words). Hende-speech has a very idealistic reason for doing as he does: he wishes to bring about an accord between Conscience and the (now thoroughly corrupt) figure of Life, so that they may "kisse her either other" (XX. 351). Naked idealism, however, is inadequate to deal with the subtle and evil enemies of Unity. And Conscience continues what Hende-speech has begun. Several parallels exist between the confrontation of Conscience and Friar Flattery and the debate of Conscience and Lady Meed in Passus III. Hende-speech's desire for a kiss of peace to terminate the battle (as if *that* were a solution to Armageddon) is reminiscent of the king's similar desire at Westminster. It is a measure of the darkness of Passus XX that this time Conscience is unable to see through the courtesy and flattery of his enemy, even though he knows much more than he did in Passus III. The friar greets Conscience "curteisly" (XX. 352), much as Lady Meed greeted the court. Conscience responds politely, out of solicitous concern for Contrition's pain:

---

11. I have discussed the handicap Conscience' courtliness is to him in greater detail in my article, "The Character of Conscience," pp. 22–25.

"Thow art welcome," quod Conscience, "canstow hele the syke?
Here is Contricioun," quod Conscience, "my cosyn, ywounded;
Conforte hym," quod Conscience, "and take kepe to his sores.
The plastres of the persoun and poudres biten to sore."

(XX. 354–57)

The repetition of the phrase "quod Conscience" sounds the warning. Conscience is indeed speaking, but it is the wrong kind of conscience. The gentleman-knight and tenderhearted companion has betrayed what he himself, as herald of the Holy Spirit, had tried so valiantly to defend.

The world's ruin as portrayed in the final passus is primarily a vision of the ruin of language. Language causes, mirrors, and is the medium within which the disintegration of the end occurs. Antichrist is the Anti-Word, just as Christ is the redeemed and redeeming Word. The two characters who are the immediate cause of Conscience' downfall (besides himself) are both personifications of concepts that often mean a false, sophistical use of language—Flattery and Hende-speech. Concept after concept is weakened, undermined, "torned . . . vp so doun." This process culminates when Contrition is doctored by friar Flattery, who heals his wounds by glossing, and does it so well that he glosses Contrition out of existence:

Tyl Contricioun hadde clene forȝeten to crye and to wepe,
And wake for his wykked werkes as he was wont to done.
For confort of his confessour Contricioun he lafte,
That is the [souereyne] salue for al synnes [of kynde].

(XX. 367–70)

The personification of Contrition is no longer Contrition. It hasn't even an opposite, distorted, or blasphemous meaning; it has no meaning at all. It is a mere shell, a shape without substance. And, considering that personifications are nothing but words, that the exploration and definition of meaning through them is a basic structural tool of the poem, this is a truly catastrophic occurrence.

Thus, Langland manages to destroy everything he has built up. Meaning is dissolved, truth is turned topsy-turvy, the medium of personification is in effect destroyed, the poem's figural allegory ends not with the New Jerusalem but with Antichrist, and Will and Conscience, who have motivated the poem's progress, are rendered impotent. The only thing left to do is what Conscience does, to strike out in search of a new world, which may be found somewhere with Piers Plowman. Yet, it is difficult to conceive in what medium this search is to be conducted, since the verbal structures which the poem has so painstakingly explored have been deprived of their value, corrupted and negated by Antichrist. And language is basic not only to poetry but to all forms of human knowledge; God is revealed through the Word, and the Word has been totally replaced in this poem by the Anti-Word.

Thus, the conclusion of the poem is unexpectedly dark, in terms of what the poem set out to accomplish, and in contrast to the sublimity it reached in Passus XVIII. From another viewpoint, however, it can be seen as ultimately positive, or at least hopeful. Granted that the search for a rhetoric in which human language can be redeemed and made truthful has proved futile, still the collapse of mortal language is not really the concluding image of the poem. Conscience continues the pilgrimage. And the apocalyptic motif of Passus XX gives an important clue to the nature of the poem's ending: the old earth, including its old language, must pass away in order that the new earth and new language may come into being. Seen from this perspective, the wordless dance of divine harmony and the equally wordless ritual of "creeping to the Cross," which end Passus XVIII, directly generate the destruction of language accomplished in Passus XIX and XX. Passus XVIII attempts to redeem human language by redefining it in divine terms, only to discover that such redefinition results in a language of *arcana verba,* hopelessly obscure as a medium for human comprehension. As a result, what the poem needs is a new language commensurate with a new heaven and a new earth. And the only way to achieve this is through an apocalypse.

Langland does not describe what the new order will be; indeed, he does not promise that Conscience will find it. But I would suggest that one term from the new language has already come into the poem—Piers Plowman. Piers is in many ways the cognitive key to the poem. The revelation of his nature is an ongoing process within it, parallel to the ongoing revelation of Christ's nature during his lifetime, which Conscience describes at the beginning of Passus XIX. In Passus V, he is an enigmatic figure, prone to error and to the partial understanding which is in keeping with his figural nature at that point in the poem. When he first enters the *Visio,* he is an evident leader, but of an ambiguous sort. Indeed, it is not at all clear whether he is anything more than a simple fourteenth-century plowman, susceptible to all the blunders of a limited human nature. But in Passus VII he is revealed, though obscurely, as a genuinely figural character, whose being has a dimension beyond the literally human. During the course of the *Vita,* Piers becomes more and more figural, and in this process his outline becomes clearer. He is identified with Peter, with Christ, with right will, with the teaching of the three Do's, with true charity. Piers is the revealer of charity and of history in Passus XVI; his is the fruit which grows on the Tree; his are the arms in which Jesus jousts, his is the pardon, and it is to him that the Holy Spirit is sent in Passus XIX. When Will first beholds the redemptive figure who enters at the beginning of Passus XIX, he sees not Christ but "Pieres the Plowman . . . paynted al blody" (XIX. 6).

It is extremely difficult to put all these manifestations together into a conceptually coherent character.[12] Piers, like Dowel, seems to be an "infinite," but if one regards them as the stages in a progressive revelation, figurally conceived, they become less mysterious. By Passus XIX, Piers Plowman, too, is a redeemed and redemptive word; consequently, one must put together the various aspects under which he appears at different points in the poem in exactly the mutually significant way in which Conscience draws together the various themes of the poem in his discourse on the names of Christ. Piers can only be understood as a *figura,* the sign (actually a series of different manifestations) which reveals partially but truthfully the divine pattern of charity acting within human time and history. To ask "who is Piers Plowman" and expect a completely articulable answer is to be as naïve and misled as Will is when he first asks "what is Dowel"—and for very much the same reasons. The question misconceives the real nature of its object, for it assumes that it has a limited, knowable nature. But Piers is the *figura* within time, "the changing aspect of the permanent"[13] progressively revealed until the end of time, the vehicle through which the ineffable is articulated within the limitations of human experience.

The old sort of word, the language of virtue and of vice, the established language of the Church itself, has proved inadequate finally to express truth, done in by its own complex verbalness, which makes it an easy prey

---

12. As, for example, Howard Troyer, "Who is Piers Plowman?," *PMLA,* XLVII (1932), 368–84, and Nevill Coghill, "The Character of Piers Plowman," *MÆ* II (1933), 108–35, attempt to do. Barbara Raw, "Piers and the Image of God in Man," comes closest to my own view of Piers, when she writes, "Piers is the embodiment of the [divine] image through history" (p. 168), though I think that even her analysis is too schematic to fit the poem exactly. See also Rosemary Woolf, "Some Non-Medieval Qualities of *Piers Plowman,*" *Essays in Criticism,* XII (1962), 111–25, who suggested that Piers is "only half understood" in the poem (p. 116).

13. Erich Auerbach, *"Figura,"* in *Scenes from the Drama of European Literature* (New York, 1959), p. 72.

for the sophistry of Antichrist. But Piers, the ineffable *figura,* the "infinite" sign of truth, who cannot be expressed fully in terms of any human concepts, seems to promise the new language and new understanding which Conscience seeks after the collapse of the old.

Yet the figure remains implicit, a dimly perceived, distant prospect, rather than an informing vision. The allegory of Antichrist is indeed figural, and Langland could have stressed its significance within the entire redemptive pattern as the destructive herald of a new, completed blessedness. But he does not; the tone and emphasis of the conclusion are negative, the positive vision evoked tentatively at best.[14] Conscience' quest for Piers Plowman seems a feeble reed in the chaotic ruin of all the poem's structures. For the ruined structure finally includes the figural vision as well: what one actually sees of the figural process within the poem ends with the victory of Antichrist. Piers has left, his whereabouts unknown. The revelation of the poem, promised by the parallels of Passus XIX–XX with the *Visio,* is the destructive reign of Antichrist. One can, of course, argue that, by making the end specifically figural, thereby invoking the promise of a new and better order after Antichrist, Langland ends the poem optimistically; it is contained within the overarching figural structure of time.[15] But that security is not to be found within the text. Instead, one is left with the lack of any real structure; the ruined world of Passus XX is painfully at odds with the harmonious heaven of Passus XVIII. On the one hand is divine harmony; on the other is chaos on the field of folk. There is no meaningful connection between the two, no rhetoric or image capable of bridging that chasm. The bridge might be found in Piers Plowman, yet the poem finally deserves its title only by faith, rather than by demonstration.

And I believe that, for a poet so urgently seeking a meaningful vision, the anguish produced by that realization motivates the continuing search not only of Conscience but of Langland himself. *Piers Plowman* is the only poem of its size in English that is so deliberately unfinished; it consciously rejects every possible informing structure. One of the poem's present

---

14. On the negativeness of the conclusion, see Sister Rose Bernard Donna, *Despair and Hope* (Washington, D.C., 1948), who argues that theological despair is not the emotion of the end of Piers Plowman; and the review of her book by E. T. Donaldson, *MLN,* LXVIII (1953), 141–42, who suggests that, while the mood may not be theological despair, it is "poetic despair."

15. As Bloomfield argues, *Piers Plowman as a Fourteenth-Century Apocalypse.*

editors has suggested that the poet died in harness, never finishing his revision of the text.[16] This seems to me completely fitting, given the terms of the poem itself. Indeed, had the revision of C been completed, there would undoubtedly have been a D- or an E-Text, until death or fatigue ended the process arbitrarily.

I began this book by subscribing my belief that *Piers Plowman* does mean something. I should better have said that *Piers Plowman* does mean, even though it doesn't mean some thing, for the meaning it evolves is finally unsusceptible of a structured statement. The poem insists constantly on the partialness of meaning, on "what the hills suddennes resists," as Donne has written, rather than on what it yields.[17] The condition of the poem is fluidity, lack of cohesion, the ultimate rejection of any single structure, however comprehensive.[18] This refusal to connect is evident on all levels of the poem, from the ellipsis of its syntax to the suddenness of its digressions, from the vision of chaos under False with which it begins to the vision of anarchy under Antichrist with which it concludes. The doctrinal statement of Lady Holy Church and the figural vision of the

---

16. E. T. Donaldson, *Piers Plowman: The C-Text and Its Poet* (New Haven, Conn., 1949), p. 197. Scholars have realized for a long time, of course, that Passus XIX–XX are essentially unrevised in the C-Text. Cf. G. H. Russell, "Some Aspects of the Process of Revision in *Piers Plowman*," in Hussey, *Critical Approaches*, pp. 27–49.

17. John Donne, *Satyre III.*

18. Charles Muscatine, *Poetry and Crisis in the Age of Chaucer* (Notre Dame, Ind., 1972), has applied the adjective "surrealistic" to the poem's art, suggesting that *"Piers Plowman* must in important ways *be* inconclusive; . . . its form and style are symptomatic of some sort of breakdown" (p. 72). He attempts to relate this breakdown to a cultural crisis of the late Middle Ages, "an immersion in the problematic character of the times" (p. 109). These remarks seem to me very suggestive, though I think that the stylistic "breakdown" occurs because of the conscious, deliberate choice of the poet, and this cannot be considered merely "symptomatic" of a vague cultural disorder in the times. As a matter of fact, Angus Fletcher, in *Allegory: The Theory of a Symbolic Mode* (Ithaca, N.Y., 1964), has argued that a "surrealistic isolation of parts" (p. 105), occurring at all levels of narrative, imagery, character, and language, is basic to the allegorical mode, "in order to force [the] reader into an analytic frame of mind" (p. 107); according to this view, Langland's refusal to connect, in most instances, would be "symptomatic" of the mode he has chosen to employ. The truth probably lies somewhere between these two positions: Langland is an allegorist profoundly conscious of the nature and limits of his chosen mode, and he is a poet intently exploring the nature and limits of vision possible to him in his own time—but a victim of neither.

triumphal, risen Christ both fail to inform the maze which is the field of folk.

Religious language, by the very nature of what it seeks to express, is understood to signify "in part," yet Langland is unique among medieval poets in his insistence on that partialness and inadequacy—it is the anguished premise of his poetry. In his acute awareness of this, he comes closer to the great medieval theologians than he does to his fellow poets. At the end of his life, the story goes, St. Thomas Aquinas, having labored to build his logically articulated, intricately connecting system of theology, was granted a vision of Christ from which he awoke saying that all he had written was straw. Less dramatically, but more in keeping with the tone of the end of *Piers Plowman*, St. Augustine writes at the end of his treatise *De trinitate*, after his own attempt to stretch language to express what cannot be expressed:

> I sought You, and desired to see with my understanding that which I believed, and I have argued and labored much. O Lord, my God, my only hope, hear me, lest through weariness I should not wish to seek You, but may ardently seek your face evermore. . . . Deliver me, O God, from the multitude of words with which I am inwardly afflicted in my soul; it is wretched in Your sight, and takes refuge in Your mercy.[19]

---

19. Augustine *De trinitate* (trans. Stephen McKenna) XV. 28.51.

Q2